ChatGPT and AI for Accountants

A practitioner's guide to harnessing the power of GenAI to revolutionize your accounting practice

Dr. Scott Dell

Dr. Mfon Akpan

ChatGPT and AI for Accountants

Group Product Manager: Aaron Tanna

Publishing Product Manager: Kushal Dave

Book Project Manager: Deeksha Thakkar

Senior Editors: Nisha Cleetus and Rounak Kulkarni

Technical Editor: Rajdeep Chakraborty

Copy Editor: Safis Editing

Proofreader: Nisha Cleetus

Indexer: Pratik Shirodkar

Production Designer: Alishon Mendonca

DevRel Marketing Coordinator: Deepak Kumar and Mayank Singh

First published: June 2024

Production reference: 1190624

Published by Packt Publishing Ltd.

Grosvenor House

11 St Paul's Square

Birmingham

B3 1RB, UK

ISBN: 978-1-83546-653-7

www.packtpub.com

Dedicated to our friends, colleagues, families, students, and veterans.

We're in this together. Helping to make a better world by providing opportunities for all to share, learn, and grow together. It is our hope and passion that by providing resources for those pursuing enhanced knowledge, our contribution will foster your success.

The journey is the reward. Thank you for committing to your own personal and professional growth and joining us on this journey.

– Dr. Scott Dell and Dr. Mfon Akpan

Contributors

About the authors

Dr. Scott Dell is a licensed CPA, insightful Wharton MBA, talented Big 4 and second-tier firm alumnus, award-winning full-time academic, successful entrepreneur, passionate career educator, proud Navy veteran, and well-respected authority and keynote speaker on GAI, including ChatGPT and ChatGPT 4o. Dr. Dell has also been a tech consultant and advocate for over 30 years. Please allow him to inspire you to apply and take advantage of the latest technologies. His knowledge and experience with ChatGPT will propel you to major success in applying and using this powerful technology.

Dr. Mfon Akpan is Assistant Professor of Accounting at Methodist University, USA. He has a passion for emerging technologies and is an expert in virtual reality technology, researching new technologies and educational methods to offer students a current, effective, and relative teaching experience.

Acknowledgements

We appreciate the supreme support of our families in giving us the opportunity to dedicate the time and resources to the development of this book. We wish to acknowledge the inspiration and encouragement received from our academic and other professional colleagues in the pursuit of making a difference in the lives of others. We also want to thank our students, who through their desire to grow while pursuing knowledge and experience, have inspired us to want to provide tools and resources that can assist them in maximizing their success.

– Dr. Scott Dell and Dr. Mfon Akpan

About the reviewer

Ashish Verma is a seasoned professional with a formidable background in finance and technology across diverse emerging markets. Having served multiple organizations as CFO in the past, he is currently dedicated to pioneering innovative solutions to enhance access to capital for women-owned and women-led businesses. Holding a chartered accountant qualification, he has enhanced his expertise through executive education in FinTech, data science, and AI.

Ashish has made significant contributions to several eminent publications, including scholarly papers on gender finance and the strategic integration of blockchain and AI in various enterprises.

I would like to express my heartfelt gratitude to my family for their unwavering support throughout the journey of reviewing this book. Their encouragement and understanding have been a source of strength and motivation for me. In particular, I am deeply grateful to my wife for her exceptional support, especially during such a significant time in our lives as we awaited the arrival of our first child. I dedicate this accomplishment to them.

Table of Contents

3

Applying AI in the Tax Realm   47

4

Enhancing Audits with AI   65

5

Integrating AI with Fraud Examination and Forensic Accounting   89

6

Turbocharging Financial Analysis and Projection   111

7

Advancing Managerial Accounting with AI   131

8

Accounting Information Systems (AIS) through the AI Lens   147

9

AI-Driven Data Analytics: Using Data Visualization Tools and Dashboards   163

10

Ethical and Secure AI Implications   179

11

Revolutionizing Corporate Governance with AI   193

12

GPT Store Feature in ChatGPT   205

13

Overcoming Resistance and Embracing Change   217

14

Lifelong Learning in the Age of AI   235

15

The Future is Now – Integrating AI into Accounting 249

Preface

ChatGPT and AI for Accountants is a comprehensive guide that explores the transformative potential of **generative artificial intelligence (GAI)** *in accounting. It provides a deep dive into how AI can enhance various aspects of accounting, from practice management and tax application to fraud examination and corporate governance.*

Who this book is for

This book is primarily designed for finance professionals and accounting business educators, students, and enthusiasts interested in understanding and applying AI in their work in their professional or personal lives. A basic understanding of the accounting environment principles is assumed. While familiarity with AI concepts can be beneficial, it is optional as the book appeals to users of the technology at all levels.

What this book covers

Chapter 1, Generative Artificial Intelligence (GAI): Understanding the Technology, provides an introduction to GAI and its potential applications in accounting.

Chapter 2, Enhancing Practice Management Using This Technology, explores how AI can streamline and optimize accounting practice management.

Chapter 3, Applying AI in the Tax Realm, discusses the use of AI for efficient and accurate tax calculations and compliance.

Chapter 4, Enhancing Audits with AI, delves into how AI can improve the audit process by providing more accurate and timely insights.

Chapter 5, Integrating AI with Fraud Examination and Forensic Accounting, examines how AI can aid in detecting and preventing fraudulent activities.

Chapter 6, Turbocharging Financial Analysis and Projection, demonstrates how AI can enhance financial analysis and forecasting.

Chapter 7, Advancing Managerial Accounting with AI, discusses the integration of AI in managerial accounting for better decision making.

Chapter 8, Accounting Information Systems (AIS) through the AI Lens, provides insights into how AI can transform traditional AIS.

Chapter 9, AI-Driven Data Analytics: Using Data Visualization Tools and Dashboards, explores the use of AI in data analytics and visualization in accounting.

Chapter 10, Ethical and Secure AI Implications, discusses the ethical considerations and security implications of using AI in accounting. It provides guidelines on how to use AI responsibly and securely.

Chapter 11, Revolutionizing Corporate Governance with AI, explores how AI can revolutionize corporate governance by providing real-time insights and predictive analytics for better decision making.

Chapter 12, Web-Enhanced ChatGPT: Powering Up with Plugins, introduces the concept of plugins in ChatGPT and how they can enhance its capabilities, particularly in the context of accounting.

Chapter 13, Overcoming Resistance and Embracing Change, addresses the common resistance to AI adoption in accounting and provides strategies for overcoming this resistance and embracing change.

Chapter 14, Lifelong Learning in the Age of AI, emphasizes the importance of continuous learning in the age of AI. It provides resources and strategies for keeping up to date with the latest developments in AI and accounting.

Chapter 15, The Future is Now: Integrating AI into Accounting, concludes the book by discussing the current state of AI integration in accounting and envisioning the future possibilities. It provides a roadmap for accounting professionals to successfully integrate AI into their work.

To get the most out of this book

Readers should have a basic understanding of accounting principles. Familiarity with AI concepts can be beneficial but is not mandatory. The book is structured in a way that gradually introduces AI and its applications in accounting, making it suitable for both beginners and those with some prior knowledge of AI.

Software/hardware covered in the book	Operating system requirements
ChatGPT	Any modern operating system with a web browser
Data Visualization Tools and Dashboards	Any modern operating system with a web browser

Disclaimer

The software and hardware requirements are designed to be as inclusive as possible. Most of the tools and platforms discussed in this book are web based, so you can access them on any device with an internet connection and a modern web browser.

Note:

The authors acknowledge the use of cutting-edge AI, such as ChatGPT, with the sole aim of enhancing the language and clarity within the book, thereby ensuring a smooth reading experience for readers. It's important to note that the content itself has been crafted by the author and edited by a professional publishing team.

Get in touch

Feedback from our readers is always welcome.

General feedback: If you have questions about any aspect of this book, email us at customercare@packtpub.com and mention the book title in the subject of your message.

Errata: Although we have taken every care to ensure the accuracy of our content, mistakes do happen. If you have found a mistake in this book, we would be grateful if you would report this to us. Please visit www.packtpub.com/support/errata and fill in the form.

Piracy: If you come across any illegal copies of our works in any form on the internet, we would be grateful if you would provide us with the location address or website name. Please contact us at copyright@packt.com with a link to the material.

If you are interested in becoming an author: If there is a topic that you have expertise in and you are interested in either writing or contributing to a book, please visit authors.packtpub.com.

Share Your Thoughts

Once you've read *ChatGPT and AI for Accountants*, we'd love to hear your thoughts! Scan the QR code below to go straight to the Amazon review page for this book and share your feedback.

https://packt.link/r/1835466532

Your review is important to us and the tech community and will help us make sure we're delivering excellent quality content.

Download a free PDF copy of this book

Thanks for purchasing this book!

Do you like to read on the go but are unable to carry your print books everywhere?

Is your eBook purchase not compatible with the device of your choice?

Don't worry, now with every Packt book you get a DRM-free PDF version of that book at no cost.

Read anywhere, any place, on any device. Search, copy, and paste code from your favorite technical books directly into your application.

The perks don't stop there, you can get exclusive access to discounts, newsletters, and great free content in your inbox daily

Follow these simple steps to get the benefits:

1.   Scan the QR code or visit the link below

https://packt.link/free-ebook/9781835466537

2.   Submit your proof of purchase
3.   That's it! We'll send your free PDF and other benefits to your email directly

1

Generative Artificial Intelligence (GAI) in Accounting

"It's slow, it's buggy, it doesn't do a lot of things very well, but neither did the very earliest computers."

– Sam Altman, OpenAI CEO and co-founder

The field of accounting, traditionally perceived as a bastion of manual processes and number crunching, is witnessing a transformative revolution – the advent of **Generative Artificial Intelligence** (**GAI**). This groundbreaking technology is not just another tool in the accountant's arsenal; it also represents a paradigm shift in how financial data is processed, analyzed, and utilized. At the heart of this transformation is the ability of GAI to automate complex tasks, glean deeper insights from vast datasets, and enhance decision-making processes. In this chapter, we embark on a journey to uncover the intricate workings, applications, and profound impact of GAI in the realm of accounting.

We begin by tracing the origins and evolution of AI in the context of accounting, providing a historical perspective that highlights the significant milestones leading to the current state of AI technology. The journey from the earliest computers, which were slow and limited in capability, to the present-day marvels of AI mirrors the evolution of accounting practices themselves.

As we delve deeper, we will explore the technical requirements to harness GAI in accounting. This includes not just the hardware and software but also the mindset needed to effectively integrate AI into traditional accounting workflows. A critical aspect of our exploration is understanding how GAI, particularly tools such as ChatGPT and its sister **Large Language Models** (**LLMs**), is making waves in the accounting sector. From the nuances of their language processing capabilities to the creative potential they unlock, these AI tools are redefining the boundaries of what's possible in accounting.

But it's not just about the capabilities of GAI. This chapter also addresses common fears and misconceptions about AI, offering a balanced view of its potential benefits and limitations. We aim to demystify AI, moving beyond the hype to a grounded understanding of its practical applications and ethical considerations.

As we proceed, we will cover a range of topics, including the roles of AI in public and private accounting tax departments, its implications for society at large, and the skills accountants need to thrive in this new AI-driven landscape. This chapter serves as your foundational guide to understanding GAI's transformative role in accounting. It's an exploration of a technology that is not just changing how we work with numbers but also reshaping the very fabric of the accounting profession.

Prerequisites

The integration of GAI into the accounting sector necessitates a robust technical infrastructure, encompassing a range of tools and software designed to harness AI's potential. This technology, while powerful, requires the right environment to thrive and deliver its full capabilities.

The essential tools for effective AI application are as follows:

- **Capable web browsers**: The first step in accessing AI tools such as ChatGPT is through a web browser. Modern browsers such as Chrome, Edge, Firefox, or Safari are essential for seamless interaction with AI platforms.

- **AI platform access**: Registration and access to AI platforms such as OpenAI are crucial. For instance, OpenAI's website provides access to various versions of GAI tools, including the widely used ChatGPT models.

- **Intellectual curiosity**: Beyond technical tools, a mindset of intellectual curiosity is fundamental. Engaging with AI technology requires an openness to explore, experiment, and adapt to new ways of processing and analyzing data.

The following are the AI-enabled accounting software that will be required:

- **Automated data processing tools**: AI-enhanced accounting software, such as QuickBooks with its AI features, automates mundane tasks such as data entry, categorization, and reconciliations, significantly reducing manual workload.

- **Advanced analysis and reporting**: Software such as Xero, integrated with AI, offers advanced data analytics capabilities. It enables accountants to extract deeper insights from financial data, produce comprehensive reports, and provide strategic advice based on data-driven predictions.

The data analysis tools are as follows:

- **Predictive analytics**: Tools such as IBM Cognos Analytics employ AI to perform predictive analysis, offering forward-looking insights that are crucial for strategic planning and decision-making.

- **Data visualization**: AI-powered data visualization tools, such as Tableau, transform complex datasets into understandable and actionable insights. These tools are crucial for accountants to communicate financial data effectively.

The data management systems are as follows:

- **Secure cloud storage**: Cloud storage solutions such as AWS or Microsoft Azure, equipped with AI, offer secure and scalable options to store vast amounts of financial data.

- **Data security and compliance**: AI integration also demands robust security protocols. Encryption, secure data transfer, and compliance with standards such as the General Data Protection Regulation (GDPR) and California Consumer Privacy Act (CCPA) are critical components of a comprehensive AI-based accounting system.

AI innovations in accounting – automated calculations and predictive analysis

The advent of AI in accounting has marked a significant leap forward in how financial data is processed and analyzed. Central to this advancement is the role of AI in automating complex calculations and providing predictive analytics, two areas that are profoundly reshaping the landscape of accounting.

Automating complex calculations

Discover how automating complex calculations can streamline processes, increase accuracy, and save valuable time, transforming the way data is analyzed and utilized.

- **Efficiency and accuracy**: AI has transformed traditional accounting calculations from being time-consuming and error-prone to efficient and highly accurate. Tools powered by AI algorithms can handle intricate calculations, such as tax estimations, depreciation schedules, and financial projections, with remarkable speed and precision.

- **Adaptive algorithms**: Modern AI systems in accounting software can adapt to changing financial environments and regulations. They continuously learn from new data, ensuring that calculations stay accurate and compliant with current tax laws and financial reporting standards.

- **Error reduction**: The automation of calculations significantly reduces the risk of human error. For businesses with complex financial structures, this ensures compliance and accuracy in their financial reporting, which is critical for both internal assessments and regulatory adherence.

Providing predictive analytics

- **Forecasting and planning**: AI's predictive analytics capabilities are a game-changer for financial forecasting and planning. By analyzing historical data patterns, AI can predict future financial scenarios, helping accountants and business leaders make more informed strategic decisions.

- **Insightful data interpretation**: AI goes beyond mere data processing; it interprets data to provide actionable insights. This involves identifying financial trends, potential risks, and opportunities, thereby guiding businesses in optimizing their financial performance.

- **Customized financial advice**: AI algorithms can tailor their analyses to specific business needs. This means that the financial advice provided by AI is not generic but customized to the unique financial situation of each business, leading to more effective tax strategies and financial planning.

The following table provides an overview of the impact of AI on accounting:

Area of impact	Description of the AI innovation	Impact on accounting practice
Automated data processing	AI algorithms automate tasks such as data entry and categorization, reducing manual effort.	Increases efficiency, reduces errors, and allows accountants to focus on higher-level tasks.
Predictive analysis	AI uses historical data to predict future financial scenarios and trends.	Enhances financial planning and strategic decision-making with data-driven insights.
Enhanced compliance monitoring	AI systems continuously monitor financial transactions for compliance with regulations.	Improves compliance accuracy and reduces the risk of regulatory penalties.
Advanced reporting capabilities	AI tools analyze financial data and generate comprehensive reports.	Provides deeper insights and clearer financial pictures for businesses and stakeholders.
Personalized financial advice	AI customizes financial advice based on individual business needs and scenarios.	Tailors financial strategies to specific company contexts, leading to more effective outcomes.

Table 1.1 - The impact of AI on accounting

In this tabular overview, we reviewed the impact of AI on accounting, including AI innovations and their impact. In the upcoming section, we will take a deep dive into case studies and real-world applications.

Case studies and real-world applications

Now, we will analyze some case studies and real-world applications that will help us understand the impact of AI.

A small business application of AI in action – revolutionizing Brewed Awakenings' finances with QuickBooks Online

Consider *Brewed Awakenings*, a cozy coffee shop in a vibrant neighborhood. As a small business with limited staff, managing finances, especially tax planning and compliance, was always a significant challenge. Here's how AI helped them overcome it:

- **The implementation of QuickBooks Online**: Brewed Awakenings implemented QuickBooks Online, an AI-powered accounting software widely used by small businesses. This software offers automated expense tracking, invoice management, and streamlined tax calculations.

- **Efficiency and accuracy in financial management**: The adoption of QuickBooks Online led to significant improvements in efficiency. The software's AI capabilities allowed for the automatic categorization of expenses and seamless integration with bank and credit card transactions, reducing manual data entry and errors.

- **Strategic financial insights**: One of the standout features of QuickBooks Online is its ability to provide predictive insights. The AI algorithms analyzed the coffee shop's financial data to forecast cash flow trends and identify potential financial risks, aiding in more informed decision-making.

- **Enhanced tax planning and compliance**: The software's tax calculation tools were particularly beneficial. QuickBooks Online helped the coffee shop accurately estimate tax liabilities, keep track of deductible expenses, and stay compliant with changing tax laws.

- **Outcome and impact**: Integrating QuickBooks Online transformed Brewed Awakenings' approach to financial management. The time saved on accounting tasks was redirected toward customer service and business growth strategies. The coffee shop not only experienced an increase in operational efficiency but also gained valuable financial insights, enabling better strategic planning and financial health.

A small business application – AI's impact on Cityscape Consulting

Consider the case of *Cityscape Consulting*, a small architectural firm specializing in urban design. With a lean team and a focus on innovative projects, managing the firm's finances, especially budgeting, accounting, and tax compliance, was a significant challenge. Here's how AI helped them overcome it:

- **Implementation of Xero – AI-powered accounting software**: To streamline its financial processes, Cityscape Consulting implemented Xero, an AI-powered accounting software tailored for small businesses. Known for its intuitive interface and smart features, Xero was an ideal choice for the firm's dynamic needs.

- **Enhancements in efficiency and accuracy**:

  - **Automated financial tasks**: Xero's AI capabilities automated several key accounting tasks. This included instant bank transaction imports, smart categorization of expenses, and reconciliations. This automation drastically reduced manual entry and the potential for human error.

  - **Real-time financial overview**: The software provided a real-time view of the firm's cash flow and financial health. With all financial data centralized, the team could access up-to-date information for quick decision-making.

- **Improved decision-making and strategic planning**:

  - **Predictive financial insights**: Xero's AI-driven analytics offered predictive insights into the firm's financial performance. This included forecasting future cash flow based on past trends, which was crucial for strategic budgeting and project planning.

  - **Tailored business advice**: The AI in Xero analyzed Cityscape Consulting's financial data to provide tailored advice. It identified cost-saving opportunities and tax deduction suggestions, alerting the firm to potential financial pitfalls.

- **Streamlining tax processes and compliance**: Xero simplified complex tax processes, ensuring that Cityscape Consulting stayed compliant with the latest tax regulations. Automated tax calculations and easy tax return filing reduced the stress and time involved in meeting tax obligations.

- **The outcome and impact on the business**:

  - **Transformed financial management**: The integration of Xero transformed Cityscape Consulting's approach to financial management. The firm experienced a notable increase in efficiency, allowing the team to devote more time to client projects and business growth.

  - **Enhanced decision-making**: The strategic insights provided by Xero's AI capabilities empowered the firm to make better-informed financial decisions. This led to more effective budget management, improved project profitability, and a stronger financial foundation for future growth.

A large corporation application – AI at GlobalTech Enterprises

In a large corporation such as *GlobalTech Enterprises*, an international technology conglomerate, accounting and financial management are inherently complex. The corporation faces challenges such as managing finances across different countries, complying with diverse tax laws, and handling large volumes of transactions. Here's how AI helped them overcome it:

- **The integration of IBM Watson in financial operations**: GlobalTech Enterprises integrated IBM Watson, an advanced AI platform known for its deep learning capabilities and natural language processing. Watson was employed to handle and analyze the enormous volume of financial data generated across various global subsidiaries.

- **Addressing complex accounting scenarios**:

  - **Automated international compliance**: Watson's AI algorithms were programmed to understand and comply with international tax laws and regulations. This automation ensured accurate financial reporting across different jurisdictions and reduced the risk of non-compliance.

  - **Predictive financial modeling**: IBM Watson provided predictive modeling capabilities, allowing GlobalTech Enterprises to forecast financial trends, market shifts, and potential risks on a global scale. This helped in strategic financial planning and investment decision-making.

  - **Efficient transaction processing**: The AI system streamlined transaction processing, handling everything from invoices to inter-company transfers efficiently. This not only improved accuracy but also freed up valuable time for the finance team to focus on strategic tasks.

- **Ethical and regulatory considerations**:

  - **Protecting sensitive information**: In an AI-driven environment, especially in a large corporation such as GlobalTech Enterprises, protecting sensitive financial data is paramount. Watson ensured strict adherence to data privacy standards such as GDPR and CCPA, employing robust encryption and secure data handling practices.

  - **Regular audits and compliance checks**: Continuous monitoring and regular audits of the AI system were conducted to ensure compliance with evolving data privacy laws and corporate governance standards. This included vulnerability checks and updates to security protocols.

- **Ethical AI usage**:

  - **Transparency in AI operations**: Ensuring transparency in how AI algorithms process and analyze data was crucial. This transparency helped maintain trust among stakeholders and ensured that financial decisions were made on an ethical basis.

  - **Bias and fairness in AI**: GlobalTech Enterprises ensured that its AI system was free from biases, particularly in areas such as credit risk assessment and fraud detection. Regular reviews and updates were made to the AI algorithms to ensure fairness and accuracy in all financial processes.

As we have analyzed the case studies, let's prepare for an AI-driven future with accounting by delving deep into the factors, which we will discuss in the following section.

Preparing for an AI-driven future in accounting

We need the necessary skills and training, and we also need to implement AI in accounting departments for an AI-driven future.

The necessary skills and training

As the accounting profession rapidly evolves with the integration of AI, accountants need to equip themselves with a new set of skills and undergo specialized training. This preparation is crucial for thriving in an AI-driven environment, where the fusion of technological savvy and traditional accounting expertise is key.

A fundamental understanding of AI and machine learning

Gaining a fundamental understanding of AI and machine learning is crucial for navigating and leveraging the advancements of the modern technological era.

- **AI literacy**: Accountants must have a basic understanding of AI, including how machine learning algorithms work and how AI systems process and analyze data. This foundational knowledge is crucial for effectively leveraging AI tools in accounting practices.

- **Machine learning concepts**: A grasp of basic machine learning concepts, such as data training, model building, and algorithmic decision-making, is essential. Understanding these concepts helps accountants interpret AI-generated insights and apply them accurately in financial scenarios.

Data analysis and management skills

Mastering data analysis and management skills is essential for making informed decisions and driving strategic success in today's data-driven world.

- **Data proficiency**: In an AI-driven environment, accountants need to be proficient in data analysis. This includes understanding data sources, ensuring data quality, and effectively structuring and interpreting large datasets.

- **Data interpretation**: Beyond number crunching, accountants should develop the ability to interpret complex data outputs from AI systems, transforming raw data into actionable financial insights.

Technology literacy and software proficiency

Developing technology literacy and software proficiency is vital for staying competitive and effective in the digital age.

- **Software familiarity**: Familiarity with AI-integrated accounting software, such as QuickBooks Online, Xero, or IBM Watson, is necessary. Accountants should be comfortable navigating these platforms and integrating them into existing workflows.

- **Adaptability to new tools**: The ability to quickly adapt to new software and tools is vital, as AI technology is continuously evolving. This adaptability ensures accountants can always leverage the most advanced features available.

Critical thinking and strategic decision-making

Enhancing critical thinking and strategic decision-making abilities is crucial for addressing complex challenges and achieving long-term success in any field.

- **Analytical skills**: AI provides valuable insights, but the final decision-making rests with the accountant. Critical thinking and analytical skills are essential for evaluating AI-generated recommendations and making informed financial decisions.

- **Strategic advisory**: Accountants should be prepared to shift from traditional roles to more advisory capacities, where they use AI-generated insights to provide strategic financial advice to clients or stakeholders.

Continuous learning and professional development

Embracing continuous learning and prioritizing professional development is key to staying adaptable and thriving in an ever-evolving global landscape.

- **Ongoing education**: The field of AI is dynamic, with constant developments. Accountants must commit to ongoing education and training to stay abreast of the latest AI advancements and applications in accounting.

- **Professional development courses**: Engaging in professional development courses, webinars, and workshops focused on AI in accounting can provide accountants with the necessary knowledge and skills to remain competitive.

The following table summarizes the skills required in an AI-driven environment:

Skill/training area	Description	Importance in AI-driven accounting
AI and machine learning understanding	A basic understanding of AI operations and machine learning concepts.	Crucial for leveraging AI tools effectively.
Data analysis and management	Proficiency in interpreting and managing large datasets.	Essential for transforming data into actionable insights.
Technology literacy and software proficiency	Familiarity with AI-integrated accounting software and adaptability to new tools.	Important for navigating AI platforms and integrating them into workflows.
Critical thinking and strategic decision-making	Ability to evaluate AI insights and make informed financial decisions.	Key to utilizing AI insights for strategic financial advice.
Continuous learning and professional development	Commitment to ongoing education in AI advancements and applications.	Necessary to stay updated with the rapidly evolving field of AI.

Table 1.2 – The necessary skills and training in an AI-driven environment

Now that we've reviewed the skills required, let's now focus on implementing AI in accounting departments.

Implementing AI in accounting departments

Successfully integrating AI into accounting departments requires a strategic approach that considers both technological and human factors. Here are key strategies to effectively implement AI in accounting workflows and departments:

Strategic assessment and planning

Navigating the integration of AI into accounting departments requires strategic assessment and meticulous planning to maximize efficiency, accuracy, and overall organizational success.

- **Identify key areas for AI implementation**: Begin by assessing current accounting processes to identify areas where AI can bring the most value, such as data entry, report generation, or compliance monitoring
- **Set clear objectives**: Define clear goals for what you want to achieve with AI, whether it's improving efficiency, enhancing accuracy, or providing better financial insights

Choosing the right AI tools

Selecting the appropriate AI tools is pivotal in successfully integrating AI into accounting departments, ensuring efficiency, accuracy, and strategic value in financial processes.

- **Select appropriate AI solutions**: Choose AI tools and software that align with your department's specific needs. Consider factors such as compatibility with existing systems, scalability, and the specific accounting tasks you want to automate or enhance.
- **Vendor evaluation and selection**: Evaluate different AI vendors and software providers. Look for vendors with robust support, a strong track record in accounting AI, and the flexibility to adapt to your organization's needs.

Training and skill development

Incorporating training and skill development programs is essential for effectively implementing AI within accounting departments, ensuring seamless integration and maximizing its potential benefits.

- **Educate and train staff**: Provide training for your accounting team on how to use AI tools. This can include formal training sessions, workshops, or online courses. Focus on both the technical aspects of the AI tools and how to interpret AI-generated insights.
- **Foster a culture of continuous learning**: Encourage an organizational culture that values continuous learning and adaptation. As AI technology evolves, so should the skills and knowledge of your accounting team.

Integration and phased implementation

Incorporating integration and phased implementation strategies is essential for effectively integrating AI into accounting departments, ensuring seamless adoption and maximizing its transformative potential.

- **Seamless Integration**: Ensure that the AI tools integrate smoothly with your existing accounting systems and workflows. This might require IT support or collaboration with the AI tool providers.

- **Phased approach**: Implement AI tools in a phased manner, starting with less complex tasks and gradually moving to more advanced applications. This allows for adjustment and fine-tuning as you go along.

Collaboration and communication

Incorporating AI into accounting departments requires effective collaboration and communication to ensure successful integration and maximize its transformative potential.

- **Collaboration between departments**: Foster collaboration between your accounting department, IT, and other relevant departments. Cross-departmental collaboration is crucial for the successful integration of AI.

- **Effective communication**: Communicate the benefits and changes brought by AI integration to all stakeholders, including accounting staff, management, and other departments. Transparency in communication helps to manage expectations and facilitate smooth adoption.

Monitoring and continuous improvement

Implementing AI in accounting departments requires a commitment to monitoring and continuous improvement to ensure efficiency, accuracy, and alignment with organizational goals.

- **Regular performance review**: Monitor the performance of AI tools regularly. Gather feedback from users and analyze how well the AI tools meet your objectives.

- **Iterative improvement**: Use the feedback and performance data to continuously improve and optimize the AI integration. Be prepared to make adjustments and updates to your AI strategy as needed.

Data governance and security

Establishing robust data governance and security protocols is paramount for ensuring the successful and ethical integration of AI within accounting departments.

- **Robust data governance**: Implement strong data governance policies to manage the data used by AI tools. Ensure compliance with data protection regulations and maintain high data quality standards.

- **Ensure data security**: Given the sensitive nature of financial data, ensure robust security measures are in place. This includes secure data storage, encryption, and regular security audits.

The following table summarizes the strategies for implementing AI:

Strategy	Key actions	Goal
Strategic assessment and planning	Assess current processes, identify AI integration areas, and set clear objectives.	Identify optimal areas for applying AI and define success metrics.
Choosing the right AI tools	Select AI solutions that align with specific needs and evaluate vendors.	Ensure that the chosen AI tools are well-suited and effective for the department's needs.
Training and skill development	Provide technical and interpretative training and foster a continuous learning culture.	Equip staff with the necessary skills and knowledge to use AI effectively.
Integration and phased implementation	Integrate AI tools with existing systems, implementing them in phases.	Ensure smooth integration without disrupting existing workflows, allowing for adjustment.
Collaboration and communication	Foster cross-departmental collaboration and maintain transparent communication.	Ensure all stakeholders are aligned and informed about AI integration.
Monitoring and continuous improvement	Regularly review performance and iteratively improve applying AI.	Optimize AI usage based on feedback and performance, adapting to evolving needs.
Data governance and security	Implement robust data governance policies and ensure strong data security measures.	Protect sensitive financial data and comply with data protection regulations.

Table 1.3 – Implementing AI in accounting departments

As AI continues to revolutionize accounting practices, its successful implementation promises to streamline processes, enhance accuracy, and empower accounting departments to deliver greater value to their organizations.

Summary

As we conclude this chapter, we will reflect on the transformative role of GAI in accounting. This chapter has provided a comprehensive overview of GAI's evolution, its technical requirements, and its groundbreaking applications in the field of accounting. We have seen how AI innovations such as automated calculations, predictive analysis, and enhanced compliance monitoring are reshaping the accounting landscape, offering increased efficiency, accuracy, and deeper financial insights.

Looking ahead, the future of AI in accounting is bright and full of potential. We anticipate further advancements in AI technologies, leading to even more sophisticated tools for financial analysis and decision-making. The role of accountants is set to evolve, with a greater emphasis on strategic advisory and data interpretation, leveraging the power of AI.

Further reading

For those interested in exploring this subject further, the following books, articles, and online resources are highly recommended:

- *Everyday AI* (Jordan Wilson): `https://www.youreverydayai.com/`
- *Padlet for Education* – access articles at `https://padlet.com/DrHeatherBrown/resources-on-chatgpt-ai-and-education-itonvxbr22rpayy3`
- *The Rundown AI* – subscribe here: `https://www.therundown.ai/subscribe`
- *Artificial Intelligence Made Simple (Devansh)* – read the newsletter at `https://artificialintelligencemadesimple.substack.com/?r=a5bgd`
- *AlphaSignal AI* – explore AI tools at `https://alphasignal.ai/`
- *Other Resources* – view all the resources at `https://www.thinglink.com/card/1736467901298246118`
- *Quora ChatGPT* – Join the discussion at `https://chatgpt5.quora.com/`
- *AI Breakfast – Weekly Curated Articles* – sign up at `https://aibreakfast.beehiiv.com/`
- *The Current by Kim Komando* – access tech insights at `https://www.komando.com/friends/?referralCode=gykckqa&refSource=copy`
- *The Neuron* – read AI news at `https://www.theneurondaily.com/`
- *AI Tool Report (Morning Brew)* – subscribe for updates at `https://aitoolreport.beehiiv.com/subscribe?ref=ai7OBtuki2`

These resources provide a wealth of information on AI in accounting and its broader impact on the industry, making them invaluable for anyone looking to deepen their understanding of this rapidly evolving field.

Q&A

Here are some thought-provoking questions and their corresponding answers:

1. How has AI changed the traditional role of accountants?

   AI has transitioned the role of accountants from predominantly number-crunching to a more strategic and advisory capacity. By automating routine tasks and providing advanced analytics, AI allows accountants to focus on offering strategic insights and decision-making support to businesses.

2. What are the ethical implications of using AI in accounting?

   The ethical implications include ensuring data privacy and security, maintaining transparency in AI-driven decisions, and preventing biases in AI algorithms. Accountants must navigate these issues carefully to uphold ethical standards and maintain public trust.

3. How can accountants prepare for an AI-driven future?

   Accountants can prepare by developing a foundational understanding of AI and machine learning, enhancing their data analysis skills, staying up to date with the latest AI advancements, and adapting to new tools and technologies.

4. What challenges do accountants face in integrating AI into their workflows?

   Challenges include the need for initial training and adaptation to new systems, ensuring data accuracy and integrity, and aligning AI integration with existing accounting processes and goals.

5. In what ways can AI enhance financial decision-making?

   AI enhances financial decision-making by providing predictive insights, identifying financial trends, and offering personalized financial advice based on data analytics. This leads to more informed and strategic financial decisions.

6. What future developments can we expect in AI and accounting?

   Future developments may include more sophisticated AI models for financial predictions, integration with blockchain for enhanced security, and AI-driven tools for more personalized and client-centric accounting services.

7. How will AI impact accounting education and training?

   AI will likely lead to a shift in accounting education and training, emphasizing technical skills in AI and data analytics, alongside traditional accounting knowledge. Educational institutions and professional bodies will need to update curricula to include AI-focused courses and certifications.

2

Enhancing Practice Management Using This Technology

"In the age of AI, being an accountant is not merely about sifting through spreadsheets and ledgers; it's about embracing and navigating the waves of a digital revolution."

– Dr. Martijn van Otterlo, assistant professor of artificial intelligence at Tilburg University in the Netherlands

As the first rays of the 21st century illuminated the horizon, they brought tectonic shifts in how industries functioned. Often viewed as a bastion of traditionalism, the accounting sector needed to be more insulated from these winds of change. Propelled by rapid technological evolutions, the age-old practices of accounting, once dominated by handwritten ledgers and manual data entries, found themselves on the brink of a revolution.

Pause and reflect for a moment. Have you contemplated the transformative potential of artificial intelligence in accounting? Throughout the annals of their profession, accountants have been the unsung heroes, meticulously ensuring accuracy, delving into the minutiae of financial records, and extracting coherent narratives from seemingly chaotic data. Yet, the burgeoning capabilities of AI compel us to envision a scenario where machines, powered with algorithms, can execute these tasks with an efficiency and precision that surpass human capabilities. This isn't a speculative scenario set in a distant, sci-fi future; it's the ground reality reshaping the accounting landscape.

This chapter offers a deep dive into the fascinating world of **Generative Artificial Intelligence (GAI)** and its profound impact on accounting practices. Far from rendering the human accountant redundant, the advent of AI signifies the dawn of a golden age for the profession. In this reimagined paradigm, accountants, equipped with the power of AI, transcend their traditional roles. They emerge as strategic visionaries, harnessing AI's prowess to deliver unparalleled value, offer foresight, and anchor informed financial decision-making.

Technical requirements

To fully benefit from this chapter, ensure you have the following:

- A stable internet connection
- A modern web browser updated with the latest features
- A basic understanding of accounting principles and practices
- Curiosity about AI and its expansive potential

Setting the stage for AI integration

In the burgeoning world of digital advancements, the saying *"A craftsman is only as good as his tools"* rings more true than ever. As we stand on the precipice of integrating AI into the accounting landscape, it becomes evident that the efficacy of these advanced systems isn't just about their innate capabilities. It's equally about the environment in which they operate. A specific technical groundwork becomes imperative to ensure that these AI tools work at their optimal capacity.

In the intricate dance of AI and accounting, the choreography is as crucial as the steps. The symphony of AI-driven solutions in accounting is best enjoyed when the orchestra – the technical setup – is in harmony. This ensures the smooth functioning of AI platforms and amplifies their accuracy, speed, and efficiency.

To set the stage for a flawless performance, here are the technical essentials you'll need:

- **A robust browser – Chrome, Edge, Firefox, or Safari**: The browser is your gateway to the vast world of AI-driven accounting tools. Modern browsers come armed with features optimized for today's web. They ensure faster loading times and enhanced security, and they are tailored to support the sophisticated functionalities that AI tools demand. Moreover, these browsers are frequently updated to incorporate the latest web standards, ensuring you always have the best seat in the house for your AI show.

- **An active account on** www.OpenAI.com: Think of OpenAI as the grand stage where the magic of AI comes alive. Registering on this platform gives you access to state-of-the-art AI models such as ChatGPT-3.5, GPT-4, and GPT-4o. Currently, you can access ChatGPT-3.5 without logging in. But it's not just about access. OpenAI's platform is designed with user experience in mind. Other platforms, including Anthropic's Claude, Alphabet/Google's Gemini, and many more appearing every day, are worthy of consideration. Even if you're not a tech wizard, the platform's intuitive design ensures that harnessing the power of AI is as easy as a few clicks.

- **Enhanced hardware**: This is not required, but certainly worth considering is hardware that includes **NPU** (**Neural Processing Unit**) chips, geared specifically for AI applications.

For those seeking the pinnacle of performance, consider this – while it's unnecessary, a high-speed, stable internet connection can elevate your AI accounting experience. Real-time data processing, instantaneous analytics, and swift financial forecasting have become the norm, ensuring you're always ahead in your accounting journey.

In summary, as we delve deeper into AI in accounting, having the proper technical setup isn't just a recommendation; it's also a requisite. It ensures that as the world of accounting undergoes its digital metamorphosis, you're not just a spectator but an active participant, ready to harness the full spectrum of possibilities that AI promises.

Reimagining scheduling in the age of AI

In today's fast-paced business ecosystem, where every second counts, managing time effectively has metamorphosed from a desirable skill to an absolute necessity. For professionals, especially those in the accounting sector, balancing many responsibilities often turns the seemingly mundane task of scheduling into a Herculean challenge. The intricacies of aligning time slots, factoring in diverse time zones, and ensuring that there are no double bookings often devolve into an intricate dance that demands time and attention.

Now, envisage a scenario where this intricate dance is seamlessly choreographed for you. A world where the repetitive toggling between emails, instant messages, and digital calendars becomes a relic of the past. This is where AI steps in, akin to a dedicated personal assistant, ever-ready and impeccably efficient. Equipped with cutting-edge algorithms, AI doesn't just recognize preferences; it also intuitively understands them. It's capable of orchestrating meetings, ensuring that there's no overlap, double-booking, or scheduling snafus. And its capabilities don't end at mere scheduling. Contemporary AI-driven scheduling systems are designed to be proactive. They dispatch reminders, adaptively reschedule appointments by responding to unforeseen circumstances, and even utilize historical data to predict optimal meeting times that align with the preferences of all participants.

The integration of such advanced scheduling mechanisms transcends the realm of mere convenience. It heralds a transformative shift, liberating countless hours previously mired in administrative tasks. For accountants, these time savings are invaluable. It provides an opportunity to divert attention to tasks that add tangible value, strategic financial planning, or intricate data analysis. Clients and coworkers also feel the ripples of this efficiency. In a world where instantaneity is prized, the swift, hassle-free scheduling offered by AI-driven tools paints a portrait of utmost professionalism. It signals respect for people's time, fostering trust and solidifying business relationships.

Furthermore, as the boundaries of the traditional workspace dissolve, giving way to remote collaborations and global partnerships, the utility of AI in scheduling becomes even more significant. It effortlessly navigates the complexities of disparate time zones, ensuring that every stakeholder, regardless of geographical location, is synchronized and informed.

In essence, scheduling and appointment coordination automation isn't just a futuristic luxury; it is also fast becoming the bedrock of modern accounting practices. For those keen on amplifying efficiency, enhancing client relationships, and positioning themselves at the vanguard of the accounting revolution, embracing AI's prowess in this domain is both a strategic move and a nod to the future. The efficiencies and advantages unlocked are significant, as the following table summarizes:

Benefit	Description
Time savings	AI automates mundane tasks, freeing accountants for value-added activities.
Increased accuracy	AI reduces human errors in calculations and data analysis.
Enhanced client interactions	Personalized and quick responses to client queries using AI-driven tools.
Cost efficiency	Reduce operational costs by automating data-driven tasks.
Scalability	AI tools can handle vast datasets, allowing firms to scale their operations.

Table 2.1: The benefits of AI in accounting

Next, let's delve into the evolution of financial forecasting with AI leading the way, showcasing the intersection of cutting-edge technology and strategic decision-making in accounting information systems.

The evolution of financial forecasting – AI at the helm

Financial forecasting has always been the backbone of sound financial planning and strategy. Historically, this intricate task hinged on delving deep into past data, meticulously dissecting market conditions, and leveraging various statistical methodologies. While these traditional tactics laid the groundwork, they often grappled with the challenge of swiftly adapting to the ever-evolving financial milieu. Then came the AI revolution.

But why is AI emerging as the beacon of modern financial forecasting? The complexities of today's financial markets demand forecasting tools that are not just advanced but also intuitively adaptive. AI's prowess isn't confined to its staggering data processing speed; its real magic lies in its ability to assimilate, learn, and evolve. From simple supervised learning to complex deep learning mechanisms and intricate neural networks, AI transcends mere data analysis. It dives into the very soul of data, discerning patterns, flagging anomalies, and even weighing in external factors such as socio-political shifts that could turn financial tides.

Harnessing the essence of this data, AI crafts a holistic view of prevailing market dynamics, facilitating the projection of future financial trajectories with an accuracy once unattainable. This reshapes the game board. Accountants are now equipped with a tool that not only offers dynamic forecasting models but also continuously refines these models. integrating fresh data. The static models of yore pale compared to these AI-driven, ever-evolving forecasting marvels.

Picture this – armed with AI-driven insights, an accountant advises a client or colleague contemplating a hefty investment. Instead of merely presenting numbers rooted in historical data, the accountant can now weave a narrative enriched by multi-dimensional analysis. This narrative encompasses everything from past investment performance to a spectrum of variables, spanning global economic shifts to nuances in industry-specific dynamics. Such profound insights transform financial advice from being merely data-centric to truly insight-driven.

In a business world teeming with razor-thin profit margins and relentless competition, pinpoint accurate financial forecasting can often be the fine line demarcating success from failure. It heralds a shift from reactive to proactive financial strategies, fine-tunes resource distribution, and spotlights potential financial icebergs well before they loom large.

In the grand tapestry of financial planning, AI has not merely simplified forecasting. It has also reimagined it, instilling it with intelligence, learning-based intuition, and unparalleled efficiency. It's a brave new world where accountants aren't just forecasters but also strategic visionaries, guiding financial narratives with unmatched precision and confidence. The step-by-step development of accurate and reliable AI forecasting models is summarized in the following table:

Step number	Process	Description
1	Data collection	Gather relevant financial data, both historical and current.
2	Data cleaning	Process and clean the data to remove anomalies or irrelevant information.
3	Algorithm training	Train the AI model using historical data to recognize patterns and relationships.
4	Model testing	Test the AI model with a subset of data to ensure accuracy.
5	Prediction generation	Use the trained model to predict future financial trends, based on the current data.
6	Review and refinement	Continually review the predictions, adjust the forecast with new reinforced data inputs, and refine the model as needed for increased accuracy.

Table 2.2: The steps in AI model development for accounting

We'll now proceed to explore the shift in client relationships propelled by AI innovation, illuminating the path to unparalleled engagement and personalized experiences in an accounting information system.

Revolutionizing client relationships with AI

The essence of any thriving business, especially in professions as intimate as accounting, is in the depth and strength of its client relationships. Clients yearn for more than just financial custodianship in a world burgeoning with data and diverse financial options. They desire a partner, a confidante who comprehends their unique financial fingerprint, foresees challenges, seizes opportunities, and architect solutions tailored for them.

As the digital zeitgeist redefines client expectations, they gravitate toward bespoke experiences and real-time resolutions. The era where one-size-fits-all financial counsel was the norm is receding. In its place emerges a clientele that's informed, digitally adept, and craves customized financial counsel that aligns with their intricate financial needs. This modern clientele prizes swift interactions, real-time insights, and a sense of being understood.

AI champions this new dynamic, bridging traditional accounting and modern client expectations. By harnessing AI, accounting professionals can sift through oceans of client data, encompassing financial trajectories to every interaction nuance with the firm. This deep dive uncovers layers of client preferences and expectations and even anticipates their future financial aspirations. Armed with this intelligence, accountants can sculpt advice that resonates with each client's unique financial narrative, fostering an aura where every client feels exclusively attended to.

However, AI's magic is not confined to customization alone. It reimagines the very fabric of client interactions. Think of AI chatbots working tirelessly, addressing client queries at all hours, offering prompt solutions, and leaving accountants with the bandwidth to untangle intricate financial conundrums. Such responsiveness is gold in client satisfaction metrics.

Imagine the profound impact when an accountant, backed by AI's predictive prowess, apprises a client about a looming market shift even before it hits the mainstream discourse. Such proactive engagement cements trust and positions the accountant as an invaluable sentinel in the client's financial odyssey.

AI's embrace transcends mere transactional engagements; it births relational symphonies. It pioneers a paradigm shift from merely dousing financial fires to sculpting strategies that add tangible value. By intertwining AI into client interactions, accountants can forge deeper trust, cultivate enduring loyalty, and etch themselves as irreplaceable custodians in their client's financial saga.

Yet, the AI revolution is not about the sheer might of the tools but their judicious application in resonating with the evolving client's requirements. AI's brilliance shines in its ability to decipher vast unstructured data. Consider **Natural Language Processing** (**NLP**) – an AI offshoot that can dissect client communications, from emails to casual chats, discerning underlying sentiments. It's like having a sixth sense, tuning into unsaid concerns or unvoiced satisfactions, empowering accountants to address them proactively.

The foresight AI offers is panoramic, spanning beyond financial landscapes to the very psyche of client behaviors. AI can predict a client's impending financial moves by decoding past engagements, transactional patterns, or even a client's digital footprints. Such insights could range from anticipating a client's significant financial plunge to sensing a waning satisfaction, prompting them to seek alternatives.

Moreover, AI's seamless integration with contemporary Customer Relationship Management (CRM) systems is transformative. These AI-empowered CRMs can automate reminders, curate content resonating with client interests, and even intuitively schedule interactions. They ensure every client touchpoint is captured and analyzed and serves as a beacon for future engagements.

Yet, beneath these layers of technological marvel lies AI's most profound offering – the amplification of human connection. While it might seem counterintuitive, AI, when wielded right, liberates accountants from repetitive tasks, channeling their energies into nurturing client relationships. It's about harmoniously fusing cutting-edge tech with the timeless human touch.

As we navigate this confluence of technology and human-centric services, AI's role in elevating client experiences is pivotal. For the avant-garde accountant, embracing AI isn't a mere trend; it's the blueprint to craft more profound, enriching client alliances in today's digital epoch.

Crafting tailored client encounters with AI

In the intricate tapestry of financial consulting, amid the staggering numbers and intricate data, human narratives resonate the most. Behind every balance sheet and financial projection lies a story – of dreams, ambitions, fears, and aspirations. A good accountant recognizes this narrative, but a great one crafts personalized financial paths and builds stories around it.

With their diverse financial history and aspirations, every client is a unique puzzle waiting to be deciphered and pieced together. While the ethos of accounting has always been precision and accuracy, modern-day challenges necessitate a more profound understanding that transcends numbers. Remembering the intricate nuances of each client's financial desires and apprehensions, especially in a bustling practice, is nothing short of Herculean. Enter AI, the modern accountant's most prized potential ally.

AI's prowess extends beyond mere number crunching. It delves into the heart of client data, dissecting past consultations, transactional patterns, feedback, and seemingly insignificant interactions. With its intuitive algorithms, AI maps out a client's needs, capturing the essence of their financial desires, risk thresholds, and long-term objectives.

Equipped with this granular understanding, accountants can sculpt financial strategies as unique as a client's fingerprint. Imagine being able to recommend a series of socially responsible investments to a client passionate about social change, or pointing out potential growth sectors in Southeast Asia to a client mulling international business expansion. AI's rigorous data analysis supports all these.

Yet, the magic of AI-driven personalization is wider than crafting bespoke financial strategies. It's the cornerstone of trust-building. Clients are more likely to invest in trust and confidence because of an accountant's deep-rooted understanding of their financial DNA. This feeling of being indeed *"seen"* and *"understood"* in a world of generic financial advice is priceless.

Furthermore, in a digital-first age, where interactions often lack the personal warmth of a handshake or a reassuring nod, AI-driven personalization adds a much-needed touch of empathy. It transforms otherwise sterile digital consultations into meaningful dialogues, replete with understanding, sensitivity, and mutual respect.

AI, often perceived as the zenith of technological advancement, finds its most profound application in adding a touch of humanity to the accounting realm. It reinforces the age-old adage that the personal touch truly counts, even in a profession dominated by numbers. Through AI-driven personalization, modern accountants don't just offer financial advice but also craft personalized financial experiences, one client at a time.

Crafting tailored client experiences with AI

In the intricate tapestry of finance and accounting, amid the sprawling spreadsheets and charts, it's crucial not to lose sight of the individual threads – the clients. They aren't just numbers or account entries but also real people, with dreams, anxieties, and distinct financial goals. The true essence of a financial consultant lies in recognizing these individual narratives and weaving them into a cohesive financial strategy.

Every client boasts a unique story with their aspirations and challenges. It's this diversity that breathes life into the world of accounting. Yet, as accountants manage an expanding clientele, the nuances of each client's story can blur together. Enter the realm of AI.

With its unmatched computational prowess, AI delves into the depths of client data like a seasoned detective. It meticulously examines previous interactions, sifts through transaction histories, scrutinizes feedback, examines market conditions, and picks up on often overlooked cues, such as the duration between proposal submission and response. Aggregating this information, AI crafts a detailed client persona, spotlighting their financial behavior, preferences, risk tolerance, and overarching goals.

Empowered with this profound understanding, accountants can curate financial strategies as unique as their clients. Picture this – AI could sift through myriad investment avenues for an environmentally conscious client to recommend the most promising green energy stocks. Similarly, AI analyses can pinpoint potential markets for entry for a client eyeing international expansion, backed by detailed economic indicators and sector-specific insights.

But AI's magic in personalization isn't confined to crafting strategies. It's also about forging connections. A client, sensing their accountant's deep-rooted understanding of their financial journey, feels a surge of trust. It's not just about financial acumen but also the comfort of knowing they're genuinely understood. In today's digital-first landscape, where screens often replace face-to-face interactions, these AI-driven personalized touchpoints recreate the warmth and intimacy of personal meetings. They elevate digital communications from mere transactions to heartfelt conversations.

In the grand scheme of accounting, while AI brings unparalleled data analytics to the forefront, its most profound impact is its ability to infuse humanity into numbers. It reiterates the age-old adage – that personal touches make the difference in finance, as in life.

Prompt responses with AI-enabled support

The digital age, characterized by instant answers and real-time updates, has reshaped client expectations. Delays are no longer just inconveniences; they're also deal-breakers. AI-driven support tools, including chatbots, step in as invaluable allies. These tools, powered by sophisticated algorithms, can instantly address many client queries, offering accurate, data-informed responses. The result is a streamlined, efficient client support experience that operates round the clock.

Efficiency unleashed – AI's role in data interpretation

In today's data-centric financial landscape, raw data is abundant. The challenge lies in interpretation – transforming this data into actionable insights.

Decoding vast data reservoirs with AI

The realm of accounting is synonymous with data. From intricate financial statements to transaction logs, the volume of data accountants grapple with is staggering. Traditional data processing methods, while effective, are often time-intensive. With its capacity to process vast datasets swiftly, AI emerges as a game-changer. It doesn't merely process; it also discerns. Recognizing patterns, extracting insights, and drawing data-driven conclusions become seamless, enabling accountants to harness insights in real time.

Real-time analytics – the AI advantage

The power of real-time data is undeniable. With AI, accountants can access real-time financial reports and in-depth analyses. This instantaneous data retrieval and processing capability facilitates quicker, more informed decision-making, empowering accountants to offer timely, strategic advice to clients. In an industry where timing can make or break financial strategies, AI's real-time analytics pave the way for proactive financial management.

Summary

In this chapter, we ventured deep into the burgeoning influence of AI within the accounting landscape. The journey illuminated the multifaceted roles that AI has commenced to play – streamlining administrative chores, crafting bespoke client experiences, and unraveling the complexities hidden within expansive data troves. The power of AI doesn't merely lie in its computational prowess but also in its ability to humanize, optimize, and revolutionize traditional accounting methodologies.

Aspects of accounting	Traditional methods	AI-driven methods
Data entry	Manual data input and prone to human error	Automated data input with validation checks reduces errors
Financial forecasting	Based on historical data and trends and less adaptive to real-time changes	Uses real-time data and machine learning to predict future trends

Aspects of accounting	Traditional methods	AI-driven methods
Fraud detection	Manual checks and balances might miss sophisticated fraudulent activities	Real-time scanning and pattern recognition to detect anomalies
Client interaction	Face-to-face meetings and phone calls, limited by office hours	24/7 AI chatbots and personalized client experiences using AI analysis
Financial analysis	Manual analysis of financial statements, which takes longer	Instant analysis using AI algorithms, providing deeper insights

Table 2.3: AI in accounting – traditional versus AI-driven methods

But this exploration is merely the tip of the iceberg. As we move into *Chapter 3, Applying AI in the Tax Realm*, we will delve into another critical dimension of accounting – taxation. Here, we will uncover how AI is poised to transform tax calculations, navigate the labyrinth of regulations, and craft innovative, adaptive tax strategies for a dynamic financial landscape. The fusion of AI and taxation promises to be intriguing and insightful, ushering in a new era of efficient and strategic tax management.

Q&A

As we wrap up this chapter, let's take a moment to reflect on the core tenets and insights we've gathered regarding the integration of AI in accounting. These questions aim to reinforce your understanding and encourage deeper contemplation on the subject:

1. In what ways is AI revolutionizing the conventional administrative processes in the accounting domain?

    AI is fundamentally reshaping administrative tasks in accounting by automating repetitive and time-consuming processes, such as data entry, invoice categorization, and reconciliations. AI-driven systems can learn from historical data, ensuring their accuracy improves. This reduces human error and frees accountants to focus on more strategic and value-added activities. Additionally, AI-powered chatbots and virtual assistants streamline client interactions, appointment scheduling, and query resolutions, further enhancing efficiency.

2. Delve into the transformative impact of real-time reporting powered by AI. How does it shape decision-making and strategic planning in modern accounting practices?

    Real-time reporting through AI provides instantaneous insights into financial data as transactions occur. This allows accountants and business leaders to make informed decisions promptly. Instead of waiting for end-of-month or quarterly reports, businesses can assess their financial health, detect anomalies, and adjust strategies. This proactive approach, facilitated by AI, ensures businesses remain agile, adapting to market dynamics and capitalizing on emerging opportunities.

3. Given the digital transformation of client relationships, why is personalizing client interactions paramount? How does AI facilitate this personalization?

    In today's digital age, clients seek experiences tailored to their unique needs and preferences. Personalized interactions signal to clients that they are valued and understood. AI facilitates this by analyzing vast client data, from transaction histories to interaction patterns. This analysis provides insights into a client's preferences, risk tolerance, and financial goals. Armed with these insights, accountants can offer highly personalized advice and solutions, enhancing client trust and satisfaction. Moreover, AI-driven tools can automate communications, sending personalized content or reminders based on a client's profile and previous interactions.

4. How does AI's capability to analyze vast datasets impact financial forecasting and client insights?

    AI's ability to process and interpret large datasets enables more profound and accurate financial forecasting. Traditional methods might rely on static models and historical data. In contrast, AI can dynamically adapt, considering various influencing factors, from broader economic indicators to industry-specific trends. This results in forecasts that are both granular and holistic. For client insights, AI can predict behavior, anticipate needs, and even gauge sentiment, allowing accountants to address concerns or capitalize on opportunities proactively.

5. What are the potential risks and ethical considerations when integrating AI into accounting, and how can they be mitigated?

    While AI offers numerous advantages, it is not without risks. One significant concern is data privacy and security. Ensuring that AI systems are secure and compliant with regulations is paramount. There's also the risk of bias in AI predictions if the system is trained on skewed or unrepresentative data. It's essential to regularly audit and update AI models to ensure fairness and accuracy. Ethical considerations arise when determining the extent of AI's decision-making autonomy, especially in areas with significant financial implications. It's crucial to maintain human oversight, ensuring that AI acts as a tool to assist accountants rather than replace their judgment. Continuous training, transparent algorithms, and robust governance frameworks can help mitigate these risks and ethical challenges.

Further reading

Please refer to the following reading materials for any additional information:

- **Books**:

  - *Python for Finance* by Yves Hilpisch: This book provides a comprehensive introduction to how to use Python for finance and financial analysis.

  - *Artificial Intelligence in Financial Markets* by Christian L. Dunis, Peter W. Middleton, and Konstantinos A. Theofilatos: This resource discusses how AI techniques can be used in trading, fund management, and risk assessment.

- **Websites and online courses**:

  - **Coursera** (`https://www.coursera.org/en-IN`): This online learning platform offers courses on AI, machine learning, and their applications in finance. Notable universities and institutions provide these courses.

  - **edX** (`https://www.edx.org`): Another online platform with courses on AI and finance. Look for courses from institutions such as MIT or Harvard that touch on these topics.

  - *Towards Data Science* (`https://towardsdatascience.com`): This publication frequently publishes articles on the intersection of AI, machine learning, and finance.

  - **OpenAI** (`https://openai.com`): While not specific to finance, OpenAI's website and blog provide a wealth of information on the latest advancements in AI.

- **Professional associations**:

  - **AICPA**: The American Institute of CPAs has resources and articles discussing the future of accounting and the role of technology, including AI

  - **ACCA**: The Association of Chartered Certified Accountants offers insights into how the accounting profession evolves with technology

- **Journals and reports**:

  - *Journal of Finance and Data Science*: This journal publishes papers on the intersection of finance and data science, including AI techniques

  - *Deloitte Insights*: *Deloitte* frequently publishes reports on the impact of AI on various industries, including finance and accounting

3

Applying AI in the Tax Realm

"Artificial intelligence is to trading what fire was to cavemen."

– an unknown stock trader

The advent of **artificial intelligence** (**AI**) in tax practices marked the beginning of a new era in taxation. This integration began with the use of basic AI algorithms to sort and analyze large volumes of financial data, thereby improving the speed and accuracy of tax computations. Early applications of AI in tax systems primarily focused on automating routine tasks such as data entry, classifying transactions, and preliminary analysis of tax implications.

The initial impact of AI on tax practices was transformative in terms of efficiency and accuracy. AI systems can process vast amounts of data at unprecedented speeds, thereby reducing the time required for tax computations and analysis. Furthermore, AI algorithms equipped with machine learning capabilities began to identify patterns and anomalies in financial data, which significantly enhanced their ability to detect errors, fraud, and discrepancies.

The introduction of AI in tax practices has also begun to change the role of tax professionals. With AI handling the mundane aspects of tax computation and data management, accountants and tax advisors started to focus more on interpreting the data, providing strategic tax advice, and ensuring compliance with the evolving landscape of tax regulations. This shift represented a move from computational tasks toward more analytical and advisory roles within the profession.

The background and evolution of tax practices from manual calculations to AI-enhanced systems demonstrate remarkable technological advancement. This evolution has not only streamlined taxation's operational aspects but also elevated tax professionals' strategic roles. As AI continues to advance, it is expected to reshape tax practices by introducing new levels of efficiency, accuracy, and strategic insight.

The role of AI in modern tax practices cannot be overlooked. In a world where financial and tax regulations are becoming increasingly complex, the need for more efficient, accurate, and insightful tax-processing tools is paramount. AI stands at the forefront of this need and offers solutions that significantly enhance various aspects of tax work:

- **Tax compliance**: AI simplifies compliance by automating the processing of vast amounts of data, ensuring accuracy, and keeping pace with changing local and global tax laws and regulations. Automation reduces the burden of manual tasks, allowing tax professionals to focus on more strategic activities.

- **Tax planning**: AI algorithms can analyze patterns and trends in financial data, providing valuable insights for tax planning. This predictive capability enables more strategic decision-making, helping businesses and individuals optimize their tax positions.

- **Tax reporting**: With AI, tax reporting becomes more efficient and transparent. AI tools can quickly compile and analyze financial data, generating comprehensive tax reports with enhanced accuracy, which is crucial for both internal decision-making and regulatory compliance.

- **Fraud detection and risk management**: AI's ability to analyze large datasets for irregularities plays a critical role in identifying potential fraud and managing tax-related risks.

- **Customized tax solutions**: AI can provide personalized tax advice based on an individual's or a company's specific financial situation, making tax practices more tailored and effective.

The integration of AI into tax practices represents a significant step forward in taxation. This chapter will explore the various dimensions of this integration, highlighting how AI not only streamlines and enhances existing processes but also opens up new possibilities for tax professionals and their clients.

In this chapter, we'll delve into the transformative role of AI in tax-related tasks and processes. As technology continues to evolve rapidly, AI has emerged as a critical element for reshaping how tax professionals approach their work. AI redefines the landscape of tax practices by automating routine tasks to provide advanced analytical capability. This chapter will explore these developments and provide you with a comprehensive understanding of how AI is integrated into various aspects of taxation.

Technical requirements

The integration of specific technical tools and software is vital to harness AI in tax-related operations. These key components include the following:

- **AI-enabled tax software**: Programs from Intuit, CCH, Lacerte, Drake, and others are critical for efficiency and accuracy. They can incorporate advanced features such as natural language processing to interpret tax legislation and machine learning to identify potential deductions and credits.

- **Data analysis tools**: Utilizing tools such as Tableau or Power BI for data visualization and SAS for advanced analytics is essential for effectively handling and interpreting vast volumes of financial data.

- **Integration software**: Platforms such as MuleSoft or Zapier can ensure seamless integration with existing financial systems such as QuickBooks or SAP, facilitating smooth data flow and minimizing manual input errors.

- **Automation software**: Tools such as UiPath for **robotic process automation (RPA)** and Blue Prism for **intelligent process automation (IPA)** can significantly streamline tax-related tasks, ranging from data entry to more complex decision-making processes.

Data management and security

Given the sensitive nature of tax data, robust data management and security systems are non-negotiable:

- **Secure data storage**: Solutions such as **Amazon Web Services (AWS)** S3 for cloud storage, equipped with encryption and robust backup facilities, are ideal for securely storing sensitive tax information

- **Data privacy compliance tools**: Tools such as OneTrust and TrustArc can help ensure compliance with data protection laws such as GDPR and HIPAA, including features for data anonymization and secure data sharing

- **Access control and authentication**: Implementing systems such as Microsoft's Azure Active Directory for access control with multi-factor authentication ensures that only authorized individuals can access sensitive tax data

- **Security audits and updates**: Regular security checks using tools such as Nessus or Qualys, combined with ongoing updates, are critical for safeguarding against potential cybersecurity threats

- **Data quality management tools**: Incorporating data management solutions such as Talend or Informatica for regular data cleansing and validation is crucial for maintaining the accuracy and consistency of tax data

AI innovations in tax compliance and reporting automated tax calculations

AI's integration of AI into tax calculations represents a significant leap in terms of accuracy and efficiency. Automation is achieved through several key functions:

- **Complex calculations and predictive analysis**: AI systems use algorithms to handle intricate calculations that are time-consuming and error-prone if performed manually. These calculations include varying tax rates, deductions, and credits across jurisdictions. Moreover, AI can predict future tax liabilities based on historical data, aiding more effective financial planning.

- **Adaptive learning for regulation changes**: AI systems are equipped with machine learning capabilities that enable them to adapt to changes in tax laws and regulations. They continuously learn from new data, ensuring that tax calculations remain accurate as the rules evolve.

- **Error reduction and consistency**: By automating the calculations, AI significantly reduces the risk of human error. This consistency is crucial for businesses with complex tax structures to ensure that they remain compliant with tax laws.

Real-time compliance monitoring

AI's role in compliance monitoring is transformative, offering real-time oversight and proactive issue identification:

- **Continuous monitoring and alert systems**: AI tools continuously analyze transaction data, flagging anomalies or discrepancies that might indicate noncompliance. This real-time monitoring allows for immediate corrective actions to be taken, significantly reducing the risk of errors and penalties.

- **Data reconciliation and pattern recognition**: AI algorithms are adept at reconciling vast amounts of data from different sources, ensuring that they align with tax reporting requirements. They can recognize patterns indicative of compliance issues such as underreporting or misclassification of income.

- **Regulatory compliance updates**: AI systems are constantly updated with the latest tax laws and regulations, helping businesses stay compliant. These updates include international tax regulations, which are particularly challenging because of their complexity and frequency of changes.

Enhanced reporting capabilities

AI profoundly enhances tax reporting and offers detailed insight and clarity:

- **In-depth data analysis**: AI can analyze more data at a deeper level than traditional methods. It can uncover hidden insights in the tax data, such as identifying tax-saving opportunities or areas of potential risk.

- **Customized reporting**: AI tools can generate customized reports tailored to the specific needs of businesses or individuals. These reports can include predictive scenarios, tax-saving strategies, and risk assessments.

- **Visualization of tax data**: AI-driven data visualization tools transform complex tax data into understandable and actionable insights. Interactive dashboards and graphical representations make it easier for decision-makers to understand tax obligations and strategies.

- **Integration with financial planning**: AI-enhanced tax reporting can be integrated into broader financial planning tools. This integration provides a holistic view of an individual's or business's financial health, thus influencing informed decision-making.

AI innovations in tax compliance and reporting have revolutionized how businesses and individuals approach their tax obligations. By automating complex calculations to enhance reporting capabilities, AI makes tax processes more accurate, efficient, and insightful. The following table highlights the key features and their respective impacts in each area:

Section	Key Features	Impact
Automated tax calculations	Complex calculations, adaptive learning, error reduction, and consistency	Improves accuracy and efficiency in tax calculations and adapts to regulatory changes.
Real-time compliance monitoring	Continuous monitoring, data reconciliation, pattern recognition, and regulatory updates	Identifies compliance issues in real time, reduces the risk of penalties, and ensures data alignment
Enhanced reporting capabilities	In-depth data analysis, customized reporting, data visualization, and integration with financial planning	Provides deeper insights, tailored reports, and visual understanding, and also aids in informed decision-making

Table 3.1 – Key features and impacts of each area

The preceding table summarizes the key features for a quick reference. Now, let's review AI in tax planning.

AI in tax planning and strategy

Let's see how AI helps with analyzing tax planning by considering some scenarios and tax benefits.

Predictive analysis for tax planning

AI's predictive analysis capabilities play a crucial role in tax planning, providing foresight into the tax implications of business decisions:

- **Forecasting tax liabilities**: AI algorithms can analyze historical financial data to forecast future tax liabilities in various scenarios. This helps businesses anticipate and plan their tax obligations.

- **Decision impact analysis**: AI models can simulate the tax impacts of different business decisions, such as expansions, investments, or restructuring, aiding in choosing the most tax-efficient strategies.

- **Tax regulation adaptation**: AI systems remain updated with current tax laws and regulations, allowing them to accurately predict how changes in legislation might affect future tax liabilities.

Scenario analysis and risk assessment

The use of AI in scenario analysis and risk assessment for tax planning is exceptionally intricate and valuable:

- **Detailed scenario simulations**: AI systems can perform comprehensive simulations of various business scenarios by incorporating a wide range of variables. These include changes in market conditions, business expansion, shifts in consumer behavior, and alterations in tax laws. By analyzing the potential tax implications of each scenario, businesses can make more informed decisions. AI models can present a range of outcomes, from best to worst-case scenarios, helping to prepare for different eventualities.

- **Advanced risk identification and profiling**: AI algorithms are capable of scanning complex datasets to identify subtle patterns and indicators of tax-related risks that might not be evident through traditional analysis. This includes detecting anomalies that could suggest noncompliance, forecasting potential future risks based on emerging trends, and identifying areas where tax strategies might be optimized to mitigate risk.

- **Dynamic risk assessment and continuous monitoring**: AI tools offer dynamic risk assessments and continually update risk profiles as new data becomes available. This real-time monitoring and updating means that businesses are always working with the most current information, allowing them to respond quickly to emerging risks or changes in the fiscal environment.

- **Strategic recommendations and decision support**: Beyond identifying risks, AI systems can provide strategic recommendations to mitigate these risks. This might include suggestions for restructuring financial holdings, altering investment strategies, and revising tax-filing approaches. These AI-driven recommendations are based on an extensive analysis of historical data, rulings by authorities, current market trends, and predictive modeling, ensuring that they are both relevant and actionable.

- **Customized analysis for business specifications**: AI tools can be tailored to understand and analyze the specific nuances of a business's tax situation. This customization means that risk assessments and scenario analyses are not just general overviews but are deeply relevant to the specific context, operations, and strategies of the business.

Optimization of tax benefits

AI is instrumental in identifying and optimizing tax benefits and credits:

- **Identification of tax credits and deductions**: AI systems can scour financial data to identify potential tax credits and deductions, ensuring that businesses take advantage of all opportunities

- **Benefit maximization strategies**: Beyond identification, AI can suggest strategies to maximize these benefits, such as the timing of expenditures or investments

- **Continuous learning and adaptation**: As tax laws and business operations evolve, AI continuously learns and adapts, ensuring the ongoing optimization of tax benefits

The following table summarizes the preceding sections for reference:

Section	Key Functions	Benefits
Predictive analysis for tax planning	Forecasting tax liabilities, decision impact analysis, and tax regulation adaptation	Aids in strategic decision-making and anticipates future tax obligations
Scenario analysis and risk assessment	Scenario simulation, risk identification and mitigation, and customized risk profiles	Prepares for various tax outcomes and minimizes tax-related risks
Optimization of tax benefits	Identification of credits/deductions, benefit maximization strategies, and continuous learning	Ensures full utilization of tax benefits and adapts to changes in tax laws

Table 3.2: AI in tax planning and strategy

Now that we've reviewed the key functions and benefits of tax planning and strategies, let's move on to a few case studies.

Case studies and real-world applications

In this section, we will review various case studies and cover scenario analysis and risk assessment.

Case study – Bean There, Done That – a local coffee shop

Let's take a closer look at our case study:

- **Background**: *Bean There, Done That* is a small, independently-owned coffee shop in Portland, Oregon. With an annual revenue of approximately $500,000, it operates with a small team and has limited resources for tax planning and compliance.

- **Challenge**: The business faced challenges in efficiently managing its tax obligations, including identifying applicable tax deductions, handling payroll taxes for a handful of employees, and navigating the complexities of the state and local taxes.

- **AI implementation**: The coffee shop implemented cloud-based AI tax software, "TaxWise AI," designed for small businesses. The AI tool is integrated with existing accounting software to provide automated tax calculations and real-time compliance monitoring.

- **Outcome**:

  - **Efficiency in tax filing**: The AI system streamlined the tax filing process, identifying all possible tax deductions, such as equipment depreciation and local tax credits for small businesses

  - **Payroll compliance**: The AI tool automatically calculates payroll taxes, ensuring compliance with federal and state regulations

  - **Strategic decision-making**: Predictive analysis features allowed owners to understand the tax implications of potential business decisions, such as expanding to a second location or changing supplier contracts

- **Impact**: The implementation of AI resulted in an estimated 20% reduction in tax-related expenditures owing to optimized deductions and improved compliance. The owners also reported a significant decrease in time spent on tax-related tasks.

Scenario analysis and risk assessment

The use of AI in scenario analysis and risk assessment for tax planning is exceptionally intricate and valuable:

- **Detailed scenario simulations**: AI systems can perform comprehensive simulations of various business scenarios by incorporating various variables. These include changes in market conditions, business expansion, consumer behavior shifts, and tax law alterations. Businesses can make more informed decisions by analyzing the potential tax implications of each scenario. AI models can present a range of outcomes, from best-to-worst-case scenarios, helping prepare for different eventualities.

- **Advanced risk identification and profiling**: AI algorithms can scan complex datasets to identify subtle patterns and indicators of tax-related risks that might not be evident through traditional analysis. This includes detecting anomalies that suggest noncompliance, forecasting potential future risks based on emerging trends, and identifying areas where tax strategies might be optimized to mitigate risk.

- **Dynamic risk assessment and continuous monitoring**: AI tools offer dynamic risk assessments and continually update risk profiles as new data become available. This real-time monitoring and updating means that businesses are constantly working with the most current information, allowing them to respond quickly to emerging risks or changes in the fiscal environment.

- **Strategic recommendations and decision support**: Beyond identifying risks, AI systems can provide strategic recommendations to mitigate these risks. This might include suggestions for restructuring financial holdings, altering investment strategies, and revising tax-filing approaches. These AI-driven recommendations are based on an extensive analysis of historical data, current market trends, and predictive modeling, ensuring that they are both relevant and actionable.

- **Customized analysis for business specifications**: AI tools can be tailored to understand and analyze the specific nuances of a business's tax situation. This customization means that risk assessments and scenario analyses are not just general overviews but are deeply relevant to the business's specific context, operations, and strategies.

A large corporation's international tax strategy

Example: *"GlobalTech Inc." with Thomson Reuters' ONESOURCE*: GlobalTech Inc. is a multinational corporation that operates in numerous countries. As a leader in technology, their operations face complex international tax scenarios as they integrate within the global tax environment:

- **Challenge**: GlobalTech must effectively navigate different tax jurisdictions, manage transfer pricing, and ensure compliance with cross-border tax regulations

- **Solution implementation**: GlobalTech has implemented Thomson Reuters' ONESOURCE, a comprehensive tax technology platform designed for complex tax management on a global scale

- **Outcome:**

  - **Automated compliance across jurisdictions**: ONESOURCE automated the tax compliance process in various countries, keeping up with changing tax laws and regulations

  - **Streamlined transfer pricing documentation**: The platform provides tools to manage and document transfer pricing, which is crucial for multinational operations, thereby minimizing the risk of disputes and penalties

  - **Data consolidation and reporting**: ONESOURCE allowed for the efficient consolidation of tax data from multiple jurisdictions, enabling streamlined reporting and analysis

  - **Risk management and strategic planning**: The system offers risk assessment tools and scenario planning capabilities, aiding GlobalTech in making strategic international investments and operational decisions

- **Impact**: The adoption of ONESOURCE resulted in significant time savings in terms of tax compliance processes, reduced compliance risks, enhanced tax-saving strategies, and enabled strategic tax planning for GlobalTech's international operations

In this section, we reviewed various case studies and tax strategies. Next, we'll do a deep dive into the ethical and regulatory considerations.

Ethical and regulatory considerations

This section delves into the ethical and regulatory aspects that are critical to AI applications in the tax domain, with a focus on data privacy and adaptation to regulatory changes:

- **Data privacy in tax AI applications**: We'll discuss the crucial need to maintain stringent data privacy and security in AI-based tax systems. Given the sensitive nature of tax data, AI systems must adhere to global data privacy standards such as GDPR and CCPA, employ advanced encryption and secure storage methods, undergo regular compliance audits, and offer transparency and control of the data. For users, measures are essential to protect personal and financial information from breaches and ensure trust and integrity in AI tax applications.

- **Navigating regulatory changes**: This section explores AI's dynamic role in adapting to and managing regulatory changes within the tax realm. AI systems are capable of real-time updates to reflect changes in tax legislation, use predictive analytics to anticipate future regulatory shifts, and offer customization to comply with jurisdictional tax laws. Moreover, AI aids in training and knowledge dissemination related to tax regulations and assists businesses in scenario planning to understand the financial impacts of potential regulatory changes.

Data privacy in tax AI applications

The integration of AI in tax applications brings data privacy and security to the forefront:

- **The sensitive nature of tax data**: Tax-related data includes sensitive personal and financial information. Protecting this data is paramount as breaches can lead to serious financial and reputational damage to individuals and businesses.

- **Data privacy standards**: AI systems in tax applications must comply with global data privacy standards such as the GDPR in Europe and CCPA in the United States. These regulations require strict data handling and user consent protocols.

- **Encryption and secure storage**: AI-driven tax systems must employ robust encryption techniques to secure data, both in transit and at rest. Secure cloud storage solutions with advanced security protocols are essential for preventing unauthorized access.

- **Regular audits and compliance checks**: Continuous monitoring and regular audits of AI systems ensure compliance with evolving data privacy laws. This includes checks for vulnerabilities and the implementation of updates to security protocols, as necessary.

- **Transparency and user control**: Users should have clear visibility of how their data is used by AI systems and retain control over it. This includes options for opt-out data collection and the ability to access and delete personal information.

Navigating regulatory changes

AI systems are uniquely positioned to adapt to and assist regulatory changes in the tax landscape:

- **Real-time updates on tax laws**: AI systems can be programmed to monitor changes in tax legislation and regulations continuously. By staying current, they can adapt calculations and compliance protocols in real time, thereby reducing the risk of non-compliance.

- **Predictive analysis for future regulations**: AI can analyze trends and predict future regulatory changes. This foresight enables businesses and tax professionals to prepare in advance, ensuring smooth transitions when new laws come into effect.

- **Customization to different jurisdictions**: For businesses operating in multiple jurisdictions, AI can customize compliance processes according to local tax laws. This is especially critical for multinational corporations that face varied and complex tax environments.

- **Training and knowledge dissemination**: AI can assist in training tax professionals and stakeholders by providing updated information on regulatory changes. This can be achieved using AI-driven training modules and real-time alerts.

- **Scenario planning for regulatory impact**: AI can model the financial impacts of potential regulatory changes, allowing businesses to conduct scenario planning. This helps with strategizing and budgeting in anticipation of new tax regulations.

This section emphasizes the importance of ethical practices and regulatory compliance in deploying AI for tax-related applications. It highlights that AI systems must maintain a balance between technological advancement and adherence to ethical and legal standards, ensuring that they serve as reliable, secure, and compliant tools in the evolving tax administration and planning landscape.

Preparing for an AI-driven future in taxation

For tax professionals to effectively utilize AI in their practice, a specific set of skills and training is essential:

- **Understanding AI and machine learning basics**: Professionals do not need to be AI experts, but a fundamental understanding of how AI and machine learning work is crucial. This includes knowledge of how these systems process data, make predictions, and learn from the inputs.

- **Data analysis and management skills**: As AI heavily relies on data, proficiency in data analysis, including understanding the data sources, quality, and structuring, is essential. The skills that are required for managing and interpreting large datasets are vital.

- **Technology literacy**: Familiarity with the latest tax software and tools that incorporate AI is necessary. This includes understanding how to integrate these tools into the existing systems and workflows.

- **Critical thinking and problem-solving**: AI provides insights and suggestions, but tax professionals need to interpret these findings and make decisions. Therefore, critical thinking and problem-solving skills are essential.

- **Continuous learning and adaptability**: The field of AI continues to rapidly evolve. Ongoing education and adaptability are key as professionals must stay updated with the latest developments in AI technology and tax regulations.

- **Ethical considerations and compliance**: Understanding the ethical implications of using AI in tax practices and ensuring compliance with data privacy and protection laws are crucial.

Implementing AI in tax departments

Here are some strategies for successfully integrating AI into tax departments and workflows:

- **Assessing current processes**: Begins by assessing current tax workflows to identify areas where AI can bring improvements, such as repetitive tasks, data analysis, or compliance monitoring.

- **Selecting the right AI tools**: Choose AI tools that align with the specific needs of the tax department. Consider factors such as scalability, ease of integration, and specific features relevant to a department's operations.

- **Training and development**: Invest in training programs for staff to familiarize themselves with the new AI tools. This training should cover both the technical aspects and best practices for using AI in tax work.

- **Phased implementation**: Implement AI tools in phases, starting with less critical areas. This approach allows you to monitor and tweak the system as needed, ensuring smoother integration.

- **Collaboration between AI experts and tax professionals**: Collaboration between AI experts and tax professionals should be encouraged to ensure that the AI system aligns with the practical needs of the department.

- **Monitoring and continuous improvement**: Regularly monitor the performance of AI tools and gather user feedback. This feedback is used to continuously improve and optimize AI systems in tax processes.

- **Data governance and security**: Implement robust data governance policies and ensure that strong security measures are in place to protect sensitive tax data.

Successfully integrating AI into tax departments requires a thoughtful and methodological approach. It begins with a thorough initial assessment of the existing tax processes. This step is crucial for identifying the specific areas where AI can be applied most effectively. Once these areas have been identified, the next critical step is to carefully select AI tools. These tools must not only align with the department's immediate needs but also have the potential to scale and evolve as requirements change.

Training and developing staff is paramount. Comprehensive programs that are designed to familiarize teams with AI tools are essential. This training ensures that the staff can use these tools effectively and understand their capabilities and limitations. The implementation of AI tools should not be abrupt but phased in. A gradual rollout allows for the necessary adjustments and fine-tuning, ensuring smoother integration into existing workflows. This phased approach also mitigates resistance to change, allowing the staff to adapt to new technologies at a comfortable pace.

Collaboration is a key component in this process. Encouraging a synergistic relationship between AI experts and tax professionals ensures that these tools are not only technically sound but also practically applicable. This collaboration fosters an environment in which AI tools can be used efficiently and effectively. Regularly monitoring and continuously improving AI systems is vital. This involves collecting and analyzing user feedback, tracking performance metrics, and making adjustments as needed. This iterative process ensures that AI systems remain relevant and effective over time.

Data governance and security protocols are non-negotiable. With tax departments handling sensitive information, robust security measures must be implemented to protect the data. This includes ensuring compliance with data protection laws and internal security policies. These strategies are designed to facilitate the seamless adoption of AI in tax departments. The aim is not only to enhance efficiency, accuracy, and compliance but also to equip the workforce with the skills and tools needed to leverage AI technologies in their tax practices effectively.

Future outlook

In the future, the field of taxation will stand on the cusp of a transformative era driven by the relentless advancement of AI. Integrating AI into taxation is not just a fleeting trend but a fundamental shift that's redefining the landscape of tax practices and policies.

Predictions and trends

The AI trajectory in taxation suggests several key predictions and trends that are likely to unfold in the coming years:

- **Increased automation and efficiency**: AI's capabilities to automate complex tax processes will continue to evolve. We can expect a future in which the majority of tax calculations and compliance checks will be automated, drastically reducing manual effort and minimizing errors. This will lead to significant efficiency gains for both tax authorities and taxpayers.

- **Enhanced predictive analysis**: AI will become more adept at predictive analysis, offering advanced foresight into the tax implications of various financial decisions. For individuals and businesses alike, this will mean more informed financial planning, with AI providing tailored advice based on personal and corporate financial data in the dynamically changing tax environment.

- **Customization and personalization**: The future will likely see AI offering highly personalized tax guidance. By leveraging data analytics and machine learning, AI can provide individualized tax-saving strategies and investment advice, taking into account a person's unique financial situation.

- **Integration with emerging technologies**: The synergy of AI with other emerging technologies, such as blockchain and the **Internet of Things (IoT)**, will further enhance the transparency, accuracy, and security of tax systems. For instance, blockchain can be used to securely store transaction records, reducing the possibility of tax fraud.

- **Proactive tax policy development**: AI's predictive capabilities will not only be limited to tax planning but also extend to policymaking. Governments could use AI to forecast the economic impact of tax policy changes, aiding the development of more effective tax legislation.

Potential developments and innovations

The horizon of AI in taxation is dotted with potential developments and innovations that could significantly impact the field:

- **AI-powered tax advisory services**: We may see an increase in AI-driven tax advisory platforms that offer real-time tax advice, similar to digital financial advisors. These platforms can provide instant recommendations on tax-related queries, making professional tax advice more accessible and cost-effective.

- **Advanced fraud detection systems**: AI's evolution will likely enhance its ability to detect and prevent tax fraud. AI systems can identify fraudulent activities with greater accuracy and speed by analyzing patterns and anomalies in large datasets.

- **Smart tax filing assistants**: The future may introduce AI assistants capable of assisting with tax filing and adapting to individual user needs. These assistants can guide taxpayers through the filing process, offer optimization tips, and even predict potential audit risks.

- **AI in international taxation**: As global business becomes increasingly complex, AI could play a crucial role in managing international tax issues such as transfer pricing and cross-border transactions. AI systems may become capable of navigating the intricate web of international tax laws, providing invaluable assistance to multinational corporations.

- **Ethical AI in taxation**: As AI becomes more entrenched in taxation, the focus on ethical AI will intensify. This includes ensuring that AI systems are transparent and fair, as well as complying with privacy and ethical standards, particularly when handling sensitive financial data.

The following table summarizes this section:

Section	Key Points	Impact on Taxation
Predictions and trends	Increased automation, enhanced predictive analysis, customization and personalization, integration with emerging technologies, and proactive tax policy development	Efficiency gains, informed financial planning, personalized tax strategies, enhanced transparency and security, and effective tax legislation
Potential developments and innovations	AI-powered tax advisory services, advanced fraud detection systems, smart tax filing assistants, AI in international taxation, and ethical AI in taxation	Accessible tax advice, improved fraud detection, user-friendly tax filing assistance, better management of international tax issues, and adherence to ethical standards

Table 3.3 – Future outlook

As AI continues to advance, its integration into the tax realm holds the promise of not only increasing efficiency and accuracy but also paving the way for innovative solutions that address complex tax challenges, ultimately reshaping the future of tax compliance and planning.

Summary

This chapter comprehensively explored the transformative impact of AI on taxation. We began by examining the innovative applications of AI in tax compliance and reporting, highlighting how automated tax calculations and real-time compliance monitoring are revolutionizing the accuracy and efficiency of tax processes. The enhanced reporting capabilities provided by AI enable deeper insights that benefit both businesses and individuals.

When we covered tax planning and strategy, we investigated the role of AI in predictive analysis, scenario analysis, and risk assessment. Here, AI's ability to forecast the tax implications of various business decisions and conduct complex risk assessments stands out as a game changer for strategic tax planning.

The case studies we covered illustrated real-world applications of AI in tax practices, from small businesses to multinational corporations. These examples underscored how AI tools such as Thomson Reuters' ONESOURCE are instrumental in navigating complex international tax laws, demonstrating AI's scalability across different business sizes and needs.

The ethical and regulatory considerations we discussed emphasized the importance of data privacy and security in AI applications. We also explored how AI systems adeptly navigate and adapt to regulatory changes, ensuring compliance in a dynamic legal landscape.

Finally, we focused on the necessary skills and strategies for implementing AI in the tax department. This included the need for ongoing training and adaptability among tax professionals, and the importance of a strategic, phased approach to AI integration in tax workflows.

Looking ahead, the potential future development of AI in taxation is vast and promising. As AI technology continues to advance, we anticipate even more sophisticated applications in tax processes. The future may hold AI systems capable of an even more nuanced understanding of tax laws and regulations, potentially offering personalized tax advice and predictions tailored to individual or business-specific contexts.

The evolving role of AI in taxation is likely to extend beyond efficiency and compliance. It can transform into a tool for strategic decision-making, offering predictive insights that could shape future tax policies and business strategies. The integration of AI with emerging technologies such as blockchain could further enhance transparency and security in tax processes.

Technological advancements must be balanced with a mindful approach toward ethical considerations, particularly around data privacy and the fair use of AI. The human element in taxation will remain crucial, with AI serving as a tool to augment rather than replace human expertise.

AI's journey in the realm of taxation is just beginning. Its full potential is yet to be realized. AI will play a pivotal role in shaping the future of tax practices, offering unprecedented opportunities for efficiency, compliance, and strategic planning in the ever-evolving taxation world.

Further reading

To learn more about AI in taxation, here is a revised list of recommended books and online resources, along with links.

Recommended books

Here are some recommended books:

- *Taxing Artificial Intelligence*, by Xavier Oberson: This book explores the concept of taxing AI as a potential solution to the challenges posed by AI in the job market. It is a fully updated edition of the author's previous work, *Taxing Robots*: `https://www.amazon.com/Taxing-Artificial-Intelligence-Xavier-Oberson/dp/1035307545`.

- *Tax and Robots (Chapter 10) - Artificial Intelligence and the Law*, edited by Jan De Bruyne, Cedric Vanleenhove: This chapter, authored by Dina Scornos, delves into the intersection of AI, law, and taxation. It is part of a broader book discussing AI's impact of AI on legal frameworks: `https://www.cambridge.org/core/books/abs/artificial-intelligence-and-the-law/tax-and-robots/DF133B5074474EAEFB64DD82AECCD629`.

- *Artificial Intelligence in Accounting: Practical Applications*, by Ng and Alarcon: Although it focuses on accounting, this book offers insights into how AI is used in financial professions, including taxation implications. This study provides practical guidance for AI applications in these fields: `https://www.routledge.com/Artificial-Intelligence-in-Accounting-Practical-Applications/Ng-Alarcon/p/book/9780367542016`.

Online resources

The following are some online resources that you may wish to consider:

- *CDE News Article – "AI in Taxation: Transforming or Replacing?"*: This study discusses the role of AI in taxation transformation: `https://cde.news/ai-in-taxation-transforming-or-replacing/`

- *AI in taxation research papers*: Platforms such as `https://scholar.google.com/` and `https://www.researchgate.net/` offer a wide range of research papers and articles on the application of AI in taxation

- *Online courses and webinars*: Websites such as `Coursera` and `Udemy` offer courses on AI applications in finance and taxation, providing both theoretical and practical insights

These resources provide a comprehensive overview of AI's role of AI in taxation, from academic insights to practical applications, and are ideal for anyone interested in understanding the current landscape and future implications of AI in this field.

Q&A

This section provides insights into various questions you may have at this point:

1. How is AI transforming the field of taxation?

   AI has revolutionized taxation by automating complex calculations, enhancing compliance monitoring, and providing predictive analytics for strategic tax planning. This transformation leads to increased efficiency, accuracy, and deeper insights into tax management for both individuals and organizations.

2. Can AI adapt to changing tax laws and regulations?

   Yes – one of the key strengths of AI in taxation is its adaptability to changes in laws and regulations. Machine learning algorithms enable AI systems to continuously learn from new data, including changes in tax legislation, ensuring that they remain current and accurate.

3. Will AI replace human tax professionals?

    AI isn't likely to replace human tax professionals entirely, but rather augment their capabilities. Although AI can handle repetitive and data-intensive tasks, the expertise, judgment, and strategic thinking of human professionals are essential, especially for complex tax planning and ethical considerations.

4. How does AI ensure data privacy and security during taxation?

    Taxation AI systems are designed with robust encryption and secure data handling practices. They comply with global data privacy standards such as GDPR and incorporate regular security audits and updates to protect sensitive tax information.

5. What are the challenges of implementing AI in tax departments?

    Key challenges include ensuring data accuracy and integrity, training staff to use AI tools effectively, integrating AI with existing systems, and maintaining pace with the rapid evolution of AI technologies. Overcoming these challenges requires strategic planning, continuous learning, and collaboration between AI experts and tax professionals.

6. What future developments can we expect regarding AI and taxation?

    Future developments may include more advanced AI-powered tax advisory services, enhanced fraud detection systems, and smarter tax filing assistants. AI's integration with blockchain technology could also enhance the transparency and security of tax processes. Ethical AI use will become a focal point to ensure fair and privacy-compliant applications.

7. How does AI assist large corporations in international taxation?

    AI aids large corporations in managing complex international tax laws by automating compliance, providing predictive analyses for strategic planning, and aiding in risk management. AI systems can customize processes according to different jurisdictional laws, helping corporations navigate the complexities of global taxation.

8. What skills are necessary for tax professionals in an AI-driven environment?

    Tax professionals require a foundational understanding of AI, data analysis skills, technology literacy, critical thinking, and problem-solving abilities. Additionally, continuous learning and adaptability are crucial to stay abreast of evolving AI technologies and tax regulations.

4

Enhancing Audits with AI

"In God we trust; all others bring data."

- W.Edwards Deming

In the meticulous and detail-oriented realm of auditing, where accuracy is paramount and there is minimal tolerance for error, **artificial intelligence** (**AI**) has emerged as a beacon of transformative potential. Traditionally characterized by manual data sifting and painstaking analysis, the auditing process is witnessing a paradigm shift owing to the integration of AI and **machine learning** (**ML**) technologies. The promise is enhanced precision, unprecedented efficiency, and deeper and more insightful analysis capabilities.

As the quote by W. Edwards Deming suggests, trust is a precious commodity, and in the world of auditing, it is earned through the relentless pursuit of data-backed truths and transparency. AI contributes significantly to this endeavor, making it indispensable for auditors to navigate the intricate tapestry of financial data and compliance requirements.

The AI audit landscape

Auditing is a pivotal function in the financial landscape, acting as a linchpin and assuring the accuracy and completeness of financial information disseminated by organizations.

Current challenges in auditing

The traditional auditing process, however, while robust, is not without its distinctive set of challenges, such as the following:

- **Volume of data**: The digital age has ushered in an era in which businesses are generating data at an unprecedented rate. In their quest to ensure financial integrity, auditors find themselves grappling with colossal datasets. The sheer volume makes manual review and analysis of all available information an arduous and often impractical task.

- **Complex transactions**: With the business environment becoming increasingly dynamic, the complexity of transactions and financial arrangements has skyrocketed. These intricacies necessitate a deeper and more nuanced understanding, often proving to be overwhelming for human auditors, who might lack the computational prowess to decode these complexities efficiently.

- **Fraud detection**: The arena of fraud detection is a battlefield in which auditors are perpetually pitted against individuals, employing sophisticated schemes to misrepresent financial records. Detecting these meticulously planned fraudulent activities remains a daunting task for auditors, who demand a combination of vigilance, expertise, and advanced analytical skills.

- **Time constraints**: Auditors constantly race against the clock. The imperative for the timely completion of audit tasks often finds itself at odds with the equally pressing demand for a thorough and meticulous analysis and review of financial statements, placing auditors under significant pressure and stress.

Against this challenging backdrop, AI has emerged as a tool and game changer. AI does not simply offer solutions; it innovatively addresses and mitigates these challenges, propelling the auditing function into a new paradigm characterized by efficiency, accuracy, and effectiveness.

How AI is transforming audits

Audits transform with AI as the catalyst, driving this change. This transformation is not superficial; it is a fundamental shift in how audits are conducted and data is analyzed.

Automated data analysis

The deluge of data in the financial sphere can indeed be overwhelming for auditors. With copious amounts of data generated every minute, manual analysis is time-consuming, susceptible to human error, and impractical. AI ingeniously addresses this bottleneck by automating much of the data-analysis processes. Here, we look at how it does this:

- **Real-time analysis**: AI is not bound by time limitations. It can analyze vast datasets in real time, offering instant insights and analysis that would take human auditors an inordinate amount of time to derive.

- **Advanced algorithms**: By applying sophisticated algorithms, AI can meticulously sift through data and precisely identify errors, discrepancies, or anomalies in financial data. These algorithms are designed to learn and adapt and become more accurate and efficient.

- **Error reduction**: Automated data analysis significantly reduces the time and effort required for verification and validation. However, the impact does not end. It enhances the accuracy of the audit by eliminating human bias or error, offering an unparalleled level of precision.

- **Efficiency and accuracy**: AI accelerates the auditing process and ensures that it is more accurate and reliable. With automated data analysis, auditors can trust the data they are working with, allowing for more accurate and insightful conclusions.

By automating data analysis, AI does not just augment the auditing process; it revolutionizes it, laying the foundation for an audit that is efficient, inherently more reliable, and accurate.

Fraud detection and prevention

In an intricate web of financial transactions, fraud detection is one of the most daunting challenges for auditors. AI and ML are equipped with predictive analytics and pattern-recognition capabilities, serving as beacons illuminating murky waters where fraudulent activities might be concealed:

- **Predictive analytics**: AI predictive analytics involves the use of statistical algorithms and ML techniques to identify the likelihood of future outcomes based on historical data. AI utilizes these analytics to predict potentially fraudulent activities before they happen or as they are happening. This proactive approach allows auditors to nip fraudulent schemes in the bud, safeguarding the organization's financial health and integrity.

- **Pattern recognition**: AI thrives on its ability to discern patterns within sprawling datasets. It meticulously analyzes transaction histories and identifies usual trends and norms in financial activities. With this knowledge, AI has become adept at spotting unusual transactions or trends that veer away from established patterns, flagging these anomalies for further scrutiny by auditors.

- **Learning from history**: AI does not function in a vacuum; it learns and evolves. By continuously learning from historical data, it develops a keen understanding of typical transaction patterns. This learning process is perpetual, with AI constantly refining and enhancing its analytical capabilities to understand the ever-changing dynamics of financial transactions and fraudulent schemes.

- **Flagging deviations**: Any deviation from the norm does not escape the AI's vigilant eye. Even subtle and sophisticated attempts at financial misrepresentation are flagged for further investigation. AI serves as an initial filter, highlighting areas that demand auditor attention, thus allowing them to focus on their expertise where it is most needed.

- **Proactive fraud prevention**: AI is not just a tool for detection; it is also an instrument for prevention. Early identification of suspicious activities enables auditors and organizations to adopt preventive measures. This proactive stance on fraud prevention minimizes financial losses and protects an organization's reputation.

- **Enhanced security protocols**: With cyber threats becoming increasingly sophisticated, AI integrates advanced security protocols to protect sensitive financial data. It plays a pivotal role in safeguarding against unauthorized access and data breaches, thereby ensuring that the audit process is accurate and secure.

AI is a powerful tool in the auditor's arsenal for fraud prevention and detection. Its capabilities extend beyond mere number crunching, offering a dynamic, responsive, and proactive approach to identifying and preventing fraudulent activities. With AI, auditors can navigate through the labyrinthine financial landscape with confidence and assurance, knowing that they have a robust and intelligent system to watch their backs.

Risk assessment

Risk assessment is a crucial aspect in the structure of the auditing process that cannot be overlooked or underestimated. AI is invaluable for auditors, providing a nuanced lens through which risks can be identified, evaluated, and understood with unparalleled depth and precision. The following are some ways in which it can assist:

- **Dynamic risk analysis**: The financial landscape is ever-changing, with risks continuing to morph and evolve. AI systems are designed to adapt to these changes dynamically and continuously update the risk profiles based on the latest available data. This dynamic approach to risk analysis ensures that auditors always work with the most current and relevant risk assessments, allowing timely and informed decision-making.

- **Nuanced understanding of risks**: AI does not just identify risks; it understands them. It considers various parameters and their interrelations, weaving a tapestry that represents the complex risk environment associated with an organization's financial statements. This nuanced understanding allows auditors to not only identify risks but also appreciate their origins, implications, and potential impacts on financial statements.

- **Targeted audit approach**: Armed with AI insights, auditors can adopt a more targeted approach to their audits and evaluations of internal controls. They can focus their attention and resources on areas identified as higher risk, ensuring that these critical sections of the financial statements receive the enhanced review and analysis that they require. This targeted approach facilitates a more efficient and effective audit process, with auditors concentrating their efforts where they matter most.

- **Optimized resource allocation**: Efficiency is at the heart of the AI's contribution to risk assessment. By identifying areas of higher risk, AI helps auditors optimize resource allocation. Instead of spreading their efforts thinly across all sections of financial statements, auditors can allocate more time and resources to high-risk areas, ensuring a deeper and more meticulous review of these sections.

- **Predictive risk modeling**: AI employs advanced algorithms and models to predict potential risks before they materialize. These predictive risk models consider various factors and variables and provide auditors with a forward-looking view of the risk landscape. This foresight enables auditors to prepare and plan for potential risks, adopt proactive measures to mitigate these risks, and protect the integrity of financial statements.

- **Interactive risk dashboards**: With AI, auditors have access to interactive dashboards that provide visual representations of the risk landscape. These dashboards allow auditors to interact with risk data, explore various risk scenarios, and understand the potential impacts of different risks on financial statements. The visual and interactive nature of these dashboards makes risk data more accessible and understandable, facilitating informed and insightful risk assessment and audit planning.

Incorporating AI into risk assessment does not simply streamline the process; rather, it transforms it. AI empowers auditors with insights and tools that allow a more nuanced, dynamic, and informed approach to risk assessment. With AI's assistance, auditors can navigate through the complex web of financial risks with confidence and precision, conducting thorough audits that reflect the intricate risk environment that characterizes today's financial landscape.

AI tools in auditing

In auditing, a suite of AI tools and applications are available, each designed meticulously to assist and support auditors as they navigate through their multifaceted and demanding tasks. These tools are not merely electronic assistants; they are sophisticated entities equipped with features such as data mining, predictive analytics, and **natural language processing** (**NLP**), all of which are instrumental in analyzing financial documents and transactions. The following table looks at a few such tools:

Tool Name	Main Functions	Application in Auditing
Audit data analytics (ADA)	Analyzes large datasets efficiently; identifies anomalies and patterns; facilitates risk assessment	Used for swift and efficient analysis of large datasets, providing deep insights and identifying anomalies and patterns crucial for risk assessment
Robotic process automation (RPA)	Automates repetitive, rule-based tasks	Frees up auditors to focus on more analytical and judgmental aspects of the audit, leading to increased productivity and efficiency
NLP	Analyzes and understands textual data; extracts relevant information; conducts sentiment analysis	Assists in analyzing financial reports, contracts, and other textual data, providing valuable insights during the audit process

Table 4.1 - Overview of AI audit tools

Let us delve deeper into the examples provided and understand their functionalities and applications in the auditing environment:

- **ADA**:

  - **Deep data insights**: ADA tools are nothing short of being revolutionary when it comes to analyzing large volumes of data. They do not just skim through the surface; they dive deep, sifting through data layers to extract insights that are not only valuable but often impossible to obtain through manual processes.

  - **Efficient analysis**: Time is essential in auditing. ADA tools understand this well. They are designed to conduct analyses quickly and efficiently, providing auditors with timely insights that can inform and guide the audit process.

- **Visual data representation**: Through interactive dashboards and visual data representation, ADA tools make data accessible and comprehensible for auditors, facilitating a better understanding and interpretation of data insights.

- **RPA**:

  - **Task automation**: RPA takes on the mantle of routine and repetitive tasks that are integral to the audit process but are time-consuming and mundane. From data entry to basic data analysis, RPA automates these tasks with precision, freeing auditors to focus on activities that require strategic thinking and analysis.

  - **Enhanced accuracy**: Accuracy is achieved through automation. RPA eliminates the risk of human error in the tasks it performs, ensuring that the data and insights generated are accurate and reliable.

  - **Streamlined workflow**: By performing routine tasks, the RPA tool streamlines the audit workflow, ensuring that tasks are completed in a systematic and timely manner, contributing to the overall efficiency and effectiveness of the audit process.

- **NLP**:

  - **Contextual understanding**: NLP tools are adept at reading and understanding text, but their true strength lies in their ability to grasp context. They can analyze textual data in financial documents and reports, communicating and understanding the nuances and implications of the language used.

  - **Sentiment analysis**: Beyond understanding text, NLP can gauge the sentiment behind words, providing insights into the tone and mood of financial documents, which can be instrumental in understanding the financial health and stability of an organization.

  - **Document summarization**: NLP tools can summarize lengthy financial documents, providing auditors with concise and comprehensive overviews of the content, making it easier for them to grasp the essence of the documents without having to sift through text pages.

The confluence of these AI tools creates an ecosystem in which data is not merely collected and analyzed; it is understood, interpreted, and utilized to inform and guide the auditing process. Each tool brings its unique set of capabilities to the table, addressing different needs and challenges within the audit environment and making the audit process more efficient, effective, insightful, and informed. The age of AI in auditing is here, and with these tools at their disposal, auditors are better equipped to conduct audits that are rigorous, accurate, and reflective of the complexities of today's financial landscape.

Benefits of AI in auditing

Incorporating AI into the auditing process is not just a matter of staying current with technological advancements; it is also an essential strategy for enhancing the quality and effectiveness of audits. The implementation of AI in auditing brings forth a cascade of benefits that are transformative and far-reaching. Let's take a closer look at these:

Increased accuracy:

- **Minimized human error**: AI operates devoid of the susceptibility to fatigue or oversight that auditors might experience. It meticulously processes and analyzes data, significantly reducing the likelihood of errors that can compromise the integrity of audit procedures, tests, and results.

- **Precision in calculations**: AI can handle complex calculations with absolute precision, ensuring that financial data and insights generated during the audit are accurate and reliable. This level of accuracy is instrumental for making informed and sound financial decisions and audit assessments.

Efficiency:

- **Swift data analysis**: The automation capabilities of AI mean that tasks, especially those related to data analysis and review, are completed expeditiously. With AI, auditors can shift through voluminous datasets in a fraction of the time it would take manually, significantly accelerating the audit process.

- **Optimized workflow**: AI not only speeds up individual tasks but also contributes to a smoother and more streamlined workflow. It allows for seamless integration and coordination of various audit tasks, ensuring that the audit process flows efficiently from one stage to the next without delays or bottlenecks.

Enhanced fraud detection:

- **Proactive fraud identification**: AI does not wait to stumble upon fraudulent activities; it actively seeks them. With its predictive analytics and pattern-recognition capabilities, AI can identify anomalous or suspicious transactions or trends, flagging them for further investigation.

- **Historical data learning**: AI learns from historical data to understand the typical transaction patterns and behaviors associated with a particular account or organization. This learning enables it to identify deviations or anomalies that could signify fraudulent activities and serve as an early warning system for auditors.

Improved risk assessment:

- **Dynamic risk analysis**: AI introduces a dynamic approach to risk analysis. It does not just look at static data; it also considers various parameters and their interrelations, providing a nuanced understanding of the risk landscape associated with an organization's financial statements.

- **Targeted audit focus**: With AI's comprehensive risk analysis, auditors can focus their attention and resources on high-risk areas. This targeted approach ensures that high-risk areas receive the scrutiny they require while resources are not wasted on lower-risk areas.

These benefits collectively contribute to faster, more accurate, insightful, and analytical audits. The use of AI in auditing represents a paradigm shift where audits are not just about compliance and verification but also about understanding, analysis, and strategic financial planning and decision-making. With AI in their toolkit, auditors are better equipped to navigate the complexities of the financial landscape, providing invaluable and indispensable services in today's fast-paced, dynamic business environment.

Diving deeper into AI audit tools

In the constantly evolving auditing landscape, AI tools are invaluable assets for auditors worldwide. These tools are designed to streamline, automate, and enhance the traditional auditing process, thereby allowing for increased audit accuracy and efficiency. Let's dive deeper into these.

Overview of AI audit tools

The advent of AI in the auditing domain marks a significant shift from conventional methods, offering advanced capabilities that auditors can leverage to efficiently navigate through the intricacies of financial data.

The introduction of AI audit tools has revolutionized how auditors approach their tasks, addressing the perennial challenges of time constraints, data volume, and complexity, which often impede the auditing process. With AI's computational power, auditors can now shift through colossal datasets in a fraction of the time it would take to accomplish manually, targeting anomalies and discrepancies with pinpoint accuracy.

AI audit tools embody diverse technologies, each contributing uniquely to the audit process. These tools bring automation to the forefront, thus minimizing the need for manual intervention in data analysis and validation. Automation accelerates the audit life cycle and introduces a level of precision that is unseen in manual methodologies. The elimination of human error, a significant factor in data misinterpretation, ensures that audit findings are reliable and reflective of the financial landscape.

AI audit tools provide auditors with insightful analytics derived from **deep learning** (**DL**) capabilities embedded within the technology. These analytics delve beneath the surface of financial transactions, uncovering patterns and trends that may escape the human eye. The insights gained through AI analytics are instrumental in forming audit strategies that are both proactive and informed, enabling auditors to anticipate and respond to financial risks through agility and foresight.

In a realm where financial transparency and accountability are paramount, AI audit tools are indispensable alliances for auditors. They facilitate a more robust and insightful audit process, empowering auditors with technology to conduct their duties with unprecedented efficiency and accuracy. Through the seamless integration of AI tools, auditors can confidently navigate the dynamic audit environment and ensure that they have the support of cutting-edge technology to guide them through the complex labyrinth of financial auditing.

ADA

ADA refers to technology that enables auditors to analyze large datasets quickly and efficiently. With ADA, auditors can review vast amounts of financial transactions and accounts, providing them with deeper insights and a better understanding of the financial data they are analyzing. ADA tools utilize various analytical procedures, including regression analysis, clustering, and classification, to identify anomalies and patterns in data. In doing so, they facilitate risk assessment and help auditors focus their efforts on areas of higher risk.

In the intricate sphere of auditing, the ability to analyze data swiftly and accurately is imperative. These ADA tools are specifically designed to address this necessity. They are not only adept at handling data of significant volume but also proficient in dissecting the data's complexity, offering auditors a clear lens through which they can examine and interpret the financial narrative unfolding within the data.

One of the standout features of ADA tools is their capacity for predictive analytics. By employing sophisticated algorithms, these tools can forecast future trends and potential risks using historical data. This predictive capability is crucial for auditors as it allows them to anticipate and prepare for future financial scenarios while evaluating the potential need for additional testing procedures, thereby enabling proactive audit planning and risk-mitigation strategies.

ADA tools also embody versatility as they are compatible with various data formats and sources. This compatibility ensures that auditors have the flexibility to seamlessly integrate data from disparate systems, thereby creating a more cohesive and comprehensive data-analysis framework. Whether dealing with structured data from databases or unstructured data from documents and emails, ADA tools can process and analyze this information efficiently.

The visual representation of data is another significant advantage of ADA tools. Through intuitive dashboards and graphic displays, auditors can visualize data trends and patterns, facilitating data interpretation and analysis. These visual elements are not only instrumental for auditors but are also valuable when communicating audit findings to stakeholders, as they provide a more accessible and understandable view of the data.

ADA tools are designed with user-friendly interfaces that do not require advanced technical expertise for navigation. Auditors can leverage these tools with minimal training, which makes ADA a practical solution for audit firms of all sizes, including those with limited resources.

Ultimately, ADA tools are indispensable assets in modern auditor toolkits. They amalgamate speed, accuracy, and depth in data analysis, providing auditors with a robust platform through which they can conduct thorough and insightful audits. Through the power of the ADA, auditors are better equipped to navigate the complex financial terrain, delivering audit results that are not only timely but also more reflective of the true financial picture of the entities they audit.

RPA

RPA is a technology that automates rule-based repetitive tasks within an audit process. RPA tools are designed to mimic an auditor's actions in gathering, processing, and analyzing data. These tools significantly reduce auditors' time on mundane and time-consuming tasks, allowing them to focus on more analytical and judgmental aspects of an audit. With RPA, auditors can increase their productivity and efficiency, leading to timely and cost-effective audits.

Within the broader framework of audit automation, RPA is a pivotal element that acts as a catalyst for enhanced operational efficiency. The power of RPA lies in its ability to execute predefined tasks without human intervention. It can shift through extensive datasets, perform calculations, generate reports, and even flag inconsistencies or anomalies in the data, all at speeds that are unattainable by a human auditor.

One of the primary advantages of RPA is its accuracy. Because it is immune to the fatigue and distraction that human auditors might experience, it performs its tasks with meticulous precision, minimizing the risk of errors. This level of accuracy is particularly crucial when dealing with financial data, in which even minor mistakes can have significant repercussions.

Furthermore, RPA is flexible and scalable. It can be easily configured to perform different tasks and scaled up or down based on the volume of data and the complexity of the audit. This scalability ensures that audit firms of varying sizes and capacities can leverage RPA to effectively streamline their audit processes.

RPA also plays a significant role in enhancing audit quality. By taking over routine and mechanical aspects of data gathering and processing, human auditors can delve deeper into the analysis and interpretation of data. This collaborative synergy between human auditors and RPA allows for a more insightful and thorough audit, contributing to the reliability and credibility of audit findings.

The implementation of RPA translates into cost savings for audit firms and their clients. With automated processes handling the heavy lifting of data, firms can allocate their human resources more strategically, focusing on areas that require critical thinking and expert judgment. This efficient allocation of resources not only reduces operational costs but also shortens the audit cycle and delivers timely results to clients.

RPA is a transformative technology in the realm of auditing. Its contributions to efficiency, accuracy, and quality are invaluable, making it an essential tool for auditors committed to delivering excellence in their engagements. Whether for a small-scale audit or a large-scale examination of multinational corporations, RPA is a reliable ally, facilitating a smooth and efficient audit process from start to finish.

NLP

NLP is a subset of AI that enables computers to understand, interpret, and generate communications in human language. In auditing, NLP tools can analyze textual data such as financial reports and contracts and extract relevant information for auditors. NLP can also help with sentiment analysis, which can be crucial in understanding the tone and content of financial disclosures, providing additional insights to auditors during their analysis.

NLP's capabilities extend beyond mere text extraction to include the comprehension and analysis of nuances in the language used in financial documents, board meetings, and analyst/earnings calls. This technology is adept at identifying subtle cues in language that might indicate potential risks or areas of concern, such as uncertainty or lack of clarity in financial disclosures. Such insights are invaluable to auditors as they can pinpoint areas that require closer scrutiny and review.

Auditors often encounter voluminous and dense documents such as regulatory filings, shareholder reports, or transaction records. Manually sifting through these pages to extract pertinent information is not only time-consuming but also prone to oversight and error. However, with NLP, auditors can swiftly and accurately navigate through these texts, isolating and extracting data crucial for their audit analysis. This accelerates the auditing process and enhances its precision and reliability.

In addition, NLP supports auditors in dealing with diverse formats and sources of textual data. Financial data is often dispersed across different documents and systems, and sometimes in unstructured forms. NLP tools are designed to handle this diversity efficiently, assimilating data from various sources into a coherent and accessible format for auditors. This capability is particularly beneficial for auditing firms with complex operations and multiple reporting structures.

Sentiment analysis, a distinctive feature of NLP, offers auditors a unique perspective. By analyzing the sentiment conveyed in financial communications and disclosures, auditors gain insights into a company's confidence level, outlook, and possibly even undisclosed challenges or issues. This analysis provides an additional layer of understanding, supplementing quantitative data with qualitative insights that contribute to a more holistic audit assessment.

Furthermore, the integration of NLP into audit processes promotes a more proactive auditing approach. Instead of reacting to issues identified through traditional audit methods, auditors equipped with NLP tools can preemptively identify potential areas of risk or concern through their analysis of language and sentiment in financial disclosures. This proactive stance enables auditors to address and mitigate risks before they escalate to significant problems.

In a continuously advancing audit environment, NLP is a powerful and indispensable tool for modern auditors. NLP enhances the scope, accuracy, and efficiency of audit processes through its ability to understand, interpret, and analyze human language in financial documents, leading to more insightful and reliable outcomes.

Selecting the right AI audit tool

Choosing an appropriate AI audit tool is paramount to the success of the audit process. Firms should consider the specific needs and objectives of their audits, the volume and type of data to be analyzed, and the desired outcomes of the audit. It is also essential to consider the tool's ease of use, integration capabilities with existing systems, and level of support and training provided by the vendor of the tool. Conducting a thorough assessment and comparing the different tools available in the market, considering their features and limitations and level of AI integration, will guide firms in selecting the AI audit tool that best suits their needs.

In the selection process, understanding the distinct challenges and requirements of the audit engagement is fundamental. Different audit engagements may demand various functionalities and capabilities from AI audit tools. For instance, an audit that focuses primarily on detecting fraud might require a tool with robust anomaly detection and predictive analytics features. Audits dealing with voluminous transaction data might require tools with powerful data analytics and processing capacities.

Compatibility with the existing technological infrastructure of an audit firm is another critical factor. The selected AI tool should seamlessly integrate with the current systems and software that the firm utilizes, minimizing disruption and facilitating a smooth transition. Integration ensures that the tool can efficiently exchange and process data with other applications, thereby enhancing the functionality of the tool and the audit team's productivity.

The user-friendliness of an AI audit tool also plays a crucial role in its successful implementation and use. Tools that offer intuitive interfaces and user experiences reduce the learning curve for auditors, promoting quicker adoption and more effective utilization. A tool that is difficult to navigate or understand can impede the audit process rather than facilitate it, leading to inefficiencies and frustrations among the audit team.

Support and training are indispensable aspects that should be considered. Vendors should provide adequate training resources and support to assist auditors in mastering the tool. Comprehensive training ensures that auditors can leverage the tool's full suite of features and capabilities, thus maximizing the value derived from its use. Continuous support from the vendor is also vital as it guarantees prompt assistance and resolution of any issues or challenges encountered while using the tool.

Furthermore, firms should weigh the cost implications of acquiring and implementing AI audit tools. While AI tools bring invaluable benefits to the audit process, they also entail investments. Firms should conduct a **cost-benefit analysis (CBA)** to ascertain how a tool's value proposition aligns with budgetary constraints and financial expectations.

Finally, considering the dynamic and rapidly evolving nature of technology, it is wise to select a scalable and adaptable tool allowing for future changes and advancements. The tool should evolve with the changing landscape of auditing and technology, accommodating new features and updates that respond to emerging audit challenges and needs.

By meticulously evaluating these factors, audit firms can ensure that they select an AI audit tool that not only meets their immediate needs but also serves as a long-term asset that contributes significantly to the efficiency, accuracy, and success of their audit engagements.

Best practices for implementing AI audit tools

Let us look at some best practices for implementing AI tools:

- **Understanding the tool**: Before implementation, auditors should have a comprehensive understanding of how the AI audit tool functions, its capabilities, and its limitations. This in-depth knowledge is fundamental as it allows auditors to leverage the tool's features fully and efficiently, thereby enhancing the audit process. Furthermore, understanding the limitations of the tool is essential as it helps set realistic expectations and prepares the audit team for potential challenges they may encounter during the audit process.

- **Training and support**: Continuous training and support are crucial for auditors to effectively use AI audit tools. Firms should invest in training programs and provide adequate support to auditors during their implementation. This support system should not only be limited to the initial stages of implementation but should also be ongoing. Continuous training programs should be developed and offered to keep auditors updated on the tool's newest features and best practices, fostering an environment of continuous learning and improvement.

- **Data quality**: The effectiveness of AI audit tools is highly dependent on the quality of the data analyzed. Ensuring that this data is accurate, complete, and reliable is fundamental for the success of AI in auditing. Auditors should work closely with their clients to establish data quality protocols and standards, ensuring that the data fed into AI audit tools is of high quality. Appropriate data governance practices, including data validation, cleansing, and enrichment, should be implemented to maintain data integrity and reliability over time.

- **Ethical considerations**: Auditors should be aware of ethical considerations related to the use of AI, including issues related to bias, transparency, and accountability. When implementing AI audit tools, firms should establish a code of ethics and guidelines to address these concerns. Ethical considerations should guide the use of AI in auditing to ensure that the audit process is fair, unbiased, and transparent, thereby building trust among clients and stakeholders.

- **Continuous improvement**: Similar to AI technology, the audit profession is continuously evolving. Firms should regularly update and improve their AI audit tools to adapt to changes in the auditing landscape and technological advancement. Adopting a culture of continuous improvement and innovation is essential. Audit firms should actively seek feedback from their auditors and clients on the tool's performance and usability using this valuable input to make iterative improvements and enhancements. Engaging with AI audit tool vendors for regular updates and staying informed about the latest technological trends and innovations in AI and auditing are also advisable.

By following these best practices, audit firms can ensure smooth and effective implementation of AI audit tools, unlocking their potential to revolutionize the audit process, drive efficiency, enhance accuracy, and deliver value to clients and stakeholders alike.

Ethical considerations in AI auditing

Let's navigate through the landscape of ethical considerations shaping the integrity and trustworthiness of audit processes driven by AI:

Ethical Consideration	Description	Importance in Auditing
Understanding and mitigating AI bias	AI tools might perpetuate or exacerbate biases present in the training data, affecting the impartiality of audit processes and outcomes	Critical for ensuring fairness and impartiality in AI-driven audit processes
Ensuring data privacy and security	With AI tools processing large volumes of sensitive data, there are heightened concerns about data security and confidentiality	Paramount for complying with data protection laws and safeguarding client data
Adhering to ethical guidelines	Developing and following ethical guidelines is crucial for maintaining the integrity and public trust in the audit profession	Necessary for navigating ethical dilemmas and challenges presented by AI in auditing

Table 4.2 – Ethical considerations in AI auditing

By dissecting these ethical considerations and understanding their pivotal role in the auditing domain, we illuminate the path to fostering ethical AI practices that uphold the core tenets of accountability, transparency, and ethical integrity in audit processes within accounting information systems.

Understanding bias in AI

Bias in AI systems, including those used in auditing, can significantly impact the fairness and impartiality of audit processes and outcomes. AI bias occurs when AI tools make assumptions based on the data on which they are trained. If the training data contains biases, the AI system is likely to perpetuate or exacerbate these biases. Additionally, the methodology and practices of the developer creating the AI may also impose inherent biases.

In the auditing sector, bias can manifest in various intricate ways, subtly influencing the AI's decision-making process. For example, an AI system might prioritize or neglect certain transactions or accounts based on biased criteria, such as the size of the company, industry type, or geographical location, which are inadvertently introduced during the training phase. This skewed focus can result in unfair or inaccurate audit outcomes, potentially harming certain businesses while favoring others.

Given the serious implications of bias, it is imperative for auditors and accounting firms to be vigilant and proactive in identifying, mitigating, and preventing bias in AI systems used for auditing. This proactive approach requires a multifaceted strategy.

First, careful selection and preparation of training data are vital. Using diverse and representative datasets helps to minimize the risk of embedding bias into the AI system. Auditors should scrutinize the data for any signs of bias or imbalance to ensure a fair representation of various business types, sizes, and sectors.

Furthermore, continuous testing and validation of AI outputs against known benchmarks and real-world scenarios are crucial. This ongoing process helps in the early identification of bias, allowing for timely adjustments and recalibrations of the AI system to correct skewed decision-making patterns.

Transparency is another cornerstone of combating AI bias in auditing. Auditors and firms must openly communicate with stakeholders, clients, and regulatory bodies about the AI tools they use, explicitly outlining their potential biases and limitations. Clear documentation of the AI system's decision-making process, criteria, and data sources can foster better understanding and trust among stakeholders.

Fostering an organizational culture that is aware of and sensitive to issues related to AI bias is essential. Training programs and awareness campaigns can equip auditors with the knowledge and skills necessary to effectively navigate challenges posed by AI bias.

In the dynamic field of auditing, where the accuracy and fairness of financial assessment are paramount, addressing AI bias is not just a technical requirement but also a fundamental ethical obligation. By taking deliberate steps to understand, mitigate, and prevent bias, auditors and accounting firms can harness the full potential of AI in auditing, thereby ensuring that it serves as an instrument of fair and impartial financial scrutiny.

Ensuring data privacy and security

Data privacy and security are paramount in the digital information age, especially in auditing, where sensitive financial data is handled. AI tools process large volumes of data, raising concerns regarding the security and confidentiality of information. Auditors and firms must adhere to strict data protection laws and industry standards in order to safeguard client data. This involves implementing robust security protocols, including data encryption, access control, and secure data storage and transmission methods. Furthermore, the use of AI should comply with privacy regulations, and clients should be informed about the extent and manner of AI's involvement in handling and analyzing their data.

In auditing, where confidential financial records and sensitive company information are routinely processed, the importance of data privacy and security cannot be overstated. The integration of AI tools into auditing practices introduces additional layers of complexity to the challenging task of securing and protecting data.

AI audit tools often require access to comprehensive datasets to function optimally, aggregating data from various sources, including confidential client information, transaction histories, and financial statements. The wide-reaching access and processing capabilities of AI tools necessitate stringent security measures to prevent unauthorized access, data breaches, and other security incidents that could compromise client data.

First, firms must be aware of and compliant with all relevant data protection legislation and regulations in their jurisdiction, such as the **General Data Protection Regulation** (**GDPR**) in Europe or the **California Consumer Privacy Act** (**CCPA**) in the US. These regulations impose strict requirements on the collection, processing, storage, and transmission of personal data, with severe penalties for non-compliance.

In addition to compliance, firms should adopt best practices in data security. Employing advanced encryption techniques is crucial for protecting data, both in transit and at rest. **Secure Sockets Layer** (**SSL**) encryption for data in transit and the **Advanced Encryption Standard** (**AES**) for data at rest are industry-standard practices that provide robust protection against unauthorized access.

Access control is another vital component of a secure AI auditing environment. Implementing a **role-based access control** (**RBAC**) system ensures that only authorized individuals have access to specific data and system functionalities. This approach minimizes the risk of internal data breaches and unauthorized access.

Secure data storage solutions, including the use of secure cloud services or on-premise servers with adequate security protocols, are essential. Firms should carefully evaluate their data storage options, considering factors such as the sensitivity of the data, regulatory requirements, and the firm's specific data access and usage needs.

Client transparency is also crucial. Clients should be fully informed of how their data is being used, processed, and protected when AI auditing tools are deployed. Clear communication helps to build trust and ensures that clients understand the measures to secure their data.

Finally, a proactive approach to security is vital. Regular security audits, penetration testing, and vulnerability assessments should be conducted to proactively identify and address potential security risks. By actively seeking to improve and fortify their data privacy and security measures, auditing firms can comply with regulatory requirements and foster trust in their clients and stakeholders, ensuring that their sensitive financial data is safe.

Ethical guidelines for AI in auditing

Developing and adhering to ethical guidelines for AI in auditing is crucial for maintaining integrity and public trust in the auditing profession. These guidelines should address bias, transparency, accountability, and data privacy issues. Firms should establish clear principles and standards to guide the ethical use of AI in auditing. This involves creating a framework for ethical considerations, training auditors on ethical issues related to AI, and establishing mechanisms for monitoring and ensuring compliance with ethical standards. Engaging with professional bodies, regulators, and stakeholders in developing and refining these guidelines can contribute to their robustness and acceptance in broader industry and society.

Ethical guidelines for AI in auditing should start with a commitment to fairness and impartiality, acknowledging the potential of AI systems to inadvertently perpetuate or exacerbate biases present in the training data. Firms must actively work to identify and mitigate these biases, ensuring that AI tools provide fair and unbiased analyses and results. This commitment should be mirrored in a firm's corporate responsibility and ethics statements, underscoring the importance of ethical AI use.

Transparency is another cornerstone of the use of ethical AI in auditing. Firms should be open to the AI tools and technologies they deploy, providing clients, regulators, and the public with insights into how they use AI, the nature of the data it analyzes, and the decisions it makes. Transparency builds trust among stakeholders and contributes to a better understanding and acceptance of AI during the auditing process.

Accountability mechanisms should be established to ensure that ethical guidelines are not merely aspirational but are actively enforced. This includes developing processes for auditing the use of AI tools, holding individuals and teams accountable for ethical AI use, and establishing clear consequences for the violation of ethical guidelines. Internal audits, reviews, and assessments of AI tool deployment and use should be conducted regularly to ensure compliance with ethical standards and guidelines.

Continuous training and education of audit professionals on ethical considerations and challenges associated with AI are paramount. As AI technologies evolve, so do ethical considerations and challenges associated with their use. Auditors should be equipped with the knowledge and skills to navigate these challenges effectively to be able to make informed and ethical decisions in their use of AI tools.

Engaging in dialogue and collaboration with external bodies, including industry associations, regulatory agencies, and ethics boards, is vital. Participating in these external engagements facilitates the sharing of best practices, insights, and updates regarding the ethical use of AI in auditing. It also helps align the firm's internal ethical guidelines with industry standards and expectations, fostering consistency and coherence in ethical practices adopted across the auditing profession.

Finally, firms should encourage a culture of ethical awareness and responsibility among professionals. Ethical considerations should be embedded in decision-making processes, with auditors encouraged to reflect on and consider the ethical implications of their actions and decisions when using AI tools. Fostering an ethical culture supports compliance with external regulations and guidelines and builds a firm's reputation as a responsible and ethical actor in the auditing space, contributing positively to public trust and confidence in the auditing profession.

The future of AI in auditing

Let's peer into the horizon of auditing as AI reshapes the landscape of this critical domain within accounting information systems. In the following table, we discover the evolving roles and competencies that define the future auditor in the era of AI-driven auditing practices:

Skill/Competency	Importance in AI-Driven Auditing
Understanding of AI and related technologies	Essential for interacting with and managing AI-driven tools and platforms effectively
Data analytics skills	Necessary for interpreting results generated by AI tools and working with large datasets

Skill/Competency	Importance in AI-Driven Auditing
Critical thinking and problem-solving	Vital for scrutinizing AI-generated insights and devising solutions to complex problems
Ethical considerations and professional skepticism	Fundamental for approaching AI tools ethically and responsibly
Continuous learning and professional development	Crucial to stay updated on the latest trends, technologies, and best practices in AI-driven auditing

Table 4.3 – Skills and competencies for future auditors

Next, let's explore the evolving audit landscape in more detail.

The evolving audit landscape

The audit landscape is in a perpetual state of evolution, responding agilely to rapid technological advancements, modifications in financial reporting and auditing standards, and the dynamic shift in global business models. In this fluid context, the imperative for audits that are not only accurate and timely but also insightful is accentuated, underscoring the critical role they play in ensuring financial transparency and accountability.

Emerging technologies are at the forefront of significant changes in the audit sector, with AI being particularly instrumental. AI is not merely another tool in the auditor's arsenal; instead, it represents a transformative force set to redefine the essence of auditing, offering unprecedented opportunities to enhance efficiency, accuracy, and insight generation.

As we navigate through the coming years, the expectation is not just incremental changes but a substantial overhaul in the way auditing functions are conceived and executed. AI's integration into the audit landscape is not a matter of if but when, and its impact will be multifaceted. On a fundamental level, AI will take on the heavy lifting associated with routine, mundane, and time-consuming tasks that have long characterized the audit process. This automation capability enables auditors to engage more deeply with the analytical aspects of auditing.

However, the influence of AI extends beyond automation. This will empower auditors with enhanced analytical capabilities, serving as a sophisticated ally in sifting through voluminous financial data to extract nuanced insights that would otherwise remain obscure. In doing so, AI acts as a catalyst, enabling auditors to delve deeper and uncover stories and trends hidden within the data, providing a richer and more informed understanding of an organization's financial health and risks.

This seismic shift caused by AI does not occur in a vacuum. This necessitates a corresponding transformation of audit methodologies and practices. Traditional approaches need to be re-evaluated and recalibrated to align with the capabilities and potential offered by AI. This realignment also extends to human capital within the audit profession. The skills profile, competencies, and expertise required of auditing professionals will undergo significant changes, with a premium placed on individuals who not only understand auditing but are also fluent in the language, applications, and possibilities of AI.

This evolution paints the picture of an audit landscape that is adaptive, forward-looking, and responsive to changing demands and complexities of the business environment. With AI as a central player in this unfolding scenario, the future of auditing appears poised for a period of exciting, transformative, and far-reaching change, promising a new era in which audits are more accurate, timely, insightful, and reflective of the complex financial tapestry they seek to examine and verify.

The role of AI in future auditing

AI is poised to play a central and indispensable role in future auditing processes, serving as a catalyst for enhanced efficiency and precision. The transformative potential of AI in auditing is multifaceted, offering a suite of capabilities set to fundamentally redefine the audit practice.

First, AI's unparalleled ability to process expansive datasets in real time constitutes a game changer for the audit profession. This real-time data processing capability will not merely streamline existing processes but will revolutionize the way auditors interact with, analyze, and interpret financial records and transactions. The ability to analyze entire populations of transactions, as opposed to relying on samples, provides auditors with a panoramic and more comprehensive view of an organization's financial landscape. This holistic perspective facilitates a deeper understanding and more accurate representation of a firm's financial position, ensuring that audits reflect a more complete financial picture.

In addition to revolutionizing data analysis, AI plays a pivotal role in proactive risk management during the auditing process. By identifying and flagging potential issues and anomalies at their nascent stages, AI enables auditors and organizations alike to address and mitigate risks before they burgeon into significant insurmountable problems. This proactive approach to risk management is facilitated by AI's advanced predictive analytics and sophisticated ML algorithms. These technologies empower AI tools to not only identify but also anticipate financial risks and irregularities with a degree of accuracy and foresight that was previously unattainable. This predictive capability provides auditors with a powerful tool for foresight, enabling them to adopt preventive measures and strategies to proactively safeguard against financial risk.

The role of AI in auditing is further amplified when considering the labyrinthine and ever-evolving regulatory environment that characterizes the financial sector. With financial regulations undergoing continuous modifications and updates, staying compliant is challenging. AI equipped with NLP serves as a valuable tool in this context. NLP enables AI tools to interpret, understand, and integrate new compliance requirements and regulatory changes. This ensures that audits are not only compliant but also aligned with the most current and relevant legal and regulatory standards, safeguarding against legal infractions and non-compliance.

Finally, and perhaps most significantly, the integration and adoption of AI within the auditing process is set to substantially enhance the value proposition offered to clients. With AI at the helm, audits are characterized by an unparalleled level of accuracy and insight driven by data analytics. These data-driven insights, borne out of AI's analytical prowess, provide auditors with a basis for delivering strategic informed advice to clients. Such counsel is invaluable for organizations seeking to understand their current financial performance and improve and optimize their financial and risk management practices. Through AI, audits will transition from retrospective analysis to a tool for prospective, strategic financial planning and decision-making, marking a significant evolution in the value and role of audits within an organization's broader financial strategy.

Preparing for the future – skills and competencies

With AI steadily becoming an indispensable component in the auditing realm, it is imperative for professionals in the field to proactively equip themselves with a novel set of skills and competencies tailored to this technological landscape. The integration of AI into auditing is not merely a supplementary addition; it represents a fundamental shift in the auditing process, necessitating auditors to have a robust understanding of AI and related technologies. This understanding is non-negotiable as it forms the basis for the effective interaction, management, and extraction of insights from AI-driven tools and platforms that are increasingly becoming the bedrock of modern auditing practices.

Auditors in the future will need to be proficient in data analytics, possessing the requisite skills for interpreting, critically analyzing, and evaluating results generated by AI tools. The ability to work adeptly with large and complex datasets, apply statistical techniques with precision, and visualize data in a manner that conveys findings clearly and compellingly are non-negotiable skills. These competencies enable auditors to communicate complex data and insights in an accessible manner, facilitating informed decision-making and strategic planning.

Critical thinking and acute problem-solving skills are of unprecedented importance in this AI-driven auditing landscape. Auditors are called upon to scrutinize AI-generated insights with a discerning eye, identifying potential issues, anomalies, or inaccuracies with precision and alacrity. Furthermore, they must be equipped to devise innovative and effective solutions to complex, multifaceted problems, navigating through the intricacies of financial data and AI-generated insights with expertise and confidence.

In a profession in which ethical considerations and professional skepticism have always been paramount, the advent of AI further accentuates the importance of these principles. Auditors must navigate AI tools and processes with a steadfast commitment to ethical considerations and approach these advanced technologies responsibly and conscientiously. Ensuring that AI-driven processes are fair, impartial, transparent, and accountable, this ethical approach safeguards against bias and ensures that AI is used to uphold the integrity and credibility of the auditing profession.

The dynamic and rapidly evolving nature of AI technologies makes continuous learning and professional development non-negotiable for auditors. Staying abreast of the latest trends, technologies, and best practices in AI-driven auditing is a perennial requirement, not a one-time effort. The future of auditing is characterized by constant change and evolution, demanding a workforce that is adaptable, tech-savvy, and unequivocally committed to excellence, ethics, and continuous improvement in delivering high-quality audit services. The auditor of the future is not just a financial expert but a technologically astute professional, equipped and ready to leverage AI for enhanced auditing practices.

Summary

In this chapter, it is essential to take a moment to assimilate and reflect on the crucial insights and extensive knowledge about the revolutionary impact of AI in auditing:

- **AI audit tool overview**: AI audit tools have emerged as irreplaceable assets in the modern auditing landscape. These tools are not merely accessories but also pivotal elements that bring unparalleled efficiency and accuracy to the table. They act as linchpins that facilitate a smoother, more streamlined approach to data analysis, fraud detection, risk assessment, and myriad other tasks integral to the auditing process. The introduction and incorporation of these advanced technological tools significantly elevate the efficacy and precision of traditional auditing methodologies, making them indispensable in the current scenario.

- **Understanding AI tools**:

  - **ADA**: ADA is a technological marvel that empowers auditors with the capability to analyze vast datasets swiftly and efficiently. This rapid analysis is not superficial; instead, it allows for deep, insightful exploration of data, shedding light on anomalies and patterns that might otherwise escape notice. Such insights are instrumental in conducting thorough risk assessments, making ADA a cornerstone of the auditing process.

  - **RPA**: RPA is an invaluable tool in the auditor's toolkit. It takes over repetitive, rule-bound tasks and executes them quickly and accurately. This automation frees auditors from the shackles of mundane tasks, allowing them to channel their expertise and focus on more analytical and judgment-intensive aspects of the audit process.

  - **NLP**: NLP is a specialized AI subset that provides the ability to analyze textual data meticulously. It does not just parse through text; it extracts relevant and crucial information and assists in conducting sentiment analysis, acting as an invaluable ally during the audit process by providing insights that are both deep and valuable.

- **Ethical considerations**: Ethical aspects must be considered when discussing AI during auditing. These considerations are not afterthoughts but integral to the process, demanding immediate attention and respect. Understanding and mitigating AI bias, ensuring the privacy and security of data, and adhering to ethical guidelines crafted for AI in auditing are non-negotiable. These ethical standards and considerations act as guiding lights, ensuring that the path of AI in auditing is not only innovative but also conscientious and responsible.

- **Future of AI in auditing**: The horizon of auditing is witnessing a transformative phase, with AI gearing up to play a central pivotal role in this transformation. In the future, glistening with promises of innovation and efficiency, auditors must brace themselves and acquire new skills and competencies. Future auditors need to be well versed in data analytics, possess razor-sharp critical-thinking abilities, approach AI tools with a deep sense of ethics and responsibility, and be committed to the path of continuous learning and professional development. The auditor of tomorrow needs to be a blend of the traditional and modern, ready to embrace the future with open arms and a prepared mind.

Closing thoughts

As we traverse and navigate through the intricate and complex tapestry of AI in auditing, the image that emerges is crystal-clear and unequivocal. AI is not merely a supplementary tool that makes the auditor's job easier. Rather, it is a transformative force: a dynamo of change that is actively reshaping, redefining, and reimagining the contours, boundaries, and essence of auditing.

AI's integration into the field is not a silent convergence but a herald of a new era. Unprecedented levels of efficiency and accuracy characterize this epoch in the annals of auditing, and it is marked by an analysis that is not just deep but also insightful. This amalgamation lays down a robust and unshakeable foundation that supports informed decision-making and strategic planning, both of which are indispensable in today's fast-paced and ever-changing business environment.

It is imperative to remember that a great power brings about even greater responsibility. Seamless adoption and integration of AI in auditing is not a task to be taken lightly. This demands a thoughtful, careful, and conscientious approach. This approach should balance the relentless pursuit of innovation with a steadfast, unwavering commitment to the principles of ethics, integrity, and professionalism that have long defined the auditing profession.

Auditors must adopt a proactive stance toward learning and development rather than being reactive. This proactive approach ensures that auditors are not only equipped with but also proficient in the skills and knowledge necessary to harness the immense power of AI effectively, efficiently, and ethically.

Standing at the cusp of this thrilling and exciting juncture, the future of auditing with AI as its partner and ally unfolds before our eyes as a landscape. However, it is not a barren or mundane landscape; it is brimming and overflowing with potential and opportunities that are just waiting to be tapped and explored.

This future is because auditors and accounting professionals engage with AI. However, this engagement is not meant to be passive, with auditors being mere recipients or beneficiaries of AI's capabilities. Instead, auditors need to step forward as active participants, contributors, and architects of a future, where auditing is defined not only by excellence and innovation but also by ethical responsibility and accountability.

As we embark on this shared and collective journey of integrating AI into auditing, it is essential to recognize that it is indeed a shared endeavor. This journey invites and welcomes collaboration, dialogue, and engagement from all stakeholders in the auditing ecosystem. From those who practice auditing to those who rely on their findings, everyone has a role to play and a contribution to make.

Together, as we navigate through the labyrinth of challenges and possibilities, and as we explore opportunities and potential that lie in wait, the future of AI in auditing promises to be not just transformative but also enriching. It promises to be a journey not just about reaching a destination but also about the learning, experiences, and insights gained along the way. For all involved, the journey of AI in auditing is set to be an adventure of discovery, learning, and growth, promising rewards and insights that are as substantial as they are transformative.

Further reading

The realm of AI in auditing is extensive and continually evolving, with new insights and practices emerging. For readers interested in deepening their understanding and staying informed about the latest developments in AI-assisted auditing, the following resources and readings are highly recommended:

- *Auditing in the age of artificial intelligence* (`https://www.audit.vic.gov.au/ sites/default/files/IMPACT-2020/Auditing%20in%20the%20Age%20 of%20Artificial%20Intelligence.pdf`): This resource was designed for auditing professionals to navigate the AI landscape. It provides essential information, tools, and best practices to help auditors effectively use AI in their work, highlighting the importance of ethics, bias mitigation, and continuous learning.

- *Ethics of Artificial Intelligence* (`https://www.unesco.org/en/artificial- intelligence/recommendation-ethics`): Focusing on ethics, this guide addresses unique challenges and considerations involved in using AI. It is a crucial resource for auditors committed to ethical practice and responsible for AI use in their profession.

- *Auditing with AI: How AI is transforming auditing* (`https://www.theaccessgroup. com/en-au/blog/act-ai-auditing/#:~:text=AI%20in%20auditing%20 processes%20can,risk%20and%20prioritise%20audit%20tasks`): Looking at the future of the auditing profession, this blog explores how AI is set to transform auditing, offering insights into the skills and competencies required of auditors in the age of AI. It provides practical guidance for auditors preparing for a future defined by AI and technology.

- *How artificial intelligence will impact accounting* (`https://www.icaew.com/technical/ technology/artificial-intelligence/artificial-intelligence- articles/how-artificial-intelligence-will-impact-accounting`): Engaging with a community of professionals, scholars, and experts in the field of AI in auditing, these platforms provide space for discussion, collaboration, and knowledge sharing among individuals interested in the transformative impact of AI on auditing.

Q&A

Next are reflective queries and answers. These answers offer a concise representation of key insights and learning points explored throughout the text:

1. How do AI audit tools enhance traditional auditing processes?

    AI audit tools significantly enhance the traditional auditing process by introducing efficiency, accuracy, and depth to data analysis and review. They automate routine tasks, thereby freeing auditors to focus on analytical and judgmental aspects of the audit, and provide deep insights by swiftly and efficiently analyzing large datasets. AI also plays a crucial role in risk assessment, fraud detection, and sentiment analysis, offering a comprehensive auditing approach.

2. What are the key ethical considerations in implementing AI in auditing?

    Ethical considerations are paramount when implementing AI in auditing. This includes understanding and mitigating AI bias, ensuring data privacy and security, and adhering to ethical guidelines crafted for AI during auditing. Auditors and firms must approach AI tools ethically and responsibly, ensuring that processes are fair, transparent, and accountable.

3. How can auditors prepare for the future integration of AI into auditing?

    Preparation for the future integration of AI in auditing requires the acquisition of new skills and competencies. Auditors must have a strong understanding of AI and related technologies, develop data analytics skills, and hone their critical thinking and problem-solving abilities. Ethical considerations continue to be fundamental, and auditors must engage in continuous learning and professional development to stay abreast of the latest trends, technologies, and best practices in AI-driven auditing.

4. What role will AI play in the auditing future?

    AI will play a pivotal role in the auditing future by introducing increased efficiency, accuracy, and proactive risk management. This facilitates the analysis of the entire population of transactions, enabling a comprehensive view of an organization's financial position and audit risks. AI will also assist in navigating complex regulatory environments and enhancing value delivered to clients through accurate data-driven insights and strategic advice.

5

Integrating AI with Fraud Examination and Forensic Accounting

"Efficiency is doing better what is already being done."

- Peter Drucker, Economist

The advent of **artificial intelligence (AI)** has ushered in a transformative era in numerous fields. Its influence on fraud examination and forensic accounting is particularly noteworthy. This chapter delves into AI's significant role in these domains, outlining how its integration enhances existing practices and paves the way for new methodologies and strategies in detecting and preventing financial fraud.

The significance of AI in fraud examination and forensic accounting

In the realm of fraud examination and forensic accounting, the utilization of AI marks a pivotal shift from traditional, often labor-intensive methods to more sophisticated, data-driven approaches. AI technologies, including machine learning algorithms and advanced analytics, offer unparalleled capabilities in processing vast amounts of data with speed and accuracy that human auditors might find unattainable. These capabilities are crucial in identifying patterns, anomalies, and trends that could indicate fraudulent activities.

AI's impact is seen in various aspects of fraud examination and forensic accounting, from automating routine tasks to providing deep insights through data analysis. For instance, AI systems can continuously monitor financial transactions to detect irregularities, reducing the time lag between the occurrence of fraud and its detection. Additionally, AI tools can learn and adapt over time, becoming more efficient in identifying complex fraud schemes that might evade traditional detection methods.

The evolving role of AI in detecting and preventing financial fraud

The role of AI in fraud examination and forensic accounting is evolving rapidly, driven by technological advancements and the increasing sophistication of financial fraud schemes. Modern AI systems are not merely tools for data analysis; they are becoming integral components in strategic planning for fraud prevention and detection. They enhance the ability to predict potential fraud scenarios, allowing organizations to implement proactive measures to mitigate risks.

AI is instrumental in enhancing the accuracy of fraud detection. By analyzing historical data, AI can identify patterns and establish benchmarks against which current transactions are compared. This not only helps in detecting known types of fraud but also in uncovering new patterns that may signify emerging fraud risks.

In conclusion, integrating AI into fraud examination and forensic accounting represents a significant leap forward in the fight against financial fraud. Its ability to process and analyze data at scale and its predictive capabilities make it an invaluable asset in detecting and preventing fraudulent activities. As this technology continues to evolve, it promises to revolutionize these fields further, making them more efficient, accurate, and proactive. This evolution signals a paradigm shift in how financial oversight and investigative processes are conducted, emphasizing the need for professionals in these fields to adapt and harness the power of AI. The subsequent sections of this chapter will explore the specific AI technologies being employed, their practical applications, and the challenges and opportunities they present in the context of fraud examination and forensic accounting in detail.

The landscape of fraud and forensic accounting

The field of fraud examination and forensic accounting has long been a bastion of financial integrity and accountability. This section provides an overview of the traditional practices in these fields and discusses their common challenges and limitations.

Traditional practices in fraud examination and forensic accounting

Fraud examination and forensic accounting have historically relied on a combination of meticulous financial analysis, investigative skills, and legal knowledge. The following are some traditional practices in these fields:

- **Detailed financial record analysis**: Forensic accountants and fraud examiners meticulously review financial records, looking for inconsistencies and anomalies that might indicate fraudulent activity

- **Interviews and interrogations**: These professionals often conduct interviews with individuals who might know what's relevant to a financial investigation, gathering information and insights that can aid in uncovering fraudulent activities

- **Legal and compliance knowledge**: A deep understanding of legal frameworks and compliance standards is crucial as these guide the investigation process and ensure adherence to regulatory requirements

- **Utilization of standard accounting and auditing techniques**: Traditional techniques such as reconciliation, sampling, and ratio analysis are employed to scrutinize financial statements and transactions

Common challenges and limitations in conventional methods

While traditional methods in fraud examination and forensic accounting have been influential to a certain extent, they face several challenges and limitations:

- **Volume and complexity of data**: The sheer volume of financial data and the complexity of financial transactions in today's digital age can be overwhelming. Traditional methods may not be sufficient to analyze large datasets effectively, leading to potential oversights.

- **Time-consuming processes**: Manual analysis of financial records is a time-consuming process that can delay the detection and resolution of fraudulent activities. This lag can result in increased financial losses and hinder the ability to take timely corrective actions.

- **Evolving nature of fraud**: As fraudulent schemes become more sophisticated, traditional methods may struggle to keep pace. New types of fraud are constantly emerging, often exploiting the latest technologies, making them harder to detect with conventional techniques.

- **Reliance on human expertise**: Traditional fraud examination and forensic accounting heavily rely on the expertise and judgment of individuals. This reliance can introduce biases and inconsistencies in the investigative process.

- **Cost-effectiveness**: Conducting thorough investigations using traditional methods can be resource-intensive and costly, especially for smaller organizations or cases involving extensive financial histories.

While traditional practices in fraud examination and forensic accounting have laid a strong foundation for financial investigation, the evolving landscape of financial transactions and the advent of sophisticated fraudulent schemes need to be reevaluated. The following table provides a concise overview of what was covered in this section:

Aspect	Traditional Practices	Challenges and Limitations
Financial record analysis	Detailed review of financial records for inconsistencies and anomalies	Overwhelmed by the volume and complexity of data in the digital age
Interviews and interrogations	Conducting interviews to gather information relevant to financial investigations	Time-consuming and may not always yield useful information

Legal and compliance knowledge	Utilizing legal frameworks and compliance standards to guide investigations	Rapid changes in laws and regulations can make it hard to stay updated
Standard accounting techniques	Employing traditional techniques such as reconciliation, sampling, and ratio analysis	May not be effective against sophisticated and novel fraudulent schemes
Reliance on human expertise	Dependence on the expertise and judgment of forensic accountants and fraud examiners	Potential for biases and inconsistencies in the investigative process
Time and resource-intensiveness	Manual processes that are resource-heavy and time-consuming	Not cost-effective, especially for smaller organizations or complex cases

Table 5.1 – Comparing traditional practices and challenges in fraud examination and forensic accounting

Transitioning from analyzing conventional methods and challenges in fraud examination, we'll turn our gaze toward the disruptive potential of AI in revolutionizing fraud detection strategies.

The emergence of AI in fraud detection

Integrating AI in fraud detection represents a significant leap in forensic accounting and fraud examination capabilities. This section provides a historical perspective on introducing AI in this domain and highlights key milestones and technological advancements.

A historical perspective on the introduction of AI in fraud detection

The journey of AI in fraud detection began with the advent of simple automated systems that were designed to flag inconsistencies in large datasets. The initial phase involved rule-based systems, where AI was programmed to identify deviations from standard patterns in transaction data. These systems, although primitive by today's standards, marked the first step toward automating fraud detection processes. Let's take a closer look:

- **1980s-1990s:** The early stages saw the implementation of basic statistical and rule-based algorithms. These systems could perform simple tasks such as identifying outliers in financial data but could not learn from data or adapt to new fraud patterns.

- **Early 2000s:** The introduction of machine learning algorithms represented a significant advancement. Unlike their predecessors, these systems could learn from data, identifying fraud patterns more effectively and adapting to new tactics employed by fraudsters.

- **2010s onwards**: The rise of big data and advanced analytics fueled a rapid evolution in AI capabilities. Deep learning and neural networks began to be employed to analyze unstructured data such as emails and social media posts, further enhancing fraud detection capabilities.

The following table breaks this down further:

Era	Milestones and Technological Advancements in AI for Fraud Detection
1980s-1990s	Introduction of basic statistical and rule-based algorithms. These systems could flag outliers but lacked adaptability to evolving fraud patterns.
The early 2000s	Implementing machine learning algorithms enables systems to learn from historical data and improve in identifying fraud patterns.
2010s onwards	Advancements in big data analytics and deep learning. The introduction of neural networks for unstructured data analysis, enhancing fraud detection capabilities.
Current trends	Natural language processing (NLP) for analyzing textual data in fraud detection. Predictive analytics for forecasting potentially fraudulent activities. Real-time analysis capabilities for immediate fraud detection. Integration with blockchain technology for securing and analyzing financial transactions.

Table 5.2 – A historical perspective of AI in fraud detection

Over the years, AI has seen a lot of advancements in fraud detection. Let's explore this a bit more.

Key milestones and technological advancements

Several key milestones and technological advancements have marked the progression of AI in fraud detection:

- **Machine learning algorithms**: These algorithms revolutionized fraud detection by enabling systems to learn from historical data and identify complex patterns indicative of fraudulent activities

- **NLP**: The ability to analyze text data opened up new avenues for detecting fraud in communication channels, such as email correspondence and financial reports

- **Predictive analytics**: AI systems equipped with predictive analytics can now anticipate potentially fraudulent activities by analyzing trends and patterns in data

- **Real-time analysis**: The development of AI systems capable of processing real-time transactions significantly reduced the time lag in detecting fraudulent activities, enabling quicker responses

- **Integration with blockchain technology**: AI's integration with blockchain technology has further strengthened fraud detection in cryptocurrency transactions and smart contracts

The emergence of AI in fraud detection has been a game-changer, transforming the landscape of forensic accounting and fraud examination. From basic rule-based systems to sophisticated machine learning models capable of real-time analysis, AI has continuously evolved to address the increasingly complex nature of financial fraud. The following sections will delve deeper into the specific AI technologies that are used in fraud examination and their practical applications.

AI technologies in fraud examination

The application of AI in fraud examination has become increasingly sophisticated, leveraging various technologies to enhance detection and prevention capabilities. This section provides an overview of these technologies and presents case studies demonstrating their application in real-world scenarios.

Here's an overview of AI technologies that are used in fraud detection:

- **Machine learning**: Machine learning algorithms are at the forefront of AI in fraud detection. These algorithms learn from historical data to identify patterns and anomalies indicative of fraudulent activities. They include supervised learning algorithms, which require labeled datasets, and unsupervised learning algorithms, which can detect unknown patterns in data.

- **Data analytics**: Advanced data analytics involves examining large datasets to uncover hidden patterns, correlations, and insights. This is particularly effective in fraud detection as it allows us to analyze transactional data at scale.

- **NLP**: NLP analyzes textual data within financial documents, emails, and communication channels. It helps in detecting fraudulent activities by identifying inconsistencies or suspicious narratives in textual data.

- **Predictive analytics**: This involves using statistical models and forecasting techniques to identify the likelihood of future outcomes based on historical data. In fraud detection, predictive analytics can indicate the probability of a transaction being fraudulent.

- **Anomaly detection**: AI systems are equipped to identify outliers or abnormal patterns in financial data that may signify fraudulent activities. Anomaly detection is crucial in identifying new and sophisticated fraud schemes.

- **Network analysis**: This involves examining the relationships and connections between different entities or transactions. Network analysis can uncover complex fraud schemes involving multiple parties or accounts.

Case studies demonstrating the application of AI in real-world scenarios

To help us better understand the role of AI in real-world scenarios, let's look at a few case studies.

Case study 1 – banking fraud detection in a major bank

A leading international bank faced challenges with traditional fraud detection methods that were proving inadequate against sophisticated schemes. To address this challenge, the bank implemented a machine-learning-based system designed to monitor and analyze customer transactions in real time. The system used a combination of supervised and unsupervised learning algorithms to identify unusual patterns that deviated from typical customer behavior.

Within months of its implementation, the AI system flagged a series of transactions involving a network of interconnected accounts. These transactions were initially deemed low risk by traditional models due to their small sizes and frequency. However, the AI system recognized a pattern resembling a "smurfing" technique, where large sums of money are broken down into smaller less suspicious amounts. Further investigation revealed a complex money laundering operation. The swift identification of this scheme by the AI system prevented significant financial loss and assisted law enforcement in apprehending the individuals involved.

This case exemplifies the power of AI in enhancing the capabilities of financial institutions to detect and prevent fraud. By leveraging advanced algorithms capable of learning and adapting to new fraud tactics, the bank was able to secure its operations and protect its customers more effectively than ever before.

Case study 2 – insurance fraud prevention in an insurance company

An insurance company grappling with fraudulent claims and decided to implement predictive analytics to improve its fraud detection processes. The AI system was trained on a vast dataset of past claims, incorporating various factors such as claim amounts, claimant history, and the nature of incidents. The goal was to identify patterns that could indicate potential fraud.

The breakthrough came when the system flagged a series of claims from a particular region that were significantly higher than the norm. These claims, although seemingly unrelated, shared subtle similarities in their documentation and timing. Upon investigation, it was discovered that a group of individuals was orchestrating accidents to file false claims. The predictive analytics tool not only identified the irregularities but also predicted future claims that were likely to be fraudulent, based on the established pattern.

This case study demonstrates the effectiveness of predictive analytics in proactively identifying and preventing insurance fraud. The AI system's ability to analyze and forecast based on historical data proved crucial in uncovering a fraudulent scheme that might have otherwise gone unnoticed.

Case study 3 – corporate financial fraud identification in a multinational corporation

A multinational corporation faced challenges with ensuring the accuracy and integrity of its financial reporting. The corporation implemented an AI system equipped with NLP to analyze its financial documents and communications to enhance its oversight. The system was designed to detect inconsistencies, anomalies, and misleading information in financial statements and reports.

The AI tool soon identified a series of discrepancies in the revenue reporting of specific business units. These discrepancies were subtle and would likely have been overlooked in a standard audit. Further investigation revealed that senior management within these units was involved in artificially inflating revenue figures, a practice known as "earnings management." This revelation led to a comprehensive internal audit that uncovered a more extensive financial misstatement scheme.

This case highlights the crucial role of NLP in corporate governance and fraud detection. By scrutinizing the language and figures that are used in financial documents, the AI system was able to uncover sophisticated fraud that traditional auditing methods had missed. The prompt detection of this fraud not only saved the corporation from potential legal and financial repercussions but also reinforced the importance of AI in maintaining corporate transparency and accountability.

Case study 4 – tackling public sector corruption with AI-driven anomaly detection

In a bid to enhance transparency and accountability, a government body implemented an AI-driven anomaly detection system to audit its procurement processes. The system was designed to analyze bidding patterns, contract allocations, and pricing data to identify any irregularities or signs of corrupt practices.

The AI tool soon flagged a series of procurement contracts that had several irregularities, including recurring patterns of contract awards to a specific set of companies and pricing anomalies compared to market standards. On closer examination, these contracts were found to be part of a collusion scheme between certain government officials and contractors. The scheme involved inflating contract prices and awarding contracts in exchange for kickbacks.

This case is a prime example of how AI can be instrumental in combating public sector corruption. The anomaly detection system's ability to analyze complex datasets and identify suspicious patterns played a key role in uncovering a corruption network, leading to significant procurement reforms and legal actions against those involved.

These detailed case studies highlight the remarkable impact and versatility of AI technologies in different sectors for fraud detection and prevention. These examples illustrate AI's practical application and effectiveness in combating various forms of financial fraud and corruption.

Integrating AI into fraud examination workflows

Integrating AI into existing fraud examination processes requires strategic planning and a focus on skill development. This section discusses the strategies for effectively implementing AI and highlights the importance of training and skill development for forensic accountants.

Strategies for implementing AI in existing fraud examination processes

Here are some strategies you can implement:

- **Assessing current processes**: Begin by thoroughly assessing current fraud examination workflows to identify areas where AI can be most beneficial. This assessment should consider the types of fraud that are commonly encountered, existing data infrastructure, and the team's technical capabilities.

- **Choosing the right AI tools**: Select AI tools and technologies that align with the specific needs identified in the assessment. This might include machine learning models for pattern recognition, NLP for text analysis, or predictive analytics for risk assessment.

- **Data preparation and management**: Ensure that the data required for AI applications is available, accurate, and well-organized. This involves setting up data collection and storage systems that are compatible with AI tools compliant with data privacy regulations.

- **Integrating with existing systems**: Integrate AI tools with existing fraud examination systems to enhance, rather than disrupt, current workflows. This might require customizing AI solutions so that they fit into the existing IT infrastructure.

- **Testing and iteration**: Implement the AI tools in phases, starting with pilot projects or specific areas of fraud examination. Use the insights gained from these initial implementations to refine and improve the integration process.

- **Continuous monitoring and updating**: AI models require regular updates and monitoring to ensure they remain effective over time. Stay abreast of new developments in AI and continually update the systems to counter new types of fraud.

Training and skill development for forensic accountants in AI applications

As the integration of artificial intelligence into forensic accounting continues to revolutionize the field, the imperative for specialized training and skill development in AI applications for forensic accountants has never been more crucial.

- **Basic AI literacy**: Train forensic accountants to develop a basic understanding of AI, including how different AI technologies work and their applications in fraud examination.

- **Specialized training programs**: Offer specialized training programs while focusing on the AI tools and systems being implemented. This could include hands-on training in using machine learning platforms or workshops on data analysis techniques.

- **Collaboration with AI experts**: Encourage collaboration between forensic accountants and AI experts. This can facilitate knowledge transfer and help forensic accountants understand how to leverage AI in their work effectively.

- **Continuous learning and adaptation**: Foster a continuous learning and adaptation culture. As AI technologies evolve, ensure that forensic accountants have access to ongoing education and resources to keep their skills up to date.

- **Ethical and legal considerations**: Include training on the ethical use of AI in fraud examination and the legal implications of using AI-driven insights in legal proceedings.

Successfully integrating AI into fraud examination workflows necessitates a comprehensive strategy encompassing technical implementation and human capital development. By equipping forensic accountants with the right tools and skills, organizations can enhance their fraud detection capabilities and stay ahead in the rapidly evolving landscape of financial fraud. The following table outlines the essential strategies for integrating AI into fraud examination workflows, highlighting the corresponding training requirements needed to equip professionals with the necessary skills to effectively leverage these advanced technologies.

Category	Strategy for AI Implementation	Training and Skill Development
Process assessment	Evaluate existing workflows to identify areas for AI integration	Basic AI literacy to understand the potential impact on workflows
Tool selection	Choose AI tools that align with identified needs and fraud types	Training on specific AI tools and technologies being implemented
Data management	Set up compatible and compliant data systems for AI applications	Workshops on data collection, management, and analysis techniques
System integration	Seamlessly integrate AI tools with current fraud examination systems	Hands-on training for integrating AI into existing systems
Testing and iteration	Implement AI in phases, starting with pilot projects	Learning to analyze initial results and refine AI applications
Continuous monitoring	Regularly update and monitor AI models for effectiveness	Ongoing education on new developments and updating AI skills
Collaboration	Facilitate collaboration between forensic accountants and AI experts	Encourage knowledge transfer and joint problem-solving initiatives
Ethical and legal training	Address the ethical and legal implications of AI in fraud examination	Include comprehensive training on ethical and legal aspects of AI application

Table 5.3 – Strategies for integrating AI in fraud examination
workflows and the associated training requirements

Next, we'll explore the role of AI in forensic analysis.

AI-powered forensic analysis

The integration of AI in forensic analysis has redefined the landscape of forensic accounting, bringing forth new techniques and tools that significantly enhance the accuracy and efficiency of investigations. This section delves into these AI-powered data analysis techniques and explores the role of AI in improving forensic investigations.

The following are some techniques and tools that you can utilize for AI-powered data analysis in forensic accounting:

- **Machine learning models**: Forensic accountants increasingly use machine learning models to identify patterns and anomalies in financial data. These models can process vast datasets quickly, detecting irregularities that might indicate fraud.

- **Predictive analytics**: This technique uses statistical models and machine learning algorithms to predict the likelihood of future events based on historical data. In forensic accounting, it helps in identifying potential areas of risk and fraud before they occur.

- **NLP**: NLP tools are used to analyze textual data within financial documents, emails, and communication channels. They are adept at detecting inconsistencies, hidden messages, or manipulative language that could point to fraudulent activities.

- **Anomaly detection algorithms**: These algorithms are specifically designed to identify outliers in data that deviate from normal patterns. Anomaly detection is crucial for uncovering novel or sophisticated fraud schemes.

- **Data visualization tools**: AI-powered data visualization tools help in presenting complex data findings in an understandable format. These tools are essential for identifying trends and patterns that might not be apparent from raw data alone.

- **Blockchain analysis**: For sectors involving cryptocurrencies and digital transactions, AI tools are used for analyzing blockchain data, providing insights into transaction patterns, and identifying potentially fraudulent activities.

AI plays a pivotal role in enhancing the accuracy and efficiency of forensic investigations. Let's look at some of the ways it can help:

- **Improved accuracy**: AI algorithms can analyze large volumes of data with a high degree of accuracy, reducing the likelihood of human error. They can identify subtle patterns and correlations that might be missed by traditional methods.

- **Increased efficiency**: AI-powered tools can process data at a speed that is impossible for human investigators, significantly reducing the time taken for forensic analysis. This rapid processing allows for more timely responses to fraud detection.

- **Adaptability to new frauds**: AI systems, particularly those using machine learning, can adapt and learn from new data. This means they become more effective over time at detecting new and evolving types of fraud.

- **Enhanced investigative capabilities**: AI tools can sift through unstructured data (such as emails or social media posts), which is often overlooked in traditional forensic investigations, uncovering hidden connections and evidence.

- **Cost-effectiveness**: By automating routine analysis tasks, AI allows forensic accountants to focus on more complex investigations, improving the overall cost-effectiveness of the forensic process.

AI-powered forensic analysis is rapidly becoming an indispensable part of forensic accounting. The advanced techniques and tools provided by AI not only enhance the accuracy and efficiency of investigations but also equip forensic accountants to stay ahead in the constantly evolving arena of financial fraud.

Ethical and legal considerations

As AI becomes more integral to fraud examination and forensic accounting, it brings with it a range of ethical concerns and legal implications. This section addresses these crucial aspects while focusing on data privacy, security, and regulatory compliance in AI implementations.

Let's address the ethical concerns and legal implications of using AI in fraud examination:

- **Bias and fairness**: AI systems, particularly those involving machine learning, can inadvertently perpetuate biases present in their training data. It's essential to ensure that AI models are designed and trained to minimize bias and promote fairness in fraud detection outcomes.

- **Transparency and explainability**: There is a growing demand for AI systems to be transparent and their decisions explainable, especially in legal contexts. Forensic accountants must be able to understand and explain how AI tools arrive at their conclusions, ensuring that the use of AI is justifiable and defensible in legal proceedings.

- **Legal responsibility and liability**: Determining legal responsibility for decisions made by AI systems can be challenging. It's vital to establish clear guidelines on liability, particularly in cases where AI-driven decisions lead to legal actions or financial repercussions.

- **Data privacy**: Implementing AI in fraud examination often involves analyzing sensitive financial data. Strict adherence to data privacy laws, such as the **General Data Protection Regulation (GDPR)** in the EU or other local data protection regulations, is essential. This includes ensuring that personal data is processed legally and ethically.

- **Data security**: The use of AI requires robust data security measures to protect against unauthorized access and data breaches. This is particularly crucial as AI systems often require access to large datasets, including confidential information.

- **Regulatory compliance**: AI tools must be compliant with existing financial and auditing standards and regulations. As the regulatory landscape evolves, particularly with the advent of AI, staying updated about these changes and ensuring compliance is crucial.

- **Ethical AI frameworks**: Developing and adhering to ethical AI frameworks can guide the responsible use of AI in fraud examination. These frameworks should encompass principles such as accountability, transparency, fairness, and respect for privacy.

- **Continuous monitoring and assessment**: Regularly monitoring and assessing AI tools is necessary to ensure they align with ethical standards and legal requirements. This includes periodic reviews of AI algorithms and their outputs for any potential ethical or legal issues.

The ethical and legal considerations regarding the use of AI in fraud examination are multifaceted and require diligent attention. Balancing the benefits of AI with ethical integrity and legal compliance is paramount. By addressing these concerns proactively, forensic accountants and organizations can harness the power of AI while maintaining trust and upholding the highest standards of their profession.

Challenges and limitations of AI in fraud detection

While AI offers significant advantages in fraud detection, it is not without its challenges and limitations. This section explores the potential obstacles to adopting AI in this field and discusses the importance of balancing AI capabilities with human expertise and judgment.

Here are some things to consider:

- **Data dependency**: AI systems, particularly those based on machine learning, require large volumes of high-quality data to function effectively. The lack of sufficient or relevant data can hinder the performance of AI models in detecting fraud accurately.

- **Algorithmic bias**: AI models can inherit biases present in their training data. This can lead to skewed results and potentially unfair or unethical conclusions, especially if the data that's used for training is not representative of the broader context.

- **Complexity and interpretability**: Some AI models, especially deep learning algorithms, are often seen as "black boxes" due to their complexity. This lack of interpretability can be a significant hurdle in environments that require transparency, such as legal proceedings or regulatory compliance.

- **Cost and resource constraints**: Implementing AI solutions can be resource-intensive, requiring significant investment in technology and skilled personnel. This can be a barrier, particularly for smaller organizations or those with limited budgets.

- **Adaptability and evolving frauds**: Fraudsters continually evolve their tactics, and there is a risk that AI systems might not adapt quickly enough to new types of fraud, especially if they are trained on outdated data sets.

- **Dependence and overreliance**: There is a risk of overreliance on AI systems, which might lead to complacency in human oversight. This dependence can be detrimental, especially if the AI system fails or is compromised.

Consider the following when balancing AI capabilities with human expertise and judgment:

- **Augmentation, not replacement**: AI should be viewed as a tool to augment human capabilities, not replace them. The role of experienced forensic accountants and fraud examiners remains crucial as they provide contextual understanding and judgment that AI currently cannot.

- **Interdisciplinary teams**: Creating teams that combine AI experts with forensic accountants can ensure a balanced approach. Such teams can leverage AI's analytical power while applying human intuition and experience to interpret findings.

- **Continuous learning and adaptation**: Both AI systems and human professionals need to engage in continuous learning. Keeping AI models updated with the latest data and fraud detection trends and ensuring that human professionals are trained in the latest AI developments is crucial.

- **Ethical oversight**: Establishing an ethical framework for AI use in fraud detection can help balance technological capabilities with moral and legal considerations. Regular ethical audits of AI systems can ensure they operate within acceptable boundaries.

- **Human-centric decision-making**: Decisions, especially those with legal or ethical implications, should be made by humans, not AI systems. AI can provide recommendations, but human professionals should make the final judgment calls.

While AI offers transformative potential in fraud detection, we must be aware of its limitations and challenges. Combining AI's analytical strengths with human expertise and ethical considerations, a balanced approach is vital for effective and responsible fraud detection.

Case studies – success stories and lessons learned

This section presents detailed case studies that exemplify successful AI integration in fraud examination and forensic accounting, highlighting the lessons learned and best practices derived from these experiences.

Case study 1: AI-driven credit card fraud detection in a major bank

Background: A leading global bank was experiencing an upsurge in credit card fraud, straining its traditional fraud detection systems.

AI integration:

- **Implementation**: The bank integrated a machine-learning-based fraud detection system that analyzed transaction patterns in real time

- **Technology**: The system used unsupervised learning algorithms to identify unusual spending behaviors and transaction patterns that deviated from a customer's typical activity

Outcome:

- **Success**: The AI system identified a sophisticated fraud operation involving cloned credit cards, which traditional methods had missed

- **Efficiency**: Fraud detection speed increased by 70%, and false positive rates decreased significantly

Lessons and best practices:

- **Continuous model training**: Regularly updating the AI models with new transaction data to keep the system effective against evolving fraud tactics

- **Blending AI with human oversight**: The bank established a protocol where AI-recommended alerts were reviewed by human analysts for final verification, ensuring a balance between AI efficiency and human judgment

Case study 2: AI in detecting payroll fraud in a multinational corporation

Background: A multinational corporation was facing internal payroll fraud, with traditional auditing methods failing to detect anomalies effectively.

AI integration:

- **Implementation**: An AI system utilizing anomaly detection algorithms was deployed to monitor payroll transactions

- **Technology**: The system used a combination of pattern recognition and anomaly detection techniques to flag irregular payroll disbursements

Outcome:

- **Success**: The AI tool uncovered a fraudulent scheme where certain employees were colluding with payroll staff to receive unauthorized bonuses

- **Transparency**: The AI system's findings led to the implementation of more transparent payroll processes

Lessons and best practices:

- **Data accuracy and integration**: Ensuring the accuracy and integration of payroll data across different departments for effective AI analysis

- **Ethical AI use**: The corporation emphasized the ethical use of AI, ensuring employees' privacy rights were respected during the analysis

Case study 3: AI-enhanced investigation of insurance claims.

Background: An insurance company struggled with the high volume of claims, which made it challenging to detect fraudulent cases efficiently.

AI integration:

- **Implementation**: The company used AI for predictive analytics to assess the likelihood of fraud in claims

- **Technology**: The system analyzed historical claims data, factoring in claimant history, incident details, and behavioral patterns

Outcome:

- **Success**: The AI model successfully predicted a high likelihood of fraud in a set of claims, which, upon investigation, were confirmed as fraudulent

- **Customer experience**: The efficiency of processing legitimate claims improved, enhancing customer satisfaction

Lessons and best practices:

- **Predictive analytics**: Utilizing predictive analytics to prioritize investigations, focusing resources more effectively

- **Regular updates and training**: Keeping the AI system updated with recent claims data and training staff to interpret AI recommendations accurately

These case studies demonstrate the powerful role of AI in enhancing fraud detection and forensic accounting practices. Key lessons include the importance of data quality, the need for continuous AI model training, balancing AI with human judgment, and adhering to ethical standards. These practices not only improve efficiency and accuracy but also foster trust and reliability in AI-integrated systems in financial oversight and fraud detection.

Future trends and developments

The application of AI in fraud examination and forensic accounting is poised for significant evolution. This section delves into predictions and future trends in AI applications within these fields, highlighting emerging technologies and their potential impacts.

The following are some predictions and future trends in AI applications:

- **Integration of AI with blockchain**: The convergence of AI and blockchain technology promises enhanced security and transparency in financial transactions. AI can analyze blockchain data to detect anomalous patterns indicative of fraud, offering a tamper-proof audit trail.

- **Advanced predictive analytics**: The next generation of predictive analytics will incorporate more sophisticated AI models, capable of analyzing a broader array of data sources, including social media and biometric data, to predict and prevent fraud more accurately.

- **Explainable AI (XAI)**: As regulatory requirements and the need for transparency grow, there will be a push toward developing AI systems that not only make decisions but also provide understandable explanations for those decisions, making AI outputs more transparent and trustworthy.

- **Autonomous fraud detection systems**: Future AI systems will become more autonomous, capable of not just detecting fraud but also taking preventative actions, such as freezing accounts or transactions, based on predefined criteria and real-time risk assessments.

- **AI and IoT for fraud detection**: Integrating AI with the **Internet of Things** (**IoT**) devices will enable real-time monitoring and analysis of transactional data from various sources, providing a more comprehensive view of potential fraud.

Preparing for an AI-driven future in fraud examination

Integrating AI into fraud examination and forensic accounting necessitates a shift in the skill set and strategies employed by professionals in the field. This section outlines the necessary skills and training for forensic accountants in an AI-driven environment and offers strategies for staying ahead in this rapidly evolving landscape.

The following are the necessary skills and training for forensic accountants:

- **Data science and analytics**: Forensic accountants will need a solid foundation in data science, including understanding data structures, statistical analysis, and the ability to interpret complex data sets. Familiarity with data visualization tools will also be crucial for effectively communicating findings.

- **Machine learning and AI principles**: A working knowledge of AI and machine learning principles is essential. This includes understanding how algorithms are trained, the basics of neural networks, and the implications of model bias and variance.

- **Programming knowledge**: While not all forensic accountants need to become expert programmers, a basic understanding of programming languages such as Python, SQL, or R, which are commonly used in data analysis and AI applications, can be highly beneficial.

- **Ethical and legal considerations in AI**: Training in the ethical use of AI, including data privacy laws and regulations, is critical. Forensic accountants should be aware of the ethical implications of using AI in investigations and ensure compliance with legal standards.

- **Continuous professional education**: The field of AI is rapidly evolving, necessitating ongoing education and training to stay current with the latest technologies and methodologies.

The following are some strategies for staying ahead in the AI and forensic accounting landscape:

- **Embrace interdisciplinary collaboration**: Collaborating with data scientists, AI experts, and technologists can provide forensic accountants with insights into the capabilities and limitations of AI tools, fostering a more comprehensive approach to fraud examination.

- **Invest in AI literacy**: Organizations should invest in AI literacy programs for their forensic accounting teams, ensuring that all members understand the basics of AI and how it can be applied to their work.

- **Adopt a culture of innovation**: Encouraging a culture of innovation within the organization can help forensic accountants remain adaptable and open to integrating new AI tools and techniques into their workflows.

- **Participate in professional networks**: Engaging with professional networks and industry groups focused on AI in fraud examination can provide valuable opportunities for learning, collaboration, and staying informed about industry best practices.

- **Leverage simulation and training platforms**: Simulation tools and AI training platforms can help forensic accountants gain hands-on experience with AI technologies in a controlled environment, building their confidence and competence in using these tools.

- **Focus on soft skills**: In an AI-driven future, soft skills such as critical thinking, communication, and ethical judgment will become increasingly important. These skills enable forensic accountants to interpret AI findings, make informed decisions, and communicate complex information to non-technical stakeholders.

Preparing for an AI-driven future in fraud examination involves acquiring new technical skills and adapting to new ways of thinking and collaborating. Forensic accountants can leverage AI to enhance their capabilities and contribute to advancing the field by embracing continuous learning, ethical considerations, and interdisciplinary collaboration. The following table outlines the manifold benefits of AI, underscoring its transformative potential across diverse sectors.

Category	Skills and Training	Strategies for Staying Ahead
Technical proficiency	Data science and analytics; understanding of machine learning and AI principles; basic programming knowledge (Python, R)	Invest in AI literacy programs; utilize simulation and training platforms
Ethical and legal knowledge	Training in ethical AI use; understanding of data privacy laws and AI regulations	Focus on continuous professional education; encourage a culture of innovation
Professional development	Continuous learning in AI advancements; familiarity with industry best practices	Engage with professional networks and industry groups; embrace interdisciplinary collaboration

Category	Skills and Training	Strategies for Staying Ahead
Soft skills	Critical thinking, effective communication, and ethical judgment	Enhance soft skills to complement AI findings interpretation; develop the ability to communicate complex AI concepts to non-technical stakeholders

Table 5.4 – Benefits of AI

In conclusion, the diverse array of benefits underscores the immense potential of AI to revolutionize industries, streamline processes, and drive innovation in the modern era.

Summary

This chapter explored the profound and multifaceted impact of AI on fraud examination and forensic accounting. Through various case studies, technical discussions, and future predictions, we have seen that AI is not just an auxiliary tool but a transformative force reshaping the landscape of financial investigations.

Here are the key insights and takeaways from this chapter:

- **Enhanced detection capabilities**: AI's ability to analyze vast datasets with unparalleled speed and accuracy has significantly improved fraud detection. Techniques such as machine learning, predictive analytics, and anomaly detection have become invaluable assets in identifying complex fraud schemes that might elude traditional methods.

- **Operational efficiency**: AI has streamlined many aspects of fraud examination, from data collection to analysis, allowing forensic accountants to focus on more strategic tasks. This efficiency gain reduces the time and resources required for investigations and enables a proactive approach to fraud prevention.

- **Adaptability to emerging fraud tactics**: The dynamic nature of AI, particularly its learning algorithms, ensures that fraud detection mechanisms evolve in tandem with new and sophisticated fraud strategies, maintaining a robust defense against financial crimes.

- **Challenges and ethical considerations**: Despite its benefits, integrating AI into fraud examination comes with challenges, including data privacy concerns, the need for transparency, and the potential for algorithmic bias. Addressing these issues is paramount to harnessing AI's full potential ethically and responsibly.

Reflecting on the transformative impact of AI

Integrating AI into fraud examination and forensic accounting marks a significant shift toward more data-driven, analytical approaches. This transformation is about adopting innovative technologies and rethinking traditional practices and strategies while considering AI's capabilities.

AI's impact goes beyond operational enhancements, driving a paradigm shift in how financial integrity is maintained and fraud is combated. As AI technologies advance, they promise even more significant potential in uncovering and preventing fraud, ensuring the integrity of financial systems, and safeguarding assets.

The journey ahead requires a balanced approach, where technological advancements are matched with ethical considerations, regulatory compliance, and continuous professional development. Forensic accountants and fraud examiners must embrace this evolving landscape, equipping themselves with the necessary skills and knowledge to leverage AI effectively.

The future of fraud examination and forensic accounting in an AI-driven era is bright and filled with opportunities for innovation and improvement. By embracing AI, professionals in these fields can enhance their capabilities, contributing to a more secure and transparent financial environment. The journey will be one of continuous learning, adaptation, and collaboration, guided by integrity, accountability, and ethical responsibility principles.

Further reading and resources

For further reading on AI in forensic accounting and fraud examination, consider exploring the following resources:

- *The Integration of Artificial Intelligence in Forensic Accounting: A Game-Changer* provides insights into how AI is reshaping forensic accounting by addressing the challenges posed by digital transactions and the complexity of modern financial systems. It discusses the adoption spectrum of technology in the industry, from data analytics to machine learning, and highlights the dynamic tension between traditional methods and the need for technological innovation (ResearchGate: `https://www.researchgate.net/profile/Upendar-Rao-Thaduri/publication/375746312_The_Integration_of_Artificial_Intelligence_in_Forensic_Accounting_A_Game-Changer_Asian_Accounting_and_Auditing_Advancement/links/655986f5ce88b87031f63eb8/The-Integration-of-Artificial-Intelligence-in-Forensic-Accounting-A-Game-Changer-Asian-Accounting-and-Auditing-Advancement.pdf`).

- *Artificial Intelligence for Audit, Forensic Accounting, and Valuation* is a comprehensive resource that covers the strategic integration of AI in accounting and auditing, discussing its potential to transform these professions. The book delves into current applications and the fragmented nature of AI implementations in these fields (Wiley Online Library: `https://www.wiley.com/en-us/Artificial+Intelligence+for+Audit%2C+Forensic+Account-ing%2C+and+Valuation%3A+A+Strategic+Perspective-p-9781119601883`).

- For an in-depth look at how AI can be leveraged for fraud detection, *Artificial Intelligence and Fraud Detection* provides a comprehensive overview of using advanced machine learning models to detect fraud across various domains, emphasizing the significant research question of fraud prevention (SSRN: `https://papers.ssrn.com/sol3/papers.cfm?abstract_id=3738618`).

These resources offer valuable insights and practical knowledge for professionals looking to leverage AI in the fight against financial fraud.

Q&A

Here are some questions and their answers to help you understand the material presented in this chapter:

1. How has AI redefined the approach to fraud examination and forensic accounting?

   AI has redefined the approach to fraud examination and forensic accounting by introducing advanced data analytics, machine learning, and automation. These technologies enable the examination of entire data sets in real time, allowing for more comprehensive and accurate fraud detection. AI systems can identify complex patterns and anomalies that may indicate fraudulent activity, significantly enhancing the traditional methods that were more manual, time-consuming, and prone to human error.

2. What ethical challenges does AI introduce in forensic accounting, and how can they be addressed?

   AI introduces several ethical challenges in forensic accounting, including bias, transparency, privacy, and accountability. To address these challenges, you can incorporate the following:

   - **Bias and fairness**: Ensure AI models are trained on diverse and representative datasets to minimize bias and implement regular audits to assess and correct discriminatory outcomes

   - **Transparency and explainability**: Develop and utilize AI models that provide transparent and interpretable results, making it easier for professionals to understand and trust AI-driven insights

   - **Privacy and data security**: Adhere to stringent data protection laws and ethical guidelines to protect sensitive information, employing secure data handling and processing practices

   - **Responsibility and accountability**: Establish clear protocols for AI usage that delineate the responsibilities of human professionals, ensuring that final decisions are subject to human judgment and oversight

3. What advancements in AI could further transform fraud examination in the future?

    Future advancements in AI transforming fraud examination include the following:

    - **XAI**: Improvements in XAI will make AI's decision-making processes more transparent and understandable, which is crucial for maintaining accountability and trust in AI-assisted investigations

    - **Federated learning**: This technique allows AI to learn from decentralized data without compromising privacy, enhancing data security in fraud examinations

    - **Quantum computing**: Though still emerging, quantum computing promises to significantly boost processing capabilities, potentially revolutionizing data analysis in forensic accounting

    - **Blockchain and AI integration**: Combining blockchain's secure and transparent transaction record-keeping with AI's analytical power could lead to more secure and efficient fraud detection systems

4. How should professionals in forensic accounting prepare for the integration of AI?

    Professionals in forensic accounting should prepare for AI integration by doing the following

    - **Developing technical skills**: Acquiring knowledge in data analytics, machine learning, programming understanding, and other related technologies to effectively use AI tools

    - **Ethical and legal training**: Staying informed about ethical considerations, data protection laws, and regulatory requirements relevant to AI in forensic accounting

    - **Continuous learning**: Embracing a mindset of continuous learning and adaptation to keep pace with technological advancements and evolving fraud tactics

    - **Collaboration and networking**: Engage with interdisciplinary teams and professional networks to share knowledge and best practices, as well as stay updated on the latest developments in AI and forensic accounting

Turbocharging Financial Analysis and Projection

"Financial analysis is a process of cleansing, adjusting, and transforming data into actionable insights. The advent of AI has taken this process from being a rear-view mirror to a powerful predictive telescope."

- Wayne R. Landsman, chief decision scientist at Moody's Analytics

Financial analysis is a critical tool for businesses and investors in today's dynamic economic environment, which is characterized by rapid changes, uncertainties, and complex global interconnections. The ability to analyze financial data accurately and project future trends is more than just a strategic advantage; it's a necessity for survival and growth. This chapter will underscore the growing importance of AI in enhancing traditional financial analysis methods, enabling organizations to navigate the complexities of the modern economy more effectively.

Financial analysis and projection are pivotal in business strategic decision-making and risk management. They provide critical insights that inform various business decisions—from day-to-day operational matters to long-term strategic planning. By accurately interpreting financial data and projecting future trends, companies can identify profitable opportunities, allocate resources more effectively, attract investors, and anticipate potential risks. In today's fast-paced and uncertain economic environment, accurately forecasting financial outcomes is invaluable. It enables businesses to stay agile, adapt to market changes swiftly, and maintain a competitive edge. Moreover, robust financial analysis and projection are crucial for risk management, helping businesses to prepare for and mitigate financial uncertainties and volatilities.

This chapter delves into the transformative role of **artificial intelligence** (**AI**) in financial analysis and projection. It explores how AI technologies have revolutionized traditional practices, bringing unprecedented efficiency, accuracy, and foresight to financial forecasting and analysis.

This chapter aims to delve into the transformative effects of advanced technologies, with a particular focus on AI in the domain of financial analysis and projection. It seeks to uncover how AI and related technologies are reshaping the landscape of financial forecasting and analysis, moving beyond traditional methodologies to more dynamic, accurate, and efficient processes. The chapter will examine the various facets of AI integration in financial analysis, including data processing, predictive analytics, and real-time reporting, and how these advancements enhance financial projections' accuracy and reliability.

Another key objective of this chapter is to offer comprehensive insights into how AI and other advanced technologies are revolutionizing traditional financial analysis and projection methods. It will explore the shift from manual, time-consuming processes to automated, sophisticated systems that leverage AI for deeper insights and more accurate forecasts. The chapter will highlight the benefits and challenges of adopting these technologies, the skills required to utilize them effectively, and the ethical considerations that arise in their application. By doing so, it aims to provide a thorough understanding of AI's current state and future potential in financial analysis and projection, equipping professionals with the knowledge to navigate and excel in this evolving field.

The conventional landscape of financial analysis and projection

This section provides a comprehensive overview of the traditional methods employed in financial analysis. It delves into the historical approaches used by financial analysts to evaluate the financial health of businesses, assess market trends, and predict future financial outcomes. These techniques often involve fundamental analysis, including examining financial statements, key ratios, industry trends, and economic indicators. The section will explore how these methods have been the cornerstone of financial decision-making, enabling analysts to draw conclusions based on historical data and established financial theories.

Alongside the methods, this section focuses on the tools integral to traditional financial projection. It will discuss using spreadsheets, statistical software, data visualization tools, dashboards, and other financial modeling tools in the industry. The discussion will include how these tools create financial forecasts and budgets, perform variance analysis, and conduct what-if scenarios. Emphasis will be placed on these tools' strengths and limitations, particularly their reliance on manual input, historical data, and linear projections. This will set the stage for understanding the contrast and evolution brought about by the advent of AI and other advanced financial analysis and projection technologies.

Challenges and limitations

Navigating the conventional landscape of financial analysis and projection presents numerous challenges and limitations, which can significantly impact the accuracy and reliability of financial decision-making.

- **Limitations of conventional methods in handling complex data**: We address the inherent limitations of traditional financial analysis methods when dealing with complex and voluminous datasets. Conventional tools and techniques, while effective for straightforward and static datasets, often struggle to cope with the vast and dynamic nature of modern financial data.

The limitations include difficulties with processing large volumes of data from diverse sources, trouble identifying subtle risks, patterns, and correlations, and the inability to update analyses in real time as new data becomes available. These constraints can lead to oversimplified analyses that may not capture the financial picture, particularly in rapidly changing market conditions.

- **Challenges in accuracy and timeliness**: The accuracy and timeliness of financial analysis and projections are critical for effective decision-making. However, traditional methods face challenges on multiple fronts. Relying heavily on historical data, these methods may not accurately predict future trends, especially in fast-paced industries or volatile global economic climates. The manual nature of traditional analysis also introduces the risk of human error, further compromising accuracy. Additionally, the time-intensive process of collecting, processing, and analyzing data manually can lead to delays in reporting, making the insights less relevant by the time they are available. This section will explore these challenges in detail, setting the context for the need for more advanced, AI-driven financial analysis and projection approaches.

The advent of AI in financial analysis and projection

This section introduces the concept of AI and its growing significance in the field of financial analysis. It begins by defining AI and its various components, such as machine learning, deep learning, and natural language processing, explaining how these technologies differ from traditional computational methods. The introduction also covers the historical context of AI's emergence in financial analysis, tracing its evolution from a novel technology to a fundamental tool in modern finance. The focus is on how AI algorithms can process vast amounts of data, learn from this data, and make predictions or identify patterns that are beyond the scope of human analysts.

AI is not just an addition to the financial analyst's toolkit; it is a paradigm shift that is fundamentally changing the landscape of financial analysis and projection. This part of the section delves into the various ways AI is transforming the field. It discusses how AI enhances the accuracy and depth of financial analysis, enables real-time data processing and interpretation, and provides predictive insights that were previously unattainable with traditional methods. The section highlights specific applications of AI in finance, such as algorithmic trading, fraud detection, credit risk assessment, and automated financial advising. It also addresses the broader implications of this shift, including how AI is democratizing financial analysis by making sophisticated tools more accessible, influencing strategic decision-making in businesses.

Areas revolutionized by AI

In financial analysis and projection, AI is making incremental improvements and revolutionizing key areas. This section highlights the significant impact of AI across various facets of financial analysis, underscoring how it is reshaping the industry.

In particular, AI is transforming portfolio management and investment recommendations. Sophisticated machine learning algorithms can analyze vast amounts of financial data to detect patterns and predict optimal asset allocation strategies. Rather than relying purely on human intuition, portfolio managers now leverage AI systems that continuously monitor the markets and adjust portfolios to maximize returns and minimize risk. The ability of these systems to process huge volumes of data empowers more informed and evidence-based investment decisions.

AI is automating routine analytical tasks to increase efficiency in financial reporting, fraud detection, and credit risk modeling. Technologies such as natural language processing parse and extract critical insights from the overwhelming amount of corporate and market data that analysts must handle. Robotic process automation also streamlines manual workflows, allowing analysts to focus on higher-value judgment-based responsibilities.

AI chatbots and robo-advisors are gaining acceptance as automated tools to engage with and deliver personalized guidance to customers. They serve as digital assistants that can interpret natural language and offer sound financial recommendations tailored to an individual's goals at scale. Their sophistication continues to improve over time through machine learning techniques.

The financial services sector has only scratched the surface of AI's disruptive capabilities. As technology advances, AI promises to reshape finance through superior data-driven insights, increased efficiency, and more intelligent customer interactions. Vital operational areas will experience fundamental changes in how analytical and advisory humans and machines perform work. AI-powered innovation stands at the brink of revolutionizing finance in the following ways:

- **Data processing and analysis**: AI has transformed the way financial data is processed and analyzed. With the ability to handle large volumes of complex data, AI algorithms can quickly sift through and analyze information, identifying trends and patterns that traditional methods might miss. This capability is particularly crucial in today's data-rich environment, where the speed and accuracy of data analysis are paramount.

- **Risk assessment and management**: AI's predictive analytics are revolutionizing risk assessment and management in finance. AI can accurately forecast potential risks by analyzing historical data and current market trends. This foresight enables financial analysts to develop more effective risk mitigation strategies, enhancing the overall stability and resilience of financial plans and investments.

- **Fraud detection and prevention**: AI has become a powerful tool in detecting and preventing financial fraud. By learning typical transaction patterns, AI systems can flag anomalies that may indicate fraudulent activities. This proactive approach to fraud detection protects financial assets and builds trust and credibility with clients and stakeholders.

- **Customized financial advice**: AI-driven tools enable more personalized financial advice. By analyzing individual client data, AI can tailor recommendations to specific needs and goals, offering a level of previously unattainable customization. This personalization transforms the client–advisor relationship, making it more data-driven and client-centric.

- **Automated reporting and compliance**: AI is streamlining financial reporting and compliance processes. Automated systems can generate reports more quickly and accurately, reducing the workload for financial analysts. Additionally, AI can track changing regulations and ensure that financial practices remain compliant, reducing the risk of legal or regulatory issues.

- **Investment analysis and portfolio management**: In investment analysis and portfolio management, AI is enabling more sophisticated and dynamic strategies. AI algorithms can analyze market conditions, predict trends, and suggest investment opportunities, helping portfolio managers make informed decisions that align with their investment goals and risk tolerance.

By exploring these areas, this chapter section provides a comprehensive view of how AI is enhancing and fundamentally changing the landscape of financial analysis and projection. The impact of AI in these areas signifies a shift toward more efficient, accurate, and personalized financial services, setting the stage for continued innovation and advancement in the field.

The following table summarizes the traditional and AI-driven financial analysis methods:

Aspect	Traditional methods	AI-driven methods
Data processing	Manual, time-consuming	Automated, efficient
Accuracy	Limited by human error and data quality	Enhanced by machine learning and algorithms
Speed	Slower due to manual processes	Real-time processing and analysis
Scalability	Limited by manual effort	Easily scalable to handle large datasets

Table 6.1 – Traditional versus AI-driven financial analysis methods

A deep dive into AI-driven financial analysis

In the landscape of AI-driven financial analysis, data analytics plays a pivotal role. This section delves into how advanced data analytics, powered by AI, transform how financial data is interpreted and utilized. It explores the shift from traditional data analysis methods to more sophisticated, AI-driven techniques that enable deeper insights and more accurate predictions. The role of data analytics in identifying trends, uncovering hidden patterns, and providing actionable insights is highlighted, demonstrating its critical importance in strategic financial decision-making. The discussion also covers how AI-driven data analytics is empowering financial analysts to make more informed decisions backed by data-driven evidence and how it is enhancing the overall efficiency and effectiveness of financial analysis processes.

This section provides an overview of the various tools and techniques employed in AI-driven data analytics. It introduces critical technologies such as machine learning algorithms, neural networks, and natural language processing, explaining how they are applied in the context of financial analysis. The section discusses specific tools such as predictive modeling, sentiment analysis, and anomaly detection, illustrating how they are used to analyze financial data, forecast market trends, and assess investment opportunities. Examples of popular software and platforms used in AI-driven financial analysis are also presented, offering insights into how these tools are integrated into financial workflows. Additionally, the section addresses the challenges and considerations in selecting and implementing these tools, such as data quality, model accuracy, and interpretability, providing a comprehensive understanding of the advanced data analytics landscape in AI-driven financial analysis.

AI tool	Application in financial analysis
Machine learning	Trend analysis, predictive modeling
Predictive analytics	Forecasting future financial trends
Natural language processing (NLP)	Sentiment analysis, report generation

Table 6.2 – AI tools in financial analysis

Predictive analytics and forecasting

This section delves into the transformative impact of AI on predictive analytics and its application in financial forecasting. It explores how AI, particularly through machine learning and deep learning models, has significantly enhanced predictive capabilities in finance. Unlike traditional forecasting methods that often rely on linear projections based on historical data, AI-driven predictive analytics can process and analyze vast, complex datasets to identify non-linear patterns and trends. This section highlights how AI models can incorporate various variables, including market trends, economic indicators, and consumer behavior, to make more accurate and nuanced financial forecasts. The ability of AI to continually learn and adapt to new data further refines these forecasts, making them more reliable over time.

Case studies and examples

To illustrate the practical applications and benefits of AI in predictive analytics and financial forecasting, this part of the section presents a series of case studies and real-world examples.

AI in a retail company's revenue forecasting

The following is a case study of a retail company that used AI to analyze sales data, market trends, and consumer preferences to forecast future revenue accurately, enabling better inventory management and marketing strategies:

- **Company**: Luxe Fashion Inc. is a global retail chain specializing in luxury apparel.

- **Challenge:** The company is struggling with overstocking and understocking issues due to inaccurate sales forecasts.

- **Solution**: It implemented an AI system that analyzed historical sales data, current market trends, and consumer preferences.

- **Outcome**: The AI system provided highly accurate revenue forecasts, allowing Luxe Fashion Inc. to optimize inventory levels and tailor marketing strategies to consumer trends. This led to a 15% reduction in inventory costs and a 20% increase in sales due to better-targeted promotions and stock availability.

Risk assessment in banking

The following is an example of how a bank implemented AI-driven predictive analytics to assess credit risk more accurately, leading to more informed lending decisions and reduced default rates:

- **Bank**: Metro Bank is a large commercial bank.

- **Challenge**: It has high default rates for personal and small business loans.

- **Solution**: It deployed an AI-driven predictive analytics system to assess credit risk based on various factors, including non-traditional data points such as social media activity and online behavior.

- **Outcome**: The AI system identified risk patterns more accurately, leading to a more informed lending process. Default rates decreased by 25% and loan approval rates increased, with the bank able to identify previously overlooked creditworthy clients.

Investment strategy in asset management

The following is a case study demonstrating how an asset management firm used AI to predict market movements and optimize investment portfolios, resulting in higher investor returns:

- **Firm**: Quantum Asset Management is a mid-sized investment firm

- **Challenge**: It has difficulties with adapting to rapid market changes and identifying long-term profitable investments

- **Solution**: It implemented an AI system to analyze market data, financial news, and economic reports to predict market trends and identify investment opportunities

- **Outcome**: The AI-driven strategy outperformed traditional methods, leading to a 30% increase in returns for investors and attracting more clients to the firm due to its innovative approach

Real estate market analysis

The following is an example of how AI was used to forecast real estate market trends, helping investors and developers make informed decisions about property investments:

- **Company**: Urban Developers is a real estate development company

- **Challenge**: It has uncertainty in choosing profitable locations and types of developments

- **Solution**: It used AI to analyze various data sources, including demographic shifts, urban development plans, and historical property value trends, to forecast real estate market trends

- **Outcome**: AI predictions enabled Urban Developers to make strategic decisions about where and what type of properties to develop, resulting in a 40% increase in ROI on their projects and establishing them as a market leader in data-driven real estate development

These case studies not only showcase the effectiveness of AI in enhancing predictive analytics and financial forecasting but also provide insights into the diverse applications of AI across different sectors within the financial industry. They underscore the growing reliance on AI-driven insights in strategic financial planning and decision-making.

Company	AI solution implemented	Outcomes achieved
Retail giant	AI for sales forecasting and inventory management	Improved accuracy, reduced costs
Major bank	AI-driven credit risk assessment	Reduced default rates, enhanced portfolio
Asset management firm	AI algorithms for market analysis	Higher returns, efficient portfolio management

Table 6.3 – Case study summary

Real-time analysis and reporting

In the fast-paced world of finance, the ability to access and analyze data in real time is crucial for effective decision-making. This section emphasizes the importance of real-time data analysis and reporting in the financial sector. It discusses how real-time data allows financial professionals to respond quickly to market changes, seize opportunities, and mitigate risks as they arise. The section highlights the limitations of traditional financial analysis methods, which often involve time lags that can render insights outdated in rapidly evolving markets and economic conditions. By contrast, real-time analysis provides a snapshot of financial performance, market conditions, and other critical metrics, enabling more agile and informed decision-making.

AI technologies have enabled real-time analysis and reporting in financial contexts. This section explores various AI tools and systems that facilitate real-time data processing and analysis. It covers how AI algorithms can continuously analyze financial data streams, from stock prices and market news to social media trends and economic reports, providing up-to-the-minute insights. The section introduces some specific AI tools:

- **Automated dashboard and reporting systems**: These systems aggregate and visualize data in real-time, allowing financial analysts to monitor key performance indicators and market trends as they unfold

- **Predictive analytics software**: This software uses AI to analyze current data and predict future trends, offering real-time forecasts that can inform immediate financial decisions

- **NLP tools**: NLP tools can instantly analyze financial news, reports, and social media, extracting relevant information and sentiments that can impact financial markets

- **Algorithmic trading platforms**: These platforms use AI to execute trades in real time based on predefined criteria, capitalizing on market opportunities the moment they arise

The section also addresses integrating these tools into existing financial systems and workflows, discussing the challenges and best practices in adopting real-time analysis and reporting capabilities. By showcasing these AI tools, the section underscores the transformative impact of real-time data analysis in modern financial decision-making, highlighting how it is becoming an essential component of a proactive and strategic approach to finance.

Challenge	AI solution
Large data volumes	AI for efficient data processing
Market volatility	Predictive analytics for trend forecasting
Fraud detection	AI algorithms for anomaly detection

Table 6.4 – Challenges and AI solutions in financial analysis

Enhancing financial projections with AI

This section explores the innovative application of AI in scenario planning within financial projections. It discusses how AI technologies, particularly advanced predictive models and machine learning algorithms, are used to develop and analyze a wide range of financial scenarios. AI's ability to process and analyze large datasets enables it to consider numerous variables and potential outcomes, making scenario planning more comprehensive and data-driven. The section highlights how AI can simulate various market conditions, economic environments, and business decisions to predict their potential impacts on financial performance. This capability enhances a business's ability to prepare for different possibilities, making strategic planning more robust and adaptable.

Stress testing is a critical component of financial risk management, and AI has significantly enhanced this process. This section delves into how AI conducts stress tests on financial models, assessing their resilience under adverse conditions. AI-driven stress testing simulates extreme market scenarios and analyzes their effects on financial portfolios, balance sheets, and overall business stability. The section will cover how AI models can identify vulnerabilities and quantify potential risks, providing valuable insights for risk mitigation strategies. It will also discuss the advantages of AI in stress testing, such as the ability to quickly adapt tests based on evolving market dynamics and the capacity to analyze complex interdependencies within financial systems. By incorporating AI into stress testing, financial analysts can better understand risk exposures and prepare more effectively for potential financial crises.

Automating projection processes

This section delves into the role of AI in automating and enhancing financial projection processes. It explores how AI technologies, particularly machine learning and data analytics, are being used to streamline and optimize the way financial projections are developed. The discussion focuses on automating repetitive and time-consuming tasks, such as data collection, data cleaning, and initial analysis, which traditionally require significant manual effort. AI's ability to process large volumes of data quickly and accurately allows for more efficient and reliable projection processes. The section also highlights how AI algorithms can identify trends and patterns in financial data that might be overlooked in manual analyses, leading to more accurate and insightful projections.

We'll discuss the benefits and some examples:

- **Increased efficiency: example—Fast Finance Solutions**: A mid-sized financial institution faced challenges with the lengthy duration of its financial projection process. By implementing an AI system, Fast Finance Solutions reduced the time required to generate financial projections from several weeks to a few days. This acceleration enabled more agile and timely decision-making, allowing the institution to respond quickly to market changes and adjust strategies accordingly.

- **Enhanced accuracy: example—Pro Revenue Corp.**: A multinational corporation specializing in consumer electronics, Pro Revenue Corp., struggled with forecasting future revenue streams. Introducing an AI-driven projection system allowed for analyzing complex market data, consumer trends, and economic indicators. This led to significantly more accurate revenue predictions, which informed strategic planning and investment decisions, ultimately driving a noticeable increase in market share and investor confidence.

- **Scalability: example—Growth Tech Enterprises**: An emerging tech start-up, Growth Tech Enterprises, experienced rapid growth and needed to scale its financial analysis capabilities. Implementing AI enabled the company to manage and analyze increasingly complex and voluminous financial data efficiently. This scalability was instrumental in supporting the company's expansion, allowing for data-driven decisions that fueled further growth, profitability, and innovation in new market segments.

These examples demonstrate the practical advantages of AI in automating financial projection processes and provide insights into how different organizations can implement similar technologies to enhance their financial planning and analysis functions.

Company	Industry/Field	Challenge Faced	AI Implementation	Outcome Achieved
Fast Finance Solutions	Financial Institution	Lengthy financial projection process	AI system for rapid data processing	Reduced projection time from weeks to days, enabling agile decision-making

Company	Industry/Field	Challenge Faced	AI Implementation	Outcome Achieved
Pro Revenue Corp.	Consumer Electronics	Inaccurate revenue forecasting	AI-driven system for market data analysis	More accurate revenue predictions, informed strategic planning, increased market share
Growth Tech Enterprises	Tech Startup	Need to scale financial analysis with growth	AI for managing complex financial data	Efficient handling of complex data, supporting company expansion and innovation

Table 6.5 – Summary of AI in automating financial projection processes

Increasing accuracy and reliability

This section examines the critical role of AI in improving the accuracy of financial projections. AI's advanced algorithms and machine learning capabilities enable a more precise analysis of financial data, leading to more accurate forecasting. The section highlights how AI can process and analyze vast amounts of data from various sources, including market trends, economic indicators, and consumer behaviors, to create a more comprehensive and nuanced financial projection. AI's ability to learn from data and adjust its models accordingly reduces the margin of error typically associated with human analysis and traditional forecasting methods. This part of the chapter will delve into the technical aspects of how AI achieves this enhanced accuracy, including its use of predictive analytics, pattern recognition, and probabilistic modeling.

The increased accuracy of financial projections due to AI directly impacts the reliability of these projections, which in turn significantly influences business decision-making. This section explores how reliable financial projections, bolstered by AI, provide a solid foundation for strategic planning, risk management, and investment decisions. It discusses how businesses can use AI-driven projections to confidently navigate market uncertainties and make informed decisions about future investments, resource allocation, and growth strategies. The section also addresses the trust and confidence stakeholders, including investors and executives, have placed in AI-enhanced financial projections. Providing real-world examples on automating projection processes with AI highlights benefits such as increased efficiency, accuracy, and scalability. This part of the section provides concrete examples to illustrate case studies and how AI's contribution to accuracy and reliability in financial projections has led to more successful business outcomes:

- **Strategic business expansion: Global Tech Innovations**:

  - **Background**: Global Tech Innovations, a leading technology firm, sought to expand its operations internationally but was unsure of the most lucrative markets to enter.

  - **AI implementation**: The company utilized AI-driven projections to analyze market data, consumer trends, and economic indicators across various geographical regions.

- **Outcome**: The AI system identified several high-potential markets for their products. Global Tech Innovations successfully entered these markets, resulting in significant growth in revenue and market share. The AI-driven approach allowed for a strategic and data-informed expansion, minimizing risks associated with international market entry.

- **Risk mitigation in investment decisions: Alpha Investments**:

  - **Background**: Alpha Investments, a prominent investment firm, faced challenges in assessing the risk profiles of diverse investment opportunities.

  - **AI implementation**: The firm integrated AI-enhanced projections into its decision-making process. The AI system was designed to analyze historical performance data, market trends, and risk factors associated with various investment options.

  - **Outcome**: With AI's advanced risk assessment capabilities, Alpha Investments was able to identify investment opportunities with the most favorable risk–reward profiles. This led to more secure and profitable investment choices, enhancing the firm's reputation and client trust.

- **Resource allocation in corporate finance: Eco Energy Corp.**:

  - **Background**: Eco Energy Corp., an energy company focusing on sustainable solutions, needed to optimize its budgeting and resource allocation amidst a rapidly changing energy sector.

  - **AI implementation**: The corporation employed AI to forecast market demand, regulatory changes, and technological advancements in the energy sector accurately.

  - **Outcome**: AI's precise forecasting enabled Eco Energy Corp. to allocate resources efficiently, focusing on the most promising projects and technologies. This strategic allocation maximized ROI and positioned the company as a leader in sustainable energy solutions.

These examples underscore the tangible benefits of AI in financial decision-making processes. They demonstrate how AI's ability to enhance the accuracy and reliability of financial projections is not just a theoretical advantage but a practical tool that drives better business decisions and outcomes. This section aims to provide readers with a clear understanding of AI's value in financial projections and the broader implications for businesses and the financial industry:

Company	Industry	Challenge	AI implementation	Outcome
Global Tech Innovations	Technology	Identifying lucrative markets for expansion	AI-driven market analysis	Successful entry and growth in new geographical areas, increased revenue and market share

Company	Industry	Challenge	AI implementation	Outcome
Alpha Investments	Investment firm	Assessing the risk profiles of investments	AI-enhanced risk assessment projections	More secure and profitable investment choices, enhanced firm reputation and client trust
Eco Energy Corp.	Sustainable energy	Optimizing budgeting and resource allocation	AI forecasting for market and technology trends	Efficient resource allocation, maximized ROI, establishment as a leader in sustainable energy

Table 6.6 – AI-driven strategies in business decision-making

Practical implications and applications

This section presents a series of case studies that illustrate the real-world applications and impacts of AI in financial analysis and projection. These case studies provide tangible examples of how AI technologies are being utilized in various industries and financial contexts, showcasing their practical benefits and the challenges encountered during implementation:

- **AI in retail financial forecasting: Trend Max Retailers**:

  - **Background**: Trend Max Retailers, a leading global retail chain, faced challenges with sales forecasting and inventory management.

  - **AI implementation**: The company implemented an AI system for advanced sales forecasting and inventory optimization.

  - **Outcome**: The AI system significantly improved forecasting accuracy, leading to better stock optimization and reduced costs. Trend Max Retailers experienced a 20% reduction in inventory costs and a 15% increase in sales due to more effective stock availability and reduced overstocking.

- **AI-driven risk management in banking: Central Trust Bank**:

  - **Background**: Central Trust Bank, a prominent banking institution, sought to enhance its credit risk assessment process.

  - **AI implementation**: The bank employed AI for in-depth credit risk analysis, utilizing machine learning algorithms to evaluate creditworthiness more comprehensively.

  - **Outcome**: The AI-driven approach led to a significant reduction in default rates and improved the overall quality of the bank's loan portfolio. Central Trust Bank also saw an increase in customer satisfaction due to more accurate and fair credit assessments.

- **Automated investment strategies in asset management: Quantum Capital**:

  · **Background**: Quantum Capital, an innovative asset management firm, aimed to improve its investment strategies.

  · **AI implementation**: The firm used AI algorithms for detailed market analysis and automated investment decision-making.

  · **Outcome**: Quantum Capital achieved higher returns for its clients, with a 25% increase in portfolio performance. The AI system enabled more efficient portfolio management and better adaptation to market changes.

- **AI in corporate financial planning: Global Dynamics Corp.**: An example of a multinational corporation that integrated AI into its financial planning process, enabling more accurate budgeting and financial resource allocation.

  · **Background**: Global Dynamics Corp., a multinational corporation, needed to enhance its financial planning process.

  · **AI implementation**: The corporation integrated AI into its financial planning, employing predictive analytics for budgeting and resource allocation.

  · **Outcome**: AI enabled more accurate and dynamic financial planning, leading to optimized resource allocation and budgeting. Global Dynamics Corp. saw a 30% improvement in financial efficiency and a significant reduction in unnecessary expenditure.

Company	Industry	Challenge faced	AI implementation	Outcome achieved
Trend Max Retailers	Retail	Inaccurate sales forecasting and inventory management issues	AI for sales forecasting and inventory optimization	A 20% reduction in inventory costs, 15% increase in sales due to better stock optimization
Central Trust Bank	Banking	Need for enhanced credit risk assessment	AI-driven credit risk analysis	Significant reduction in default rates, improved loan portfolio quality
Quantum Capital	Asset management	Improving investment strategies	AI algorithms for market analysis and automated investment decisions	A 25% increase in portfolio performance, more efficient portfolio management
Global Dynamics Corp.	Multinational corporation	Enhancing the financial planning process	AI for predictive analytics in budgeting and resource allocation	A 30% improvement in financial efficiency, reduction in unnecessary expenditures

Table 6.7 – AI in financial analysis and projection: case studies

Best practices and strategies

This part of the section outlines the best practices for integrating AI into financial analysis and projection processes. It covers key considerations such as ensuring data quality and integrity, selecting the right AI tools and platforms, and aligning AI initiatives with business objectives. The discussion includes the importance of stakeholder engagement, training and upskilling of financial teams, and establishing clear governance and ethical guidelines for AI use.

Effective implementation of AI in financial analysis requires strategic planning and execution. This section provides strategies for successfully integrating AI into financial workflows. It emphasizes the need for a phased implementation approach, starting with pilot projects for testing and learning before scaling AI solutions across the organization. The section also discusses the importance of continuously monitoring and evaluating AI systems, adapting and refining AI models as business needs evolve, and staying abreast of technological advancements in AI to ensure that financial analysis methods remain cutting-edge and competitive.

By combining case studies with best practices and strategies, this section offers a comprehensive guide for professionals looking to harness the power of AI in financial analysis and projection, ensuring they are well-equipped to navigate the challenges and maximize the benefits of this transformative technology.

Skill/competency	Description
Data literacy	Understanding and interpreting data
AI proficiency	Knowledge of AI tools and applications
Critical thinking	Analyzing AI outputs and making decisions

Table 6.8 – Skills and competencies for financial analysts in the AI era

Ethical and regulatory considerations

This section focuses on the critical issues of data security and privacy in the context of AI-driven financial analysis. With AI systems processing vast amounts of sensitive financial data, ensuring the security and confidentiality of this data is paramount. The discussion will cover the risks associated with data breaches, unauthorized access, and data misuse in AI applications. It will also explore the strategies and technologies used to safeguard data, such as encryption, secure data storage, and access control mechanisms. Additionally, the section will address compliance with data protection regulations such as GDPR and how AI systems can be designed and operated to uphold the highest data privacy standards. This chapter highlights the importance of robust data security and privacy measures in maintaining trust and integrity in AI-driven financial analysis.

Transparency and accountability are critical concerns in deploying AI for financial decision-making. This section explores how businesses and financial institutions can maintain transparency in their AI-driven processes and ensure accountability for the decisions made by AI systems. It discusses the challenges of "black box" AI models—where the decision-making process is not easily understandable—and the importance of developing interpretable and explainable AI models. The section also covers the ethical implications of AI decisions, particularly in high-stakes financial contexts, and the need for clear guidelines and frameworks to govern AI use. Additionally, it addresses the role of regulatory bodies in overseeing AI applications in finance and the importance of adhering to industry standards and ethical principles. This section emphasizes transparency and accountability and underscores the need for responsible AI practices that foster trust and confidence among users, stakeholders, and the broader public.

Strategy/best practice	Description
Align with objectives	Ensure AI initiatives align with business goals
Pilot projects	Start with small-scale implementations
Continuous learning	Keep up with AI advancements

Table 6.9 – AI implementation strategies and best practices

Preparing for an AI-driven future in financial analysis

This section outlines the essential skills and competencies that financial analysts need to thrive in an AI-driven environment. It emphasizes the importance of data literacy, including understanding data sources, data processing, and data interpretation in the context of AI. The section also highlights the need for proficiency in AI and machine learning concepts and familiarity with AI tools and platforms commonly used in financial analysis. Additionally, it discusses the growing importance of soft skills, such as critical thinking, problem-solving, and adaptability, in an ever-evolving technological landscape.

To equip financial analysts with these necessary skills, this section explores the various training and development initiatives organizations can undertake. It covers the design of targeted training programs, workshops, and continuous learning opportunities to keep pace with technological advancements. The discussion also includes strategies for fostering a culture of learning and innovation within financial teams.

Strategies for successful implementation

This section provides a roadmap for organizations looking to integrate AI into their financial analysis processes. It discusses the importance of aligning AI initiatives with business objectives, conducting thorough needs assessments, and choosing the right AI solutions. The section also delves into the practical implementation aspects, including infrastructure setup, data management, and integration with existing systems.

Implementing AI in financial analysis comes with its set of challenges. This section addresses common obstacles, such as data quality issues, resistance to change, and budget constraints. It offers strategies to overcome these challenges, such as stakeholder engagement, phased implementation approaches, and ROI analysis. Additionally, it highlights how organizations can leverage AI to create new opportunities and competitive advantages in financial analysis.

Future outlook

This section offers predictions and insights into future trends in AI as it relates to financial analysis. It discusses potential advancements in AI technologies and how they might shape financial practices.

Potential developments and innovations

The landscape of AI-driven financial analysis is poised for significant advancements and innovations. As technology evolves, we can anticipate several key developments:

- **Quantum computing in financial modeling**: The integration of quantum computing with AI could revolutionize financial modeling and analysis. Quantum computers, with their immense processing power, could handle complex financial simulations and scenarios much more efficiently than current systems.

- **Explainable AI (XAI) for transparency**: As AI models become more complex, the need for transparency grows. XAI aims to make AI decision-making processes clear and understandable, which is crucial for trust and accountability in financial decisions.

- **AI-driven personalized financial services**: Advancements in AI could lead to highly personalized financial advice and services, tailored to individual customer profiles, preferences, and financial goals, transforming the customer experience in banking and investment.

- **Blockchain and AI integration**: Combining blockchain technology with AI could enhance security and transparency in financial transactions and record-keeping, leading to more robust and trustworthy financial systems.

- **Predictive analytics for real-time decision-making**: Future AI systems will likely offer even more advanced predictive capabilities, enabling real-time financial decision-making and forecasting, with a focus on predictive rather than reactive financial management.

Summary

AI is revolutionizing financial analysis and projection by significantly enhancing accuracy, efficiency, and predictive power. AI-driven tools and algorithms can process vast amounts of data in real-time, uncovering patterns and trends that traditional methods might overlook. This allows for more precise forecasting and risk assessment. Additionally, AI enables automated decision-making and reduces human error, leading to more reliable financial outcomes. The transformative impact of AI also democratizes financial analysis, making advanced analytical capabilities accessible to smaller firms and individual investors, thereby leveling the playing field in the financial sector.

In closing, the chapter reflected on the future trajectory of financial analysis in the context of AI. It emphasized the potential for AI to continue driving innovation, efficiency, and accuracy in financial practices.

Further reading

Books:

- *Artificial Intelligence in Finance: A Python-Based Guide* by Yves Hilpisch
- *Machine Learning for Asset Managers* by Marcos López de Prado

Academic articles:

- *Big Data and AI Strategies: Machine Learning and Alternative Data Approach to Investing* by J.P. Morgan
- *The FinTech Opportunity* by Thomas Philippon, published in the NBER Macroeconomics Annual

Online platforms:

- Coursera and edX offer courses such as *AI in Finance* and *Machine Learning for Finance*
- See the Financial Times' AI hub for the latest news and insights on AI in finance

Q&A

1. How is AI transforming traditional financial analysis?

   AI is revolutionizing financial analysis by introducing a level of automation and efficiency that goes far beyond traditional methods. It accomplishes this through several key innovations:

   - **Enhanced data processing**: AI algorithms can process vast volumes of financial data at unprecedented speeds, significantly reducing the time and effort required for data analysis.

   - **Advanced predictive analytics**: AI employs sophisticated machine learning models to predict market trends, investment outcomes, and financial risks, offering insights that were previously unattainable with standard statistical methods.

   - **Real-time decision-making**: AI enables financial analysts to make informed decisions quickly thanks to its ability to analyze real-time data. This capability is a significant leap from traditional methods, which often rely on historical data analysis.

2. What are the ethical considerations in AI-driven financial analysis?

   When utilizing AI in financial analysis, several ethical considerations must be considered:

   - **Data privacy**: Ensuring the confidentiality and security of financial data is paramount, as AI systems often handle sensitive personal and business information

- **Algorithmic transparency**: There is a need for a clear understanding of and transparency in how AI algorithms make decisions to maintain trust and accountability

- **Bias and fairness**: It's crucial to ensure that AI-driven decisions are free from biases and do not perpetuate unfair practices, which requires regular auditing and refinement of AI models

3. How can one stay up to date with AI advancements in finance?

Staying abreast of AI advancements in finance involves taking a proactive approach:

- **Continuous learning platforms**: Utilize online courses and platforms, such as Coursera, edX, or courses offered through trade associations, that offer specialized courses in AI and finance

- **Industry conferences**: Attending finance and technology conferences can provide insights into the latest trends and developments

- **Financial technology publications and forums**: Regularly reading reputable fintech publications and participating in professional forums can help keep professionals informed about the latest AI advancements

4. What skills are essential for financial analysts in the era of AI?

In the era of AI, financial analysts need to develop a blend of technical and soft skills:

- **Data analytics proficiency**: Being able to interpret and analyze data is crucial in an AI-driven environment

- **AI and machine learning understanding**: A foundational knowledge of AI and machine learning concepts is essential to understanding how these technologies impact financial analysis

- **Ethical reasoning**: Analysts must be equipped to navigate the ethical implications of using AI in finance

- **Adaptability**: The ability to adapt to rapidly changing technologies and methodologies is critical for staying relevant in the field

5. What is the future outlook for AI in financial analysis?

The future of AI in financial analysis is poised for significant advancements:

- **Sophisticated predictive models**: AI is expected to develop more nuanced and accurate predictive models, offering deeper insights into financial markets

- **Integration with emerging technologies**: Technologies such as blockchains may increasingly integrate with AI, enhancing security and transparency in financial transactions

- **Personalization and customer-centric services**: AI will likely focus more on personalizing financial services, tailoring insights and recommendations to individual customer needs and preferences

7

Advancing Managerial Accounting with AI

"If implemented the right way, AI has the potential to significantly improve efficiency and reduce costs for the accounting industry while freeing up professionals' time to focus on higher-level, value-added engagements."

- *The AI Revolution: Transforming Accountants' Roles*

By Sean P. Breheney, CPA, MBA, PKF O'Connor Davies – September 12, 2023

AI has brought about a paradigm shift in managerial accounting by automating repetitive, high-volume tasks such as data entry, reconciliation, and financial transaction analysis, all of which have traditionally been performed manually. This automation improves efficiency and reduces costs while freeing accounting professionals to focus on higher-level, value-added engagements, enhancing their role from mere number crunchers to strategic advisors.

The advent of machine learning, a subset of AI, has further accelerated this transformation. Machine learning algorithms are designed to learn from data, enabling tasks that previously consumed a significant portion of an accountant's time to be automated. By adopting these processes, accounting firms and accounting departments can expedite decision-making while reducing associated costs, even allowing smaller firms to implement these advanced processes on a smaller scale using pre-built software.

Despite concerns about AI potentially replacing many aspects of human work in accounting, it offers a more intuitive approach to data analysis. AI can reduce the impact of human error and provide more accurate, precise, and consistent results. It also aids in regulatory compliance by recognizing patterns and detecting anomalies that suggest noncompliance, thereby playing a crucial role in reducing fraud risk within the audit industry.

The integration of AI in accounting is not just about technological adoption but also about adapting to new roles and opportunities that AI presents. With routine tasks being automated, accountants can explore new specialties and add higher levels of value in other practice areas, focusing on the human element that distinguishes them from their peers.

As AI continues to evolve and impact the accounting industry, it's clear that its role is not to displace accountants but to enhance their capabilities and allow them to thrive in a changing landscape. The future of accounting lies in embracing AI, adapting to its developments, and leveraging the opportunities it provides to advance the profession. Here's a quick comparison between traditional and AI-enhanced approaches in accounting:

Task	Traditional Approach	AI-Enhanced Approach	Impact
Data analysis	Manual data aggregation and analysis	Automated data processing and real-time analysis	Increased efficiency and accuracy
Forecasting	Based on historical trends and manual calculations	Predictive analytics and machine learning models	Improved accuracy and strategic foresight
Reporting	Static reports generated periodically	Dynamic, real-time reporting with interactive dashboards	Enhanced decision-making support
Compliance	Manual monitoring and reporting	Automated compliance checks and reporting	Reduced risk of errors and non-compliance

Table 7.1: Traditional versus AI-enhanced managerial accounting tasks

Next, we'll explore the role of AI in budgeting and forecasting.

AI in budgeting and forecasting

The incorporation of AI in budgeting and forecasting represents a significant leap forward in managerial accounting. AI's ability to analyze large datasets and predict future trends brings a new level of precision and efficiency to financial planning.

Expanding on AI's effectiveness in financial planning through case studies

Let's look at a few case studies to better understand AI's effectiveness.

Case study 1 – retail chain sales forecasting

A leading retail chain implemented AI to refine its budgeting and sales forecasting for over 500 stores nationwide. The AI system integrated historical sales data, local economic indicators, seasonal trends, and promotional activities to predict sales at a granular level for each store. By identifying patterns and correlating them with upcoming marketing campaigns and seasonal changes, the AI provided forecasts that were significantly more accurate than previous models. This enabled the chain to optimize stock levels, reducing both understock and overstock situations, leading to improved customer satisfaction and a reduction in storage and markdown costs. The adaptability of the AI model allowed for rapid adjustments to forecasts in response to real-time market changes, ensuring that each store operated at peak efficiency.

Case study 2 – manufacturing resource optimization

A global manufacturing firm specializing in consumer electronics utilized AI to enhance its forecasting for raw material procurement and product demand. The AI model drew from a diverse set of inputs, including global market trends, raw material price fluctuations, geopolitical events, and historical production efficiency data. By accurately forecasting material costs and product demand, the company was able to streamline its manufacturing process, aligning production volumes closely with market demand. This optimization led to a significant reduction in inventory holding costs and minimized the risk of stockouts or excess inventory, thereby safeguarding the firm's profit margins and market competitiveness.

Case study 3 – financial services revenue projections

In the dynamic world of financial services, a prominent investment firm leveraged AI to revolutionize its revenue forecasting and client advisory services. The AI system analyzed vast data arrays, including historical investment performance, market volatility indicators, regulatory changes, and macroeconomic trends. By providing highly accurate revenue forecasts, the firm could tailor its investment strategies to capitalize on market opportunities more effectively. Furthermore, the AI's predictive insights enabled the firm to offer personalized investment advice to clients, enhancing client satisfaction and loyalty. The firm's proactive approach, powered by AI-driven analytics, secured its competitive edge and set new industry standards for financial advisory services.

These expanded case studies illustrate AI's profound impact on budgeting and forecasting within diverse sectors. By harnessing the power of AI, businesses can achieve heightened accuracy in financial planning and gain strategic insights that drive decision-making and competitive advantage. As AI technology continues to evolve and integrate into various business functions, its role in enhancing financial efficiency and strategic foresight will undoubtedly become more pronounced, marking a new era in managerial accounting.

Now that we've illustrated how AI enhances financial planning effectiveness through real-world applications, let's delve into the transformative role of AI in another critical domain: cost management.

Cost management through AI

AI is revolutionizing cost management in business, offering unprecedented opportunities for identifying cost-saving opportunities and achieving operational efficiencies. By analyzing vast datasets and identifying patterns and inefficiencies that might escape human notice, AI is enabling businesses to optimize their spending and resource allocation in ways never before possible.

AI's utility in identifying cost-saving opportunities

AI algorithms, particularly those based on machine learning, can sift through complex data to identify inefficiencies, waste, and opportunities for cost reduction across various business operations. For instance, AI can analyze procurement data to identify trends and anomalies, such as unusually high costs for certain materials or services, suggesting areas where negotiations or supplier changes could yield savings.

Moreover, AI can optimize energy usage in manufacturing processes or building management by analyzing usage patterns and adjusting systems in real time for maximum efficiency. Predictive maintenance, another AI application, anticipates equipment failures before they occur, preventing costly downtime and extending the lifespan of machinery.

Next, we'll look at a few examples of operational efficiencies that have been achieved through AI.

Example 1 – supply chain optimization

A multinational corporation utilized AI to overhaul its supply chain, resulting in substantial cost reductions and increased agility. The AI system analyzed historical supply chain data, including supplier performance, transportation costs, and inventory levels, to identify bottlenecks and inefficiencies. By implementing AI-driven recommendations, the company optimized its routing, reduced inventory levels through just-in-time inventory practices, and improved supplier selection, saving millions in operational costs annually.

Example 2 – energy consumption reduction in data centers

A leading tech company employed AI to manage energy consumption in its vast data centers. The AI system monitored real-time data from cooling systems, servers, and external weather conditions to dynamically adjust cooling requirements. This not only reduced energy consumption by a significant margin but also decreased the carbon footprint of the company's data centers, aligning with its sustainability goals.

Example 3 – AI-driven workforce optimization

A service-based enterprise harnessed AI to optimize its workforce allocation, addressing the common issue of overstaffing or understaffing across its various locations. The AI analyzed customer traffic patterns, service demand, and staff performance to create optimal scheduling, ensuring that customer service levels remained high while minimizing unnecessary labor costs. This strategic workforce management led to enhanced employee satisfaction due to better work-life balance, reduced overtime costs, and improved overall service quality.

Integrating AI into cost management practices offers a clear pathway to operational efficiency and financial optimization. By leveraging AI's analytical prowess, businesses can uncover hidden cost-saving opportunities, streamline operations, and allocate resources more effectively. As AI technology continues to advance, its role in driving cost efficiency and operational excellence will undoubtedly expand, further solidifying its value in strategic cost management.

Now that we've showcased the tangible impacts of AI in uncovering cost-saving opportunities and optimizing operational efficiencies, let's focus on another critical aspect: performance management.

Performance management with AI

Integrating AI into performance management is transforming how businesses monitor and manage their financial performance. AI tools are being employed to provide deeper insights, automate analysis, and enhance the decision-making process regarding financial health and operational efficiency.

Utilizing AI tools for performance monitoring and management

AI systems excel in aggregating and analyzing data from diverse sources, offering a comprehensive view of an organization's financial performance. These tools can process real-time data, from sales figures and production costs to market trends and customer feedback, providing a holistic view of performance almost instantaneously.

As an example, AI-driven analytics platforms can track financial metrics against historical performance, benchmarks, and forecasts, identifying variances that require attention. Predictive analytics can forecast future trends based on current data, allowing organizations to anticipate changes in financial performance and adjust strategies proactively.

AI's role in enhancing KPI evaluation and OKR targets

Evaluating **key performance indicators** (**KPIs**) and **objectives and key results** (**OKRs**) is crucial in gauging an organization's success in meeting its operational and strategic goals. AI significantly influences this process by offering advanced data processing capabilities and insights generation:

- **Automated KPI and OKR tracking**: AI tools automate the process of tracking KPIs and OKRs, continuously analyzing data streams to provide up-to-date information on performance metrics. This automation ensures that decision-makers have access to the latest data without manual intervention.

- **Advanced data analysis**: Beyond simple tracking, AI can delve into the "why" behind the numbers while employing machine learning to identify patterns, correlations, and causations within the data. This can reveal underlying factors affecting KPIs, offering actionable insights for improvement.

- **Predictive insights for KPIs**: AI's predictive capabilities can forecast future performance based on current and historical data trends. This allows organizations to set more informed targets and adjust their strategies to address anticipated challenges or capitalize on emerging opportunities.

- **Personalized dashboards and reporting**: AI allows you to customize dashboards and reports so that you can focus on the KPIs most relevant to specific users or departments. This personalization ensures that stakeholders have direct access to the metrics that matter most to their responsibilities and goals.

Let's look at some case examples.

Case 1 – retail chain inventory management

A retail chain used AI to optimize inventory levels across its stores, tying inventory KPIs directly to sales forecasts and supplier performance. The AI system provided predictive insights that helped adjust inventory in real time, reducing overstock and stockouts while significantly improving cash flow and customer satisfaction.

Case 2 – financial services risk assessment

A financial services firm implemented AI to enhance its risk management KPIs, analyzing client portfolios and market conditions to assess risk exposure accurately. The AI system's insights allowed for more nuanced risk mitigation strategies, protecting assets while identifying growth opportunities.

AI is redefining performance management by offering advanced tools for real-time monitoring, in-depth analysis, and predictive financial performance forecasting. By enhancing the evaluation of KPIs, AI empowers organizations to make data-driven decisions, optimize operations, and strategically align their resources for maximum effectiveness. As AI technologies continue to evolve, their role in performance management is set to become even more integral, driving efficiency and strategic insight across all levels of an organization.

AI-enabled strategic decision-making

The advent of AI has significantly bolstered strategic planning and decision-making processes in businesses. By offering advanced data analysis, predictive modeling, and scenario planning, AI is empowering organizations to make more informed, strategic financial decisions.

AI's support in strategic planning and decision-making

AI's capacity to process and analyze vast amounts of data surpasses human capabilities, enabling a more nuanced understanding of market trends, consumer behavior, and financial forecasts. This analytical power supports strategic planning by providing a data-driven foundation for decision-making, ensuring strategies are aligned with predictive market insights and operational capabilities:

- **Predictive modeling**: AI excels in forecasting future market trends, customer demand, and revenue potentials by analyzing current and historical data. These predictive models allow businesses to anticipate changes and adapt their strategies proactively.

- **Scenario planning**: AI can simulate various strategic scenarios based on different assumptions and external factors, such as economic changes, market trends, or competitive actions. This helps organizations evaluate potential outcomes and make strategic decisions that hedge against risks while capitalizing on opportunities.

- **Optimization algorithms**: AI uses optimization algorithms to identify the most efficient allocation of resources, whether it's capital investment, workforce distribution, or supply chain logistics, ensuring that strategic decisions maximize operational efficiency and profitability.

For a better understanding, let's look at some real-world instances of AI-facilitated strategic financial decisions.

Instance 1 – multinational corporation market expansion

A multinational corporation utilized AI to assess the viability of entering new markets. The AI system analyzed economic indicators, consumer behavior data, and competitive landscapes across various regions. By identifying the most promising markets and forecasting potential revenue, the corporation strategically allocated resources to its expansion efforts, resulting in successful market penetration and significant revenue growth.

Instance 2 – tech startup product development

A tech startup harnessed AI to guide its product development strategy. Through sentiment analysis and trend forecasting, the AI tool identified emerging consumer needs and technological trends. This insight allowed the startup to prioritize its R&D investments, leading to the development of a highly successful product line that met market demand and outpaced competitors.

Instance 3 – financial services portfolio management

A financial services firm integrated AI into its portfolio management strategy. By employing AI-driven risk assessment and market analysis, the firm was able to optimize its investment portfolio balancing risk and reward more effectively. The AI's predictive insights into market movements and asset performance enabled the firm to make strategic shifts in its investment strategy, enhancing portfolio returns while maintaining risk tolerance levels. AI-enabled strategic decision-making transforms how organizations approach planning and resource allocation. By leveraging AI's predictive insights and analytical capabilities, businesses can navigate the complexities of modern markets with greater confidence and precision. These real-world instances underscore AI's potential to drive strategic financial decisions that propel businesses forward, highlighting the technology's integral role in future corporate strategy development.

Having explored the transformative role of AI in facilitating strategic financial decisions, let's shift our focus to the critical realms of risk management and compliance.

Risk management and compliance

The integration of AI into risk management and compliance has revolutionized the approach businesses take to navigate financial risks and adhere to regulatory standards. AI's advanced analytical capabilities and real-time processing power offer a proactive and efficient means to assess, mitigate, and monitor financial risks while ensuring compliance.

AI's application in financial risk assessment and mitigation

AI systems employ predictive analytics, machine learning algorithms, and data mining techniques to identify potential financial risks before they materialize. By analyzing vast datasets, AI can detect subtle patterns and correlations that may indicate emerging risks, from credit risks to market volatility and operational inefficiencies:

- **Credit risk analysis**: AI models assess the creditworthiness of borrowers by analyzing traditional financial metrics and incorporating alternative data sources, such as social media activity or transaction histories, to predict the likelihood of default more accurately

- **Market risk management**: AI tools monitor market conditions and global economic indicators in real time, helping firms to anticipate market movements and adjust their investment strategies accordingly to maximize gains and minimize losses

- **Operational risk identification**: By analyzing internal processes and historical incidents, AI can identify operational vulnerabilities and recommend corrective actions to prevent future occurrences

AI's role in ensuring compliance with financial regulations

Compliance with financial regulations is a critical aspect of risk management. AI enhances regulatory compliance by automating the monitoring and reporting processes, ensuring that financial institutions adhere to laws and standards efficiently and effectively:

- **Automated regulatory reporting**: AI systems can automate the process of extracting, processing, and submitting required regulatory filings, reducing the likelihood of errors and ensuring timely compliance

- **Fraud detection and anti-money laundering** (**AML**): AI-driven systems analyze transaction patterns to identify suspicious activities that may indicate fraud or money laundering, facilitating prompt investigation and reporting to regulatory authorities

- **Compliance monitoring**: AI continuously scans for changes in regulatory requirements across jurisdictions and updates compliance frameworks accordingly, ensuring that businesses remain compliant amid a constantly evolving regulatory landscape

Let's explore some real-world applications to understand this better.

Banking sector compliance automation

A leading bank implemented AI to streamline its compliance processes, particularly in AML and **know-your-customer** (**KYC**) regulations. The AI system enhanced the accuracy and speed of customer verification processes and suspicious activity reports, significantly reducing manual workload and improving compliance efficiency.

Insurance risk assessment

An insurance company utilized AI to revolutionize its risk assessment models and incorporated a wider range of data points, including environmental and social factors, to predict claims more accurately. This not only improved risk pricing but also ensured compliance with emerging regulatory standards focused on holistic risk assessment.

AI's role in risk management and compliance is transformative, offering businesses a powerful tool to navigate the complex landscape of financial risks and regulatory requirements. By leveraging AI, organizations can achieve a higher level of precision in risk assessment, enhance operational efficiencies, and maintain compliance with greater ease, ultimately safeguarding their financial health and reputation. As AI technology continues to evolve, its impact on risk management and compliance is poised to deepen, further embedding AI as an essential component of modern financial strategies.

Now that we've examined the pivotal role of AI in ensuring compliance with financial regulations through real-world applications within the banking and insurance sectors, we must pivot our attention toward the critical domain of ethical and legal considerations.

Ethical and legal considerations

As businesses leverage AI for regulatory compliance and risk assessment, understanding and addressing ethical considerations and legal frameworks become paramount to fostering trust, transparency, and accountability:

Ethical Consideration	Mitigation Strategy	Implementation
Data privacy	Implement robust data encryption and access controls	Ensure compliance with data protection regulations
Algorithmic bias	Regularly audit AI systems for bias and adjust algorithms	Diversify training data and incorporate fairness criteria
Transparency	Develop explainable AI (XAI) models	Provide clear documentation and rationale for AI-driven decisions

Table 7.2: Ethical considerations and mitigation strategies in AI implementation

The integration of AI into managerial accounting raises significant ethical and legal considerations. As AI systems take on more complex tasks, including decision-making processes previously reserved for humans, it becomes crucial to address the ethical implications and navigate the evolving legal landscape surrounding AI applications.

Ethical implications of utilizing AI in managerial accounting

Let's delve into the key ethical considerations associated with utilizing AI in managerial accounting while focusing on aspects such as data privacy, transparency, bias mitigation, and accountability to ensure ethical practices in leveraging AI for financial decision-making:

- **Data privacy and security**: With AI systems processing vast amounts of sensitive financial data, ensuring the privacy and security of this data is paramount. Ethical considerations include safeguarding against unauthorized access and ensuring that data usage complies with privacy regulations such as GDPR.

- **Transparency and explainability**: The "black box" nature of some AI systems can lead to a lack of transparency in how decisions are made. Ethical practices necessitate making these processes more transparent and understandable, ensuring that stakeholders can trust and verify AI-driven decisions.

- **Bias and fairness**: AI systems can inherit biases from their training data, leading to unfair or discriminatory outcomes. Ethically, it's essential to audit AI systems regularly for bias and take corrective actions to ensure fairness in decision-making processes.

- **Accountability**: Determining accountability for decisions made by AI systems is a complex ethical issue. Organizations must establish clear guidelines on accountability, ensuring that human oversight is maintained in critical decision-making processes.

Navigating the legal aspects of AI applications

Now, let's explore the critical legal considerations associated with AI applications in managerial accounting by focusing on regulatory adherence, intellectual property rights, contractual implications, and the evolving legal frameworks that shape the deployment of AI technologies in the financial realm:

- **Regulatory compliance**: AI applications in managerial accounting must comply with existing financial regulations and standards. This includes ensuring that AI-driven processes meet auditing standards, financial reporting requirements, and industry-specific regulations.

- **Intellectual property rights**: As AI systems can generate reports, forecasts, and other intellectual outputs, clarifying the ownership of these outputs is crucial. Legal considerations include understanding how global and local intellectual property laws apply to AI-generated content.

- **Contractual obligations**: The use of AI in service delivery may affect contractual obligations with clients and suppliers. Legal frameworks should address how AI impacts these relationships and the delivery of contractual commitments.

- **Emerging legislation**: The legal landscape for AI is continually evolving, with new laws and regulations being proposed to address the unique challenges posed by AI technologies. Staying informed about and compliant with these emerging legal frameworks is essential for organizations using AI in managerial accounting.

The ethical and legal considerations surrounding AI in managerial accounting are complex and multifaceted. Addressing these concerns requires a proactive approach, including implementing robust data protection measures, ensuring transparency and fairness in AI applications, and maintaining compliance with current and emerging regulations. By navigating these ethical and legal challenges responsibly, organizations can harness the benefits of AI in managerial accounting while upholding the highest standards of integrity and accountability.

Future trends in AI and managerial accounting

As we peer into the horizon of AI's evolution in managerial accounting, the emergence of future trends promises transformative possibilities for financial management practices. Let's explore the rapidly-increasing landscape of innovative technologies and trends poised to shape the future of AI applications in managerial accounting, unraveling their potential impact on financial decision-making processes:

Trend	Description	Potential Impact
Predictive analytics	Advanced models for forecasting financial outcomes	Enhanced strategic planning and risk management
Blockchain integration	Secure, transparent transaction records	Improved audit trails and fraud prevention
Natural language processing (NLP)	Automated analysis of textual financial data	Greater insights from qualitative data sources

Table 7.3: Future trends in AI for managerial accounting

The intersection of AI and managerial accounting is poised for significant evolution, driven by advancements in AI technologies. These developments promise to reshape the landscape of managerial accounting, bringing new capabilities and challenges.

Emerging AI technologies and their impacts

Let's explore the transformative impacts of emerging AI technologies and their potential to reshape the future of managerial accounting:

- **XAI**: Future AI systems in managerial accounting will likely focus on enhancing the transparency and understanding of AI decision-making processes. XAI aims to make AI's conclusions more interpretable and trustworthy, which is crucial for financial decision-making and compliance.

- **Advanced predictive analytics**: Leveraging more sophisticated machine learning models, predictive analytics will offer deeper insights into financial forecasting, risk assessment, and market trends, enabling more strategic planning and decision-making.

- **AI-enhanced automation**: Beyond automating routine tasks, AI will increasingly automate more complex managerial accounting functions, such as strategic budget allocation and financial risk management, with higher precision and efficiency.

- **Integration of AI with blockchain**: The combination of AI and blockchain technology promises enhanced security and transparency in financial transactions and record-keeping, potentially revolutionizing areas such as contract management and compliance auditing.

- **NLP**: NLP technologies will improve their ability to analyze textual financial data, such as reports and communications, providing richer insights into market sentiment and competitor analysis.

Strategies for staying ahead in the AI landscape

Let's explore the key skills and resources that are crucial for navigating the nuances of AI in managerial accounting:

Skill	Description	Resources for Development
Data analysis	Ability to interpret and derive insights from data	Online courses, workshops, and certifications in data science
AI literacy	Understanding of AI technologies and applications	Webinars, seminars, and professional development programs
Strategic thinking	Capacity to contribute to business strategy using AI insights	Leadership and strategy training tailored to accountants

Table 7.4: Skills and resources for navigating AI in managerial accounting

Next, let's delve into actionable approaches for staying ahead in the rapidly evolving AI landscape of financial management:

- **Continuous learning and adaptation**: Professionals in managerial accounting should commit to ongoing education in AI technologies and their applications in the field to remain relevant and competitive

- **Strategic investment in AI**: Organizations should strategically invest in AI technologies that align with their specific needs and goals, ensuring that AI initiatives drive value and support strategic objectives

- **Cross-disciplinary collaboration**: Collaborating with AI experts, data scientists, and technologists can provide managerial accountants with deeper insights into the capabilities and limitations of AI tools, fostering more effective implementation

- **Ethical and responsible AI use**: Emphasizing the ethical use of AI, including considerations for data privacy, security, and fairness, is essential for maintaining trust and integrity in AI applications

- **Agility and flexibility**: Adopting an agile approach to AI integration, where strategies and technologies can quickly adapt to new developments and insights, will be key to navigating the rapidly evolving AI landscape

The future of AI in managerial accounting is rich with possibilities, offering opportunities to enhance efficiency, accuracy, and strategic insight. By staying informed about emerging technologies, adopting a strategic approach to AI integration, and emphasizing ethical considerations, managerial accountants can not only navigate but thrive in the AI-enhanced future of the field.

Summary

This chapter explored the transformative role of AI in advancing managerial accounting, highlighting how AI technologies are reshaping traditional practices and paving the way for a new era of efficiency, accuracy, and strategic insight.

Here are the key insights from this chapter:

- **Enhanced decision-making**: AI's ability to analyze vast datasets significantly improves decision-making processes in managerial accounting, providing deeper insights and predictive analytics that drive strategic planning

- **Operational efficiency**: The automation of routine tasks through AI leads to unprecedented operational efficiency, allowing managerial accountants to focus on more value-added activities and strategic roles

- **Risk management and compliance**: AI revolutionizes risk assessment and compliance monitoring, offering sophisticated tools to identify potential risks and ensure adherence to financial regulations with greater precision

- **Ethical and legal considerations**: The integration of AI into managerial accounting brings forth ethical and legal challenges, necessitating a careful balance between leveraging AI's capabilities and ensuring data privacy, security, and ethical decision-making

- **Future trends**: Emerging AI technologies, such as XAI and AI-enhanced automation, promise to further impact managerial accounting, emphasizing the need for continuous learning and adaptation

Reflections on the future of managerial accounting in an AI-driven era

The future of managerial accounting in an AI-driven era is marked by the promise of greater innovation and the potential for reshaping the profession in fundamental ways. As AI continues to evolve, it will offer even more sophisticated tools for financial analysis, strategic planning, and decision support, further embedding AI as a crucial component of managerial accounting.

This future also requires a new mindset among managerial accountants. Embracing AI means not only adapting to new technologies but also rethinking traditional roles and processes. The accountants of the future will need to blend technical AI knowledge with strategic business acumen, ethical judgment, and interpersonal skills to navigate the complexities of an AI-enhanced business environment.

The ethical and responsible use of AI will remain at the forefront, ensuring that advancements in AI contribute positively to the profession and society at large. This includes addressing challenges related to data governance, privacy, and the equitable use of AI technologies.

The integration of AI into managerial accounting is not just a technological upgrade but a strategic enabler that can drive the profession toward more insightful, proactive, and value-driven practices. As we look to the future, the role of managerial accountants will continue to evolve, guided by the opportunities and challenges presented by AI, shaping a dynamic and forward-looking field ready to meet the demands of the modern business landscape.

Further reading and resources

To gain a comprehensive understanding and explore AI in managerial accounting further, consider the following resources that delve into various aspects of this dynamic field:

- *Artificial Intelligence for Audit, Forensic Accounting, and Valuation*, by Al Naqvi, explores AI's application across various accounting disciplines, offering practical insights: `https://onlinelibrary.wiley.com/doi/book/10.1002/9781119601906`

- *The Impact of Artificial Intelligence on the Professional Services Sector* delves into AI's transformative effects on services, including accounting, highlighting future trends and challenges: `https://www.linkedin.com/pulse/impact-ai-professional-services-tareq-wehbe/`

- *Artificial intelligence-based decision-making in accounting and auditing: ethical challenges and normative thinking* reviews ethical challenges in AI-based decision-making within accounting, providing a comprehensive framework for understanding these issues: `https://www.emerald.com/insight/content/doi/10.1108/AAAJ-09-2020-4934/full/pdf?title=artificial-intelligence-based-decision-making-in-accounting-and-auditing-ethical-challenges-and-normative-thinking`

These resources cover AI's practical applications, ethical considerations, and broader impacts on the accounting profession.

Q&A

The following are some reflective questions and insights that can be gleaned:

1. How has AI redefined the role of managerial accountants?

   AI has shifted the focus from traditional bookkeeping to strategic analysis and decision support, enabling accountants to contribute more significantly to business strategy.

2.   What are the ethical considerations in implementing AI in accounting practices?

Ethical concerns include ensuring data accuracy, preventing algorithmic biases, and maintaining transparency in AI-driven decisions to uphold trust and integrity.

3.   How can professionals adapt to the evolving AI landscape in managerial accounting?

Continuous learning, upskilling in AI and data analytics, and staying informed about technological advancements are crucial for adapting to the changing field.

8

Accounting Information Systems (AIS) through the AI Lens

"Innovation in AI is making accounting a lucrative profession for accountants who can leverage its value."

- Jeff Dernavich, VP of Product, LeaseQuery

This chapter embarks on an exploratory journey toward integrating **artificial intelligence** (**AI**) into **accounting information systems** (**AIS**). We'll delve into how this integration is not merely an enhancement but a transformative shift in the accounting landscape. This chapter aims to unravel the complexities and potential of AI-driven AIS, providing insights into how these systems are reshaping financial data processing, analysis, and reporting.

The incorporation of AI into AIS marks a significant milestone in the evolution of accounting practices. AI technologies bring unprecedented efficiency, accuracy, and capabilities to AIS, transforming them from mere data-recording systems into powerful analytical tools. We'll discuss the growing relevance of AI in modern AIS, highlighting how AI-driven innovations enable accountants to gain deeper insights, forecast financial trends more accurately, and make more informed strategic decisions. The integration of AI not only enhances existing functionalities but also opens new avenues for predictive analytics, risk assessment, and decision support in accounting.

The background and evolution of AIS

The AIS journey is a fascinating tale of evolution from rudimentary manual processes to sophisticated, software-based systems. Initially, accounting was predominantly a manual task involving ledger books, where accountants manually recorded financial transactions. This era was characterized by intensive labor, a high propensity for human error, and significant time consumption for data entry and reconciliation.

The need for more efficient and accurate accounting processes became evident as the business world became more complex. This necessity paved the way for introducing mechanical and electronic calculators, significantly speeding up calculations, but still requiring manual data entry and management.

This fundamental transformation began with the advent of computers. In the mid-20th century, as computers became more accessible, AIS began transitioning to computer-based methods. Early systems required more extensive and often limited essential bookkeeping functions. However, this marked the beginning of a new era in accounting, one where efficiency and accuracy started to take center stage.

The development of software applications in the late 20th century brought a more sophisticated AIS. With incredible speed and reduced errors, these systems could handle various accounting tasks, from transaction recording to generating financial statements. The introduction of databases and networking allowed for the centralization and easy sharing of financial data, further enhancing the efficiency of accounting processes.

The advent of AI in AIS

The integration of AI into AIS is a relatively recent development; It has already begun to significantly impact the field. AI technologies, including machine learning, **natural language processing** (**NLP**), and data analytics, have begun to transform AIS from mere data-recording tools into intelligent systems capable of complex analysis and decision-making support.

AI's initial impact on AIS can be observed in several key areas, such as the following:

- **Automated data processing**: AI algorithms have enabled the automation of routine tasks such as data entry, categorization, and reconciliation. This automation saves time and reduces the likelihood of human errors.

- **Predictive analytics**: AI has introduced predictive capabilities into AIS. By analyzing historical data, AI can forecast future trends, helping businesses in budgeting, financial planning, and risk management.

- **Fraud detection**: AI systems are equipped to identify anomalies and patterns indicative of fraudulent activity. This capability enhances the security and integrity of financial information.

- **Enhanced decision-making**: AI-driven AIS provides valuable insights and recommendations, supporting more informed and strategic decision-making. They can analyze vast amounts of data to uncover insights that would be difficult, if not impossible, for humans to detect.

- **Compliance and reporting**: AI has streamlined the compliance and reporting processes. It can keep track of changing regulations and ensure that financial reporting adheres to the latest standards, thus reducing the compliance burden on businesses.

The advent of AI in AIS represents a significant leap forward, transitioning accounting systems from passive record-keeping tools to those that actively participate in financial analysis and strategic planning. This integration is still in its early stages, and the full potential of AI in AIS is yet to be fully realized. However, its initial impact has already set the stage for a more data-driven, efficient, and intelligent accounting approach:

Importance of AI in Modern AIS	Key Points
Automated data processing	AI algorithms enable automation of routine accounting tasks such as data entry, saving time and reducing errors
Predictive analytics	AI allows AIS to analyze historical data and forecast future financial trends to support planning and risk management
Fraud detection	AI can identify suspicious patterns and anomalies indicative of fraud, improving the security of financial data
Enhanced decision-making	AI provides valuable insights and recommendations to support more informed business decisions
Compliance and reporting	AI helps ensure reporting adheres to the latest standards and keeps up with changing regulations, easing the compliance burden

Table 8.1: Importance of AI in AIS

Traditional AIS versus AI-enhanced AIS

Exploring the transition from traditional AIS to AI-enhanced AIS unveils the significant shifts in technological capabilities and operational efficiencies within financial management. We will explore this next.

Traditional AIS

Traditional AIS has been pivotal in managing financial data, processing transactions, and generating reports. These systems, primarily software-based, have automated various accounting tasks, reducing the manual labor and errors associated with paper-based processes. The conventional AIS functionalities include ledger management, account reconciliation, financial reporting, and compliance tracking. They are instrumental in streamlining financial operations, ensuring data accuracy, and providing timely financial information.

Despite its benefits, traditional AIS has limitations. They often rely on static rule-based processes that lack the flexibility to adapt to rapidly changing financial environments. These systems can struggle with handling unstructured data such as free-text notes in transactions or complex financial instruments. In addition, traditional AIS may not efficiently handle large volumes of data, leading to slower processing times and potential bottlenecks. The lack of predictive capabilities in these systems means that they primarily focus on recording and reporting past transactions and offer limited insights into future trends or potential risks.

AI-enhanced AIS

AI-enhanced AIS represents a significant leap forward from traditional systems. By integrating AI, these advanced systems introduced functionalities that were previously unattainable. AI in AIS includes machine learning algorithms for predictive analytics, NLP for handling unstructured data, and intelligent automation for streamlining complex tasks. These features enable the AI-enhanced AIS to learn from data patterns, predict future trends, and provide deeper insights into financial health.

Advantages over traditional systems

The integration of AI into AIS offers several advantages over traditional systems:

- **Predictive analytics**: AI-enhanced AIS can analyze historical data to forecast future trends, helping businesses anticipate and prepare for potential financial challenges.

- **Enhanced data processing**: AI algorithms can handle large volumes of diverse data types, including unstructured data, with greater speed and accuracy. This leads to a more comprehensive and insightful financial analysis.

- **Automated decision-making**: AI in AIS can automate complex decision-making processes such as credit risk assessments or fraud detection by identifying patterns and anomalies that might be invisible to human analysts.

- **Customized financial insights**: AI-driven systems can tailor financial reports and insights into specific user needs, thereby providing more relevant and actionable information.

- **Continuous learning and improvement**: AI-enhanced AIS continuously learns from new data, improving its accuracy and effectiveness over time. This adaptability ensures that systems remain relevant and valuable in a dynamic financial landscape.

AI-enhanced AIS not only retains the core functionalities of traditional systems but also introduces advanced capabilities that transform how financial data is managed, analyzed, and utilized for strategic decision-making.

Let's look at a quick side-by-side comparison:

Feature	Traditional AIS	AI-Enhanced AIS
Predictive analytics	No	Yes
Unstructured data handling	Limited	Extensive
Decision automation	Manual	Automated
Customizable insights	Fixed	Flexible
Adaptability	Static	Continuous learning

Table 8.2: Comparison of traditional AIS and AI-enhanced AIS

Embarking on a journey through the realm of AI transformations within AIS unveils a landscape where automated data processing and analysis redefine operational efficiencies and accuracy, reshaping the very core of financial management practices. We will explore this next.

AI transformations in AIS

Automated data processing and analysis powered by AI has revolutionized how routine tasks are managed in AIS, particularly in data processing and analysis. Automation through AI significantly reduces the manual effort required for data entry and reconciliation, which is traditionally time-consuming and prone to human error:

- **Automated data entry**: AI systems can automatically input data into accounting systems from various sources, including invoices, bank statements, and other financial documents. This automation is often facilitated by technologies such as **optical character recognition (OCR)** and machine learning algorithms, which can accurately recognize and categorize financial information.

- **Intelligent reconciliation**: AI enhances the reconciliation process by quickly and accurately matching transactions from different sources, such as bank statements and ledgers. Machine learning algorithms can identify discrepancies and anomalies, thus flagging them for review purposes. This not only speeds up the reconciliation process but also improves its accuracy.

- **Advanced data analysis**: Beyond handling routine tasks, AI can analyze financial data to uncover trends, patterns, and insights that might not be evident through traditional analysis. This capability allows for a more in-depth financial analysis, aiding strategic planning and decision-making.

Enhanced decision-making with predictive analytics powered by AI plays a crucial role in enhancing decision-making processes within AIS. By leveraging historical data, AI can forecast future financial trends and provide valuable insights for strategic decision-making:

- **Financial forecasting**: AI algorithms can process vast amounts of historical financial data to predict future trends. This forecasting can range from revenue and expense trends to cash flow projections, helping businesses plan more effectively.

- **Risk assessment**: AI-driven predictive analytics can assess risks by analyzing patterns and trends in financial data. This assessment is particularly useful for identifying potential financial pitfalls, allowing businesses to take proactive measures to mitigate risks.

- **Customized financial advice**: AI can provide personalized financial advice based on a company's specific financial history and goals. This tailored approach ensures that the advice is relevant and actionable.

Time reporting and compliance powered by AI significantly enhances the capabilities of AIS in terms of real-time reporting and maintenance of regulatory compliance, both of which are critical in today's fast-paced business environment:

- **Real-time financial reporting**: AI systems can process and analyze financial data in real time and provide up-to-date financial reports. This immediacy allows businesses to make informed decisions quickly and respond effectively to market changes.

- **Automated compliance monitoring**: AI can monitor changing financial regulations and ensure that a company's financial practices are compliant. This is particularly important given the complexity and frequency of changes in financial regulations. AI systems can automatically update reporting standards and compliance requirements, thereby reducing the risk of non-compliance.

- **Fraud detection and prevention**: AI can monitor financial transactions in real time to detect unusual patterns that may indicate fraudulent activity. By identifying these activities early, AI systems can help prevent financial fraud and maintain the integrity of financial data.

The integration of AI into AIS transforms the landscape of accounting and financial management. It not only automates routine tasks but also provides advanced analytical capabilities, enhances decision-making with predictive insights, and ensures real-time reporting and compliance, thereby significantly increasing efficiency and accuracy in financial management.

Case studies in AI-enhanced AIS

Let's look at a couple of case studies to explore AI-enhanced AIS, starting with a small business accounting firm called *Bella's Boutique*.

Background: *Bella's Boutique*, a small but trendy clothing store in downtown San Francisco, faced challenges in managing accounting efficiently. With limited staff and resources, the boutique struggled with time-consuming manual data entry, error-prone financial reconciliations, and delayed reporting.

AI implementation: The boutique integrated an AI-enhanced AIS specifically designed for small businesses. The system features automated data entry using OCR to scan invoices and receipts, intelligent reconciliation algorithms, and real-time financial reporting.

Outcomes:

- **Operational efficiency**: The AI system automated routine accounting tasks, reducing the time spent on data entry by 70%. Staff could focus more on customer services and strategic business growth.

- **Improved accuracy**: AI-driven reconciliation minimizes errors in financial records and ensures accurate financial statements.

- **Real-time financial insights**: The boutique could access real-time financial reports, helping the owner make timely decisions on inventory purchases and sales strategies.

The next case study is of a large financial management corporation, *TechGlobal Inc.*

Background: *TechGlobal Inc.*, a multinational technology corporation, has faced complexities in financial management due to its size, diverse product lines, and global operations. The corporation required a sophisticated solution for strategic financial planning and analysis.

AI implementation: *TechGlobal Inc.* adopted a comprehensive AI-enhanced AIS that includes advanced predictive analytics for financial forecasting, AI-driven risk assessment models, and automated compliance monitoring systems.

Outcomes:

- **Strategic financial planning**: The AI system provides predictive insights into market trends, enabling TechGlobal to make strategic decisions about product development and market expansion

- **Risk management**: The AI-enhanced risk assessment tools allowed the corporation to identify potential financial risks early, particularly in its international operations, leading to more effective risk-mitigation strategies

- **Regulatory compliance**: With operations in multiple countries, automated compliance monitoring ensured that TechGlobal adhered to various international financial regulations, reducing the risk of non-compliance penalties

The AI system enabled TechGlobal's financial analysts to conduct in-depth analyses of financial data, uncovering insights that informed the corporation's investment decisions and resource allocations.

In both case studies, integrating AI into AIS significantly transformed financial management processes. According to *Bella's Boutique*, AI brought efficiency and accuracy to its operations, which is crucial for its growth and sustainability. In contrast, AI provides sophisticated tools for strategic planning, risk management, and compliance, which are essential for its global operations and competitive edge in the technology industry. These examples illustrate the versatility and impact of AI on AIS across different business scales.

Challenges and considerations in AI-enhanced AIS

As AI continues to reshape AIS, a critical examination of the associated challenges and considerations becomes imperative. In this section, we'll delve into key areas such as data security, privacy, ethical and regulatory concerns, and strategies for effectively addressing these pivotal issues within AI-enhanced AIS.

Data security and privacy

In the realm of AI-enhanced AIS, data security and privacy have emerged as paramount concerns. The integration of AI into AIS involves processing vast amounts of sensitive financial data, making it a prime target for cyber threats and data breaches. Ensuring the security and confidentiality of these data is crucial, not only to maintain the integrity of financial systems but also to uphold the trust of clients and stakeholders.

The following are some challenges in data security:

- **Vulnerability to cyberattacks**: AI systems, with their complex algorithms and extensive data networks, can be susceptible to hacking, phishing attacks, and other forms of cybercrime

- **Data breach risks**: Storing and processing large volumes of financial data increases the risk of data breaches, potentially leading to significant financial and reputational damage

- **Insider threats**: The risk of data misuse or unauthorized access by internal users within an organization

Now, let's cover some strategies for ensuring data privacy:

- **Encryption and secure data storage**: Implement advanced encryption methods for data at rest and in transit and use secure servers and cloud services

- **Access control mechanisms**: Establish stringent access controls and authentication protocols to ensure that only authorized personnel can access sensitive financial data

- **Regular security audits**: Frequent security audits and vulnerability assessments should be conducted to identify and rectify potential security loopholes

Ethical and regulatory considerations

The integration of AI into AIS also raises significant ethical and regulatory considerations. As AI systems increasingly influence financial decision-making and reporting, ensuring that these systems operate within ethical boundaries and comply with existing regulations becomes critical.

The following are some ethical concerns to consider:

- **Bias and fairness**: AI systems may inherit biases present in their training data, leading to unfair or discriminatory financial decisions

- **Transparency**: The black-box nature of some AI algorithms can lead to a lack of transparency in financial decision-making processes

- **Accountability**: We can determine accountability for decisions made by AI systems, especially in cases of errors or financial discrepancies

Now, let's look at some regulatory compliance considerations:

- **Adherence to financial regulations**: AI systems must comply with existing financial regulations and standards, such as **Generally Accepted Accounting Principles (GAAP)** and **International Financial Reporting Standards (IFRS)**

- **Data protection laws**: Compliance with data protection laws such as the **General Data Protection Regulation (GDPR)** and **California Consumer Privacy Act (CCPA)**, particularly concerning the handling of personal and financial data

- **Reporting standards**: Maintaining accuracy and integrity in financial reporting, as mandated by regulatory bodies such as the **Securities and Exchange Commission (SEC)** and the **Financial Accounting Standards Board (FASB)**

Strategies for addressing ethical and regulatory challenges

In the dynamic landscape of AI-enhanced AIS, navigating the ethical and regulatory terrain demands proactive strategies and vigilant oversight. Here, we'll explore key approaches to addressing these critical challenges:

- **Ethical AI frameworks**: Developing and implementing ethical guidelines and frameworks for AI use in AIS, focusing on fairness, transparency, and accountability

- **Continuous monitoring and auditing**: Regularly monitoring and auditing AI systems to ensure compliance with ethical standards and financial regulations

- **Stakeholder engagement**: Involving various stakeholders, including regulatory bodies, in discussions and decision-making processes related to AI integration in AIS to ensure a balanced and comprehensive approach

The following table delves into the intricacies of data security, privacy, ethical considerations, and regulatory compliance in AI-enhanced AIS through a detailed exploration of key aspects, challenges, and considerations in the evolving landscape of financial management:

Aspect	Challenges	Considerations
Data security and privacy	Ensuring that sensitive financial data is protected from breaches and unauthorized access in AI systems	Implement robust encryption and access controls, and ensure compliance with data protection laws such as GDPR
Ethical and regulatory compliance	Addressing potential biases in AI algorithms and ensuring decisions made by AI are fair and transparent	Develop ethical guidelines for AI use, ensure transparency in AI decision-making processes, and adhere to regulatory standards

Table 8.3: Challenges and considerations in AI-enhanced AIS

By addressing these challenges and considerations, organizations can harness the benefits of AI in AIS while mitigating risks and upholding ethical and regulatory standards.

Future trends and developments in AI-enhanced AIS

In this section, we will explore the cutting-edge innovations and trends shaping the landscape of AIS, propelling the evolution toward greater efficiency, insight, and adaptability in the digital age.

Emerging technologies in AIS

As we venture deeper into the 21st century, the landscape of AIS is rapidly evolving thanks to the continual advancements in AI. The future of AIS is poised to be shaped by several emerging technologies, each with the potential to revolutionize how accounting tasks are performed and information is processed. Let's look at a few:

- **Predictive analytics and machine learning**: One of the most significant advancements is the integration of predictive analytics and machine learning algorithms. These technologies enable the AIS to process vast amounts of financial data and predict future trends and financial outcomes with high accuracy. This predictive capability is crucial for financial forecasting, risk assessment, and decision-making.

- **NLP**: NLP is another emerging technology that is expected to enhance AIS by automating the interpretation and analysis of unstructured data such as emails, memos, and reports. This significantly reduces manual data entry and increases the efficiency and accuracy of accounting information processing.

- **Blockchain technology**: The incorporation of blockchain technology into AIS could offer unprecedented levels of security and transparency. Blockchain can be used for secure and tamper-proof recording of transactions, making it an invaluable asset in compliance and auditing processes.

- **Robotic process automation** (**RPA**): This involves the use of software bots to automate routine tasks and overcome various repetitive and time-consuming tasks in AIS. This not only speeds up the processes but also minimizes human error, leading to more reliable accounting records.

Preparing for an AI-driven future in accounting

For accounting professionals, an imminent AI-driven future necessitates a shift in skill sets and knowledge bases. Professionals must focus on several key areas to remain relevant and competent in an increasingly automated environment:

- **Embracing technological literacy**: Accountants need to become technologically literate, understanding not only the basics of AI and its applications in AIS but also the underlying principles that drive these technologies.

- **Focus on analytical and strategic skills**: As AI takes over routine data processing tasks, the role of accountants will evolve to focus more on analytical and strategic aspects. Professionals should hone their data analysis, interpretation, and strategic decision-making skills.

- **Continuous learning and adaptation**: The field of AI is continuously evolving. Therefore, accounting professionals must commit to lifelong learning, staying abreast of the latest technological developments, and understanding how they impact AIS and accounting practices.

- **Ethical considerations and AI governance**: With the increased use of AI in accounting, ethical considerations and AI governance will become paramount. Professionals must be equipped to address issues related to data privacy, the ethical use of AI, and compliance with regulations governing AI technologies.

Summary

This chapter delved into the transformative impact of AI on AIS, highlighting the emerging technologies shaping the future of accounting. From predictive analytics to blockchain, these advancements promise to enhance the efficiency, accuracy, and security of accounting processes.

As we look toward an AI-driven future in accounting, it is evident that professionals must adapt by embracing new technologies, developing analytical and strategic skills, and committing to continuous learning. The integration of AI into AIS is not just a technological upgrade but a paradigm shift that calls for a holistic approach encompassing technical proficiency, ethical considerations, and strategic foresight.

Closing thoughts

The future of AIS, influenced by AI, holds immense potential for innovation and growth in the accounting sector. While challenges and uncertainties lie ahead, the opportunities presented by AI-enhanced AIS are vast. As accounting professionals and organizations navigate this evolving landscape, their success hinges on their ability to adapt, innovate, and ethically integrate AI technologies into their practices. The journey ahead is not just about keeping pace with technology, but also about leveraging it to drive forward-thinking, ethical, and strategic accounting practices that can thrive in the AI era.

Future outlook

As we look to the future of AIS, the integration of AI is poised to bring about transformative changes. This section outlines the key predictions and trends expected to shape the evolution of AIS in the era of AI:

- **Advanced predictive analytics**: The integration of AI in AIS will lead to more sophisticated predictive analytics, enabling businesses to anticipate future financial trends, customer behavior, and market dynamics more accurately.

- **Automated accounting processes**: AI is expected to automate a vast range of accounting tasks, including data entry, invoice processing, and compliance checks, leading to increased efficiency and reduced human errors.

- **Enhanced decision-making**: AI-driven AIS will provide deeper insights and analytics, aiding more informed and strategic decision-making. Accountants can leverage AI to analyze complex financial scenarios and make predictions based on large datasets.

- **Customization and personalization**: AIS will become more tailored to the specific needs of businesses, adapting to unique accounting practices, and providing personalized financial advice through AI algorithms.

- **Fraud detection and risk management**: AI will significantly improve fraud detection capabilities within an AIS. AI can identify potential risks and fraudulent activities more effectively than traditional methods by analyzing patterns and anomalies in financial data.

- **Real-time financial reporting**: With AI, financial reporting is expected to become real time, allowing businesses to access up-to-the-minute financial information, leading to more dynamic and responsive financial management.

- **Interactive user interfaces**: AI will revolutionize the user experience in AIS with more interactive and intuitive interfaces, making complex financial information more accessible to non-expert users.

- **Integration with other business systems**: AIS will increasingly integrate with other business systems (such as CRM and ERP), enabling a more holistic view of business operations and financial health.

- **Ethical and regulatory challenges**: As AI becomes more prevalent in AIS, ethical considerations and regulatory compliance become more complex. Ensuring the ethical use of AI and adhering to evolving regulations are critical.

- **Continuous learning and adaptation**: Professionals in the field need to engage in continuous learning to keep pace with AI advancements, ensuring that they remain adept at using AI-enhanced systems effectively.

- **A shift in professional roles**: The role of accounting professionals will evolve, with greater emphasis on strategic planning, interpreting AI-generated insights, and managing AI-driven systems.

The future of AIS is intrinsically linked to the advancement of AI technologies. These predictions and trends highlight a shift toward more efficient, intelligent, and data-driven accounting practices. As AIS evolves, it will not only transform how financial data are processed and analyzed but also redefine the role of accounting professionals in the business ecosystem. The challenge and opportunity for businesses and accountants alike is to adapt to these changes, harnessing the power of AI to drive innovation and efficiency in financial management.

Further reading/resources

If you're keen to deepen your understanding of AI in AIS, the following resources offer a wealth of information, ranging from foundational concepts to advanced applications. These resources include books, scholarly articles, and online platforms, all of which provide a comprehensive view of the intersection of AI and AIS.

Books:

- *Artificial Intelligence in Practice: How 50 Successful Companies Used AI and Machine Learning to Solve Problems*, by Bernard Marr and Matt Ward, provides case studies from various industries on the practical application of AI, offering insights that can be applied to AIS

- *Accounting Information Systems*, by Marshall B. Romney and Paul J. Steinbart, is a comprehensive resource for understanding the fundamentals of AIS, which is foundational for appreciating the impact of AI integration
- *Data-Driven Innovation: Big Data for Growth and Well-Being*, by OECD, discusses the broader implications of data-driven innovations such as AI in fields such as accounting and finance

Scholarly articles:

- *The Impact of Artificial Intelligence on Accounting*, in the Oxford Research Encyclopedia of Economics and Finance, provides an academic perspective on how AI is transforming accounting practices.
- *Artificial Intelligence in Accounting: A Review*, in the Journal of International Technology and Information Management, discusses the current state and potential future of AI in accounting

Online resources:

- *AI in Accounting – Coursera Specialization*: Online courses that offer insights into AI applications in accounting
- *Journal of Emerging Technologies in Accounting*: An academic journal featuring articles on the latest technology trends in accounting, including AI
- *American Institute of CPAs (AICPA) Resources*: The AICPA offers various articles, webinars, and resources on the intersection of AI and accounting
- *Deloitte Insights on AI in Accounting*: Deloitte provides thought leadership articles and reports on AI applications in accounting and finance
- *Accounting Today*: A leading publication that often features articles on AI and technology in the accounting industry

Podcasts and webinars:

- *Journal of Accountancy Podcast*: This covers a range of accounting topics, including episodes of AI and technology in accounting
- *AICPA webinars*: The American Institute of CPAs frequently hosts webinars on accounting technology, including AI

These resources offer a range of perspectives, from practical applications to theoretical discussions, providing a well-rounded view of AI in the context of AIS. Recall that the field of AI is rapidly evolving, so staying up-to-date with the latest publications and resources is essential.

Q&A

The following are some reflective questions and insights that can be gleaned:

1. How is AI transforming traditional AIS?

   AI has revolutionized AIS by automating routine tasks, enhancing data analysis, and improving decision-making processes. Automation of repetitive tasks, such as data entry and reconciliation, frees accountants to focus on more strategic activities. AI's predictive analytics capabilities enable more accurate forecasting and risk assessment, whereas machine learning algorithms can uncover insights from vast datasets more efficiently than traditional methods.

   Insight: The transformation is not just about efficiency; it is about enabling a more strategic role for accountants where they can focus on interpreting data and advising on business decisions rather than just compiling and verifying financial records.

2. What are the potential risks and challenges associated with implementing AI in AIS?

   The major risks include data privacy concerns, the potential for algorithmic bias, the need for significant investment in technology and training, and the risk of job displacement in some areas of accounting. Ensuring data security and complying with evolving regulations around AI are also critical challenges.

   Insight: Addressing these challenges requires a balanced approach that includes robust data governance, continuous monitoring of AI systems for bias and errors, and ongoing training of staff to adapt to new technologies.

3. Can AI fully replace the role of human accountants in AIS?

   Although AI can automate many tasks, it cannot replace the nuanced judgment and strategic thinking provided by human accountants... yet. AI is a tool that enhances accountants' capabilities, allowing them to focus on the more complex and strategic aspects of their roles.

   Insight: The future of accounting is collaborative, where AI will handle routine tasks and data analysis, while human professionals will focus on interpretation, strategic decision-making, and client relations.

4. How can accounting professionals prepare for an AI-driven future in AIS?

   Accounting professionals should focus on developing skills in areas such as data analysis, strategic thinking, and understanding AI and machine learning. Embracing continuous learning and staying up-to-date with technological advancements in the field are crucial.

   Insight: The key to success in the AI-driven future is adaptability. Accountants who can adapt to new technologies, understand how to work alongside AI, and leverage it to enhance their strategic capabilities are in high demand.

5. What ethical considerations arise regarding the use of AI in AIS?

    Ethical considerations include ensuring the accuracy and fairness of AI algorithms, protecting the privacy and security of financial data, and using AI transparently in financial reporting and auditing.

    Insight: The ethical use of AI in AIS requires a framework that includes clear guidelines, regulatory compliance, and an emphasis on transparency and accountability in AI-driven decisions.

9

AI-Driven Data Analytics: Using Data Visualization Tools and Dashboards

"Visualization gives you answers to questions you didn't know you had."

– Dr. Ben Shneiderman, University of Maryland

In today's data-driven world, the volume, velocity, and variety of data have surpassed the capability of traditional analytics methods to provide timely and actionable insights. AI-driven data analytics has emerged as a pivotal solution, leveraging machine learning, natural language processing, and other AI technologies to sift through massive datasets, identify patterns, predict trends, and offer prescriptive insights. This AI-enhanced approach accelerates the analytical process and increases its accuracy and relevance, enabling organizations to make more informed decisions swiftly.

Parallel to the advancements in data analytics, there has been a significant evolution in data visualization tools and dashboards. Traditionally, these tools offered static representations of data, requiring manual updates and offering limited interactivity. However, the integration of AI has transformed these tools into dynamic platforms that can provide real-time data insights, predict future trends, and even suggest actionable strategies. AI-driven visualization tools now offer more intuitive interfaces, advanced analytical capabilities such as predictive modeling and anomaly detection, integration with third-party applications, and customizable dashboards tailored to specific user needs and industry requirements.

This synergy between AI-driven analytics and advanced visualization tools has not only democratized data access across organizational levels but also fostered a culture of data-driven decision-making. By making complex data more accessible and understandable, AI-enhanced visualization tools empower stakeholders to leverage data insights directly, fostering a more agile and responsive organizational environment.

As we delve deeper into this chapter, we will explore the mechanisms through which AI drives data analytics, examine the innovative features of modern visualization tools, and highlight real-world applications that showcase the transformative power of AI in unveiling insights hidden within data.

The role of AI in data analytics

Artificial Intelligence (**AI**) technologies have revolutionized the field of data analytics by introducing sophisticated machine learning models and predictive analytics capabilities. These advancements enable the extraction of meaningful insights from vast and complex datasets, transforming raw data into actionable intelligence.

Enhancing data analytics with AI technologies

Let's explore data-driven decision-making with the transformative capabilities of AI technologies in enhancing data analytics:

- **Machine learning models**: Machine learning, a core component of AI, allows systems to learn from data, identify patterns, and make decisions with minimal human intervention. In data analytics, machine learning models can classify, predict, and cluster data, providing deeper insights into customer behavior, operational efficiencies, and potential market trends.

- **Predictive analytics**: AI-driven predictive analytics use historical data to forecast future events. These models can predict customer churn, sales trends, and inventory demands, allowing businesses to make proactive decisions and strategic plans.

- **Natural Language Processing** (**NLP**): NLP enables AI systems to understand and interpret human language, making it possible to analyze textual data such as customer reviews, social media posts, and open-ended survey responses. This provides a richer understanding of consumer sentiment and market needs.

Case studies illustrating AI's impact on data analysis

Let's explore some real-world examples showcasing the profound impact of AI on data analysis through compelling case studies.

Case study 1 – Retail sales forecasting

In a transformative initiative, a leading global retail chain deployed AI-driven analytics to overhaul its sales forecasting methodology. The retailer integrated machine learning models to sift through years of historical sales data, alongside real-time inputs on market trends and detailed consumer behavior analytics. The AI system was trained to recognize patterns correlating specific events, promotions, and consumer preferences with sales outcomes across various regions and product categories. By implementing this AI-driven approach, the retailer achieved a granular level of sales forecasting accuracy, enabling precise inventory management that significantly reduced overstock and stockouts. Moreover, the insights gained from AI analytics informed targeted marketing campaigns, leading to a more personalized shopping experience. The culmination of these efforts resulted in a notable increase in sales, enhanced customer loyalty, and a marked reduction in operational costs due to streamlined inventory processes.

Case study 2 – Healthcare patient care optimization

A renowned healthcare provider embarked on an AI journey to revolutionize patient care. Utilizing predictive analytics, the provider analyzed extensive datasets encompassing patient medical records, treatment histories, and clinical outcomes. The AI models employed were adept at identifying effective treatment protocols for individual patients, considering a multitude of factors such as medical history, genetic information, and lifestyle choices. This AI-powered personalized care approach not only elevated patient outcomes by ensuring the most effective treatments were administered but also optimized the allocation of medical resources. As a result, the healthcare provider saw a significant reduction in the administration of unnecessary tests and procedures, contributing to cost savings and more focused, efficient patient care.

Case study 3 – Financial fraud detection

In response to the escalating challenges of financial fraud, a prominent banking institution integrated AI into its fraud detection framework. The institution leveraged advanced machine learning algorithms to conduct a deep analysis of transactional data across millions of accounts, learning to spot intricate patterns and anomalies indicative of fraudulent activity. This real-time anomaly detection system enabled the bank to swiftly identify and mitigate potential fraud threats, often before the customers were even aware. The proactive nature of this AI-driven fraud detection system not only safeguarded the financial assets of the bank's clientele but also bolstered customer trust and confidence in the institution's security measures. The bank reported a substantial decrease in fraud-related losses and an improvement in operational efficiency due to the reduced need for manual fraud investigation processes.

These case studies underscore the profound impact AI has on enhancing data analysis across diverse sectors. By harnessing the power of AI, businesses in retail, healthcare, and finance have not only optimized their operational efficiencies but have also set new benchmarks in customer satisfaction, patient care, and financial security. As AI technologies continue to advance, their role in data analytics will further expand, driving innovation and strategic advancements across industries. Let's discover the latest advancements in data visualization tools, revolutionizing the way we interpret and communicate complex data insights.

Advancements in data visualization tools

Integrating AI into data visualization tools has marked a significant leap forward in how data is interpreted and presented. These advancements offer more than just aesthetic improvements; they provide deeper insights, predict trends, and enable more informed decision-making processes.

Latest AI-integrated data visualization tools and capabilities

AI-integrated visualization tools leverage machine learning algorithms to automate the analysis and presentation of complex datasets. These tools can do the following:

- **Automatically generate insights**: AI can identify and highlight significant patterns, outliers, and correlations in the data, offering instant insights without manual intervention.

- **Predictive visualization**: Beyond depicting historical data, AI-enhanced tools can forecast future trends, providing predictive visualizations based on existing data patterns.

- **NLP**: Some advanced visualization tools incorporate NLP, allowing users to query data using natural language and receive visualizations in response, making data analysis more accessible to non-technical users.

- **Dynamic and interactive dashboards**: AI-driven tools can create dashboards that update in real time and adjust based on user interactions, offering personalized insights tailored to individual user needs.

Let's delve into a comprehensive comparison between traditional visualization tools and their AI-enhanced counterparts, illuminating the evolution of data representation and analysis:

Feature	Traditional Tools	AI-Enhanced Tools
Data analysis	Primarily manual, requiring significant user input to identify trends and patterns	Automated analysis, with AI identifying trends, patterns, and anomalies without explicit instructions
Insights generation	Dependent on user expertise to derive insights from visualizations	Automatic insights generation, highlighting key data points and trends directly within the tool
Interactivity	Limited to predefined queries and filters	Dynamic interactivity, with the ability to adjust visualizations based on real-time data and user queries
Predictive capabilities	Focus on historical data representation	Predictive analytics are incorporated, offering forecasts and trend predictions within visualizations
Accessibility	Often requires technical expertise to navigate and interpret	Enhanced by NLP, allowing users to interact with data using natural language, broadening accessibility

Table 9.1 – Traditional versus AI-enhanced visualization tools: a comparative analysis

This comparative analysis underscores the transformative impact of AI on data visualization tools. AI-enhanced tools simplify the data analysis process and democratize data access, enabling a broader range of stakeholders to leverage data insights for strategic decision-making. As AI technologies continue to evolve, the capabilities of visualization tools will expand, further bridging the gap between complex datasets and actionable insights. Let's dive into the building and leveraging of AI-powered dashboards, revolutionizing data-driven decision-making with unparalleled insights and agility.

Building and utilizing AI-powered dashboards

Building and utilizing AI-powered dashboards effectively can transform raw data into actionable insights, enhancing decision-making processes across various business functions. Here's a step-by-step guide to creating and leveraging these advanced tools:

1. **Define objectives**: Clearly identify the goals and KPIs that the dashboard aims to track. This ensures that the dashboard is aligned with business objectives and user needs.

2. **Data integration**: Aggregate data from various sources into a centralized platform. Ensure that the data is clean, accurate, and structured for analysis.

3. **Select the right tools**: Choose AI-powered dashboard tools that suit your business requirements, considering factors such as scalability, ease of use, and integration capabilities.

4. **Design for clarity**: Design the dashboard layout to present data clearly and intuitively. Use visual hierarchies to guide users to the most important information.

5. **Incorporate AI analytics**: Integrate AI models for predictive analytics, trend analysis, and anomaly detection. These models can provide automated insights and forecasts directly within the dashboard.

6. **Customization and interactivity**: Enable customization options for users to explore data based on their specific queries. Interactive elements such as filters, drilldowns, and sliders can enhance user engagement.

7. **Testing and feedback**: Test the dashboard with end users to gather feedback on its usability and effectiveness. Iterate on the design based on this feedback to ensure that it meets user needs.

8. **Deployment and training**: Roll out the dashboard to the intended users, providing necessary training and resources to help them utilize it effectively.

9. **Monitor and update**: Continuously monitor the dashboard's performance and user engagement. Update it regularly to reflect new data sources, business objectives, and user feedback.

The following table is your definitive guide to crafting and harnessing the potential of AI-powered dashboards for transformative data visualization and decision-making:

Step/Best Practice	Description	Key Points
1. Define objectives	Establish clear goals for what the dashboard should achieve, aligning with business strategies and user needs.	- Identify key metrics and KPIs - Understand user roles and requirements
2. Data integration	Gather and consolidate data from diverse sources, ensuring cleanliness and structure for analysis.	- Use ETL processes -Ensure data accuracy and consistency
3. Select the right tools	Choose dashboard tools that offer AI capabilities and meet your specific business needs.	- Consider scalability, user-friendliness, and integration features - Evaluate AI and ML functionalities
4. Design for clarity	Design the dashboard to present data intuitively, using visual hierarchies and layouts.	- Prioritize important metrics - Use whitespace effectively
5. Incorporate AI analytics	Embed AI models to automate insights generation, such as predictions and anomaly detection.	- Integrate predictive analytics for forecasting - Utilize AI for real-time anomaly alerts
6. Customization and interactivity	Enable users to interact with and personalize the dashboard based on their queries.	- Offer filters and drill-down capabilities - Allow users to save custom views
7. Testing and feedback	Involve end users in testing to gather feedback and refine the dashboard's design and functionality.	- Conduct user testing sessions - Iterate design based on feedback
8. Deployment and training	Deploy the dashboard to users, providing necessary training and support.	- Organize training sessions - Provide documentation and support
9. Monitor and update	Regularly review the dashboard's performance and user engagement, updating as needed.	- Track usage metrics - Refresh with new data and features

Table 9.2 – Guide to creating and utilizing AI-powered dashboards

The integration of AI-powered dashboards marks a significant stride toward data-driven excellence, empowering organizations to extract actionable insights swiftly and efficiently, thereby fostering innovation and driving sustainable growth.

Best practices for dashboard design and user interaction

You can optimize dashboard design and user interaction with our curated selection of best practices, ensuring seamless navigation and maximized usability for enhanced data interpretation and decision-making:

- **Simplicity is key**: Avoid clutter by focusing on essential metrics. A clean, uncluttered design aids in quicker data comprehension.

- **Consistent design**: Use consistent color schemes, fonts, and visual elements to make the dashboard intuitive and easy to navigate.

- **Use visuals wisely**: Choose the correct type of chart or graph for each data type. For example, use line charts for trends over time and bar charts for comparisons.

- **Prioritize actionable insights**: Highlight actionable insights prominently on the dashboard. Use AI-driven alerts or notifications to draw attention to critical data points.

- **Responsive design**: Ensure that the dashboard is responsive and accessible across devices, especially for users who need access on the go.

- **Provide context**: Include tooltips, legends, and brief descriptions to help users better understand the data and visuals.

- **User-centric customization**: Users can customize views and save their preferences for more personalized data exploration.

Practice	Description	Implementation Tips
Simplicity	Keep the dashboard uncluttered for easier data comprehension.	- Limit the number of widgets - Focus on essential data
Consistent design	Use uniform color schemes and visual elements for intuitive navigation.	- Standardize fonts, colors, and chart styles - Maintain layout consistency
Visuals selection	Match data types with appropriate visual representations.	- Use bar charts for comparisons - Use line charts for trend data
Actionable insights	Ensure that insights that drive action are front and center.	- Highlight critical metrics - Use alerts for key changes
Responsive design	Make the dashboard accessible on various devices.	- Test on multiple screen sizes - Ensure mobile accessibility

Practice	Description	Implementation Tips
Contextual help	Provide explanations for data and visuals to aid understanding.	- Include tooltips and legends - Include brief descriptions for complex charts
User customization	Allow users to tailor the dashboard to their needs.	- Enable the saving of preferred views - Offer customizable widgets

Table 9.3 – Best practices for dashboard design and user interaction

By following this guide and adhering to best practices in dashboard design and user interaction, organizations can create effective AI-powered dashboards that visualize data efficiently and uncover deeper insights, driving informed strategic decisions.

Case studies – AI-driven analytics and visualization in action

The transformative potential of AI-driven data analytics and visualization tools is best illustrated through real-world applications across various industries. These case studies highlight how businesses leverage AI to derive actionable insights, enhance decision-making, and achieve strategic advantages.

Case study 1 – E-commerce personalization

Background: A leading e-commerce platform sought to personalize the shopping experience for its users to increase engagement and sales.

Solution: The platform implemented AI-driven analytics to understand user behavior, preferences, and purchase history. By analyzing this data, the platform could predict individual customer preferences and recommend products accordingly.

Visualization: AI-powered dashboards provide a real-time view of customer engagement metrics, product performance, and personalized marketing campaign results.

Outcome: The personalized recommendations led to a significant increase in user engagement, higher conversion rates, and an uplift in sales. The dashboards allowed the marketing team to adjust strategies in real time, optimizing marketing spend and ROI.

Case study 2 – Healthcare patient monitoring

Background: A hospital aimed to improve patient care and outcomes by monitoring patient data more effectively.

Solution: The hospital deployed AI models to analyze real-time patient data from various monitoring equipment, predicting potential health issues before they became critical.

Visualization: Custom dashboards visualized patient health trends, flagged anomalies, and alerted medical staff to potential issues, facilitating timely intervention.

Outcome: The proactive approach to patient care reduced emergency incidents, improved patient outcomes, and optimized staff allocation, demonstrating the power of AI in enhancing healthcare services.

Case study 3 – Manufacturing process optimization

Background: A manufacturing company faced challenges with production inefficiencies and quality control.

Solution: The company introduced AI-driven analytics to monitor production processes, identify inefficiencies, and predict equipment failures.

Visualization: Dashboards provided a comprehensive overview of the production line, highlighting inefficiencies and predictive maintenance alerts, enabling proactive management.

Outcome: The optimization led to reduced downtime, improved production efficiency, and higher product quality, showcasing the impact of AI-driven insights in manufacturing.

Case study 4 – Financial services fraud detection

Background: A financial institution needed to enhance its fraud detection capabilities to protect its customers and assets.

Solution: AI algorithms were employed to analyze transaction patterns and behaviors, detecting anomalies indicative of fraudulent activities.

Visualization: Interactive dashboards presented real-time transaction monitoring, fraud alerts, and investigation outcomes, streamlining the fraud detection process.

Outcome: The institution significantly reduced fraud incidents, safeguarding customer trust and financial assets and highlighting AI's role in securing financial transactions.

These case studies across e-commerce, healthcare, manufacturing, and financial services illustrate the versatile applications of AI-driven data analytics and visualization. By harnessing AI, businesses can unlock deep insights, predict trends, and make informed decisions, driving operational excellence and strategic growth. As AI technologies continue to advance, their applications in analytics and visualization are expected to become even more integral to industry success.

Challenges in implementing AI-driven analytics and visualization

Let's explore the complexities and hurdles faced in the implementation of AI-driven analytics and visualization, as we navigate through the challenges that shape the landscape of data-driven innovation and decision-making:

- **Data privacy and security**: With AI relying heavily on data, ensuring the privacy and security of this data becomes paramount. Organizations must adhere to regulations such as GDPR, ensuring that data is collected, stored, and processed in compliance with legal standards.

- **Complexity of AI systems**: AI models can be complex and require specialized knowledge to develop, deploy, and maintain. This complexity can pose challenges in integrating AI into existing IT infrastructures and workflows.

- **User adoption**: Introducing new technologies often faces resistance. Ensuring that end users, who may not have a technical background, can effectively use AI-powered dashboards is crucial for adoption. Training and user-friendly design play key roles here.

- **Data quality and accessibility**: AI systems are only as good as the data they process. Ensuring high-quality, clean, and accessible data is a significant challenge, particularly for organizations with legacy systems and siloed data.

- **Interpretability and trust**: AI's "black box" nature can lead to skepticism about its decisions. Making AI processes transparent and understandable is essential for building trust among users.

Ethical considerations in automated data analysis and presentation

Let's delve into the ethical dimensions of automated data analysis and presentation as we navigate the intricate terrain of responsible AI usage, ensuring that innovation aligns with ethical principles and societal values:

- **Bias and fairness**: AI systems can inadvertently perpetuate or amplify biases present in their training data. Ensuring fairness and avoiding bias in AI-driven insights is a critical ethical consideration.

- **Transparency**: Stakeholders should know how AI-driven insights are generated. This includes understanding the data sources, models used, and any assumptions made during analysis.

- **Accountability**: When AI systems guide decision-making, establishing clear lines of accountability is crucial. Organizations must determine who is responsible for the outcomes of AI-driven decisions.

- **Informed consent**: When personal data is used, obtaining informed consent from individuals whose data is being analyzed is an ethical imperative.

- **Impact on employment**: Automating tasks previously performed by humans raises concerns about job displacement. Organizations should consider the social impact of implementing AI and explore ways to reskill and redeploy affected employees.

Navigating AI-driven analytics and visualization's challenges and ethical considerations requires a balanced approach, combining technical solutions with ethical principles. Organizations must invest in data governance, user training, and transparent AI practices to overcome these challenges, ensuring that AI-driven systems are used responsibly and effectively to enhance decision-making and business outcomes.

Future trends in AI-driven data analytics and visualization

Let's explore the predictions on upcoming advancements in AI technologies for data analytics and visualization:

- **Augmented analytics**: The next wave of AI in data analytics is expected to focus on augmented analytics, where AI not only automates data analysis but also augments human intelligence with insights and recommendations, making analytics more accessible to a broader range of business users.

- **Explainable AI (XAI)**: As AI models become more complex, there's a growing demand for transparency and interpretability. XAI aims to make AI decisions more understandable, fostering trust and enabling users to make informed decisions based on AI insights.

- **Real-time data processing**: Advances in AI and computing power are expected to enhance the capabilities for real-time data processing and visualization, enabling businesses to react instantly to market changes and operational issues.

- **Integration with IoT**: The integration of AI-driven analytics with **Internet of Things** (**IoT**) devices will likely enhance real-time monitoring and visualization of data from various sources, providing more granular insights into operations, customer behavior, and market trends.

- **Advanced NLP**: NLP technologies will become more sophisticated, allowing users to interact with data visualization tools using natural language, making complex data analysis more accessible to non-technical users.

Let's now discover the potential new features and capabilities of future data visualization tools and dashboards:

- **Adaptive dashboards**: Future dashboards will become more adaptive, automatically adjusting content and visualizations based on user interactions, preferences, and roles, providing a personalized experience for each user.

- **Immersive visualization**: With the advancement of **Virtual Reality** (**VR**) and **Augmented Reality** (**AR**), data visualization tools may offer immersive experiences, allowing users to explore data in a 3D space, enhancing comprehension and engagement.

- **Predictive and prescriptive visualizations**: Beyond showcasing historical data, future tools will offer more predictive and prescriptive visualizations, suggesting potential future scenarios and recommending actions based on AI analysis.

- **Automated storytelling**: AI will enhance the storytelling aspect of data visualization, automatically generating narratives that explain the insights revealed by the data, making reports more engaging and easier to understand.

- **Enhanced collaboration features**: Data visualization tools will likely incorporate more advanced collaboration features, enabling teams to work together on data analysis projects in real time, share insights easily, and make collective decisions based on data.

The future of AI-driven data analytics and visualization holds immense potential, with advancements that promise to make data more accessible, insights more actionable, and decision-making more informed. As these technologies evolve, businesses will have unprecedented opportunities to leverage data for strategic advantage, driving innovation and growth in an increasingly data-driven world.

Trend/Feature	Description	Impact on Data Analytics and Visualization
Augmented analytics	Integration of AI to enhance human decision-making with automated insights and recommendations	Makes analytics more accessible and intuitive, extending its benefits across various business functions
XAI	Efforts to make AI decisions more transparent and understandable to users	Builds trust and allows for informed decision-making based on AI-generated insights
Real-time data processing	Enhancements in processing power to analyze and visualize data in real time	Enables immediate responses to market changes and operational issues, providing a competitive edge
Integration with IoT	Combining AI analytics with data from IoT devices for comprehensive monitoring	Offers detailed insights into operations and customer behaviors, driving operational efficiency and customer satisfaction
Advanced NLP	Improved natural language interactions with data visualization tools	Lowers the barrier to data analysis, making it accessible to a wider audience without technical expertise

Table 9.4 – Future trends in AI-driven data analytics and visualization

In anticipation of future trends, the intersection of AI-driven data analytics and visualization promises continued innovation, paving the way for unprecedented insights and transformative advancements in various fields.

Summary

In this chapter, we dove deep into the transformative role of AI in data analytics and visualization, exploring the integration of advanced AI technologies that enhance the way data is analyzed, interpreted, and presented. From the advent of AI-driven analytics enhancing decision-making processes to the evolution of data visualization tools empowered by AI, the landscape of business intelligence is undergoing a profound shift.

We discussed the significant advancements in data visualization tools, noting how AI integration has led to more intuitive, predictive, and interactive dashboards. These tools not only present data more effectively but also unearth deeper insights, facilitating informed strategic decisions. The exploration of real-world case studies across various industries illustrated the practical applications and benefits of these AI-driven technologies, showcasing their potential to drive efficiency, innovation, and competitive advantage.

The journey toward fully leveraging AI in data analytics and visualization is not without challenges. Issues such as data privacy, the complexity of AI systems, user adoption, and ethical considerations require careful navigation to ensure that the benefits of AI are realized responsibly and inclusively.

Looking ahead, the future of data analytics and visualization in an AI-driven era appears promising. With emerging trends such as augmented analytics, XAI, and the integration of AI with IoT devices, the potential for AI to further revolutionize this field is vast. New features and capabilities, such as adaptive dashboards, immersive visualization, and enhanced collaboration tools, are set to make data analytics and visualization even more accessible, engaging, and impactful.

As we embrace this AI-driven transformation, it's clear that the way we interact with data is changing fundamentally. The continuous evolution of AI technologies will undoubtedly bring forth new opportunities and challenges, but the potential to enhance decision-making, streamline operations, and uncover new insights makes this journey an exciting frontier in the realm of data analytics and visualization.

Further reading and resources

For further exploration of AI-driven data analytics and visualization, consider these resources, which discuss various aspects of the field, offering insights, methodologies, and case studies:

* *Data Science for Business: What You Need to Know about Data Mining and Data-Analytic Thinking* by Foster Provost and Tom Fawcett:

  This book provides a comprehensive introduction to data science, focusing on the principles and methods that are vital for understanding data analytics and visualization in a business context (https://www.amazon.com/Data-Science-Business-Data-Analytic-Thinking/dp/1449361323)

- *Storytelling with Data: A Data Visualization Guide for Business Professionals* by Cole Nussbaumer Knaflic:

  Cole Nussbaumer Knaflic teaches you how to leverage the power of storytelling with data to make complex information more accessible and actionable (`https://www.amazon.com/Storytelling-Data-Visualization-Business-Professionals/dp/1119002257`)

- *Applied Artificial Intelligence: A Handbook for Business Leaders* by Mariya Yao, Adelyn Zhou, and Marlene Jia:

  This handbook is a practical guide for business leaders looking to understand how AI can be leveraged in various operations, including data analytics and decision-making processes (`https://www.amazon.com/Applied-Artificial-Intelligence-Handbook-Business/dp/0998289027`)

- *Python Data Science Handbook: Essential Tools for Working with Data* by Jake VanderPlas:

  For those interested in the technical side of data analytics and visualization, this handbook thoroughly introduces Python for data science, covering essential libraries and tools, including NumPy, pandas, Matplotlib, and more (`https://www.amazon.com/Python-Data-Science-Handbook-Essential/dp/1491912057`)

These resources offer a blend of theoretical insights and practical applications, catering to professionals looking to deepen their understanding of AI-driven data analytics and visualization.

Q&A

As we wrap up this chapter, let's take a moment to reflect on the core tenets and insights we've gathered in this chapter. These questions aim to reinforce your understanding and encourage deeper contemplation on the subject:

1. How does AI transform traditional data analytics?

   AI automates and enriches data analysis processes, enabling the handling of vast datasets with complexity beyond human capability. It brings predictive analytics, pattern recognition, and even prescriptive insights, which were previously challenging or impossible to achieve.

2. What ethical considerations arise with AI-driven visualization?

   Ethical concerns include data privacy, the potential for bias in AI algorithms, and the transparency of the decision-making processes. Ensuring ethical AI involves rigorous testing, bias mitigation strategies, and clear communication about how AI-derived insights are generated.

3. How can businesses ensure user adoption of AI-powered dashboards?

    User adoption can be enhanced by involving end users in the design process, offering comprehensive training, and ensuring that dashboards are intuitive and responsive to user needs. Customization and interactivity also play significant roles in encouraging regular use.

4. What future advancements can we anticipate in AI-driven analytics and visualization?

    Future advancements may include more sophisticated machine learning models that offer finer insights, the integration of AI with emerging technologies such as AR/VR for immersive data experiences, and advancements in NLP to facilitate more natural interactions with data analytics systems.

10

Ethical and Secure AI Implications

"We all have to work to ensure that AI is developed in a way that is ethical and aligned with human values. Ensuring that the technology is secure and that user privacy is protected will be fundamental to achieving this goal."

-Tim Cook, CEO of Apple

The advent of **artificial intelligence** (**AI**) has ushered in transformative changes across various sectors, from healthcare and education to finance and security. However, with great power comes great responsibility. Introducing AI technologies necessitates carefully examining the ethical and security implications of their development and deployment. This chapter seeks to delve into the critical role that ethics and security play in shaping the landscape of AI, ensuring that these groundbreaking technologies are harnessed for the greater good while mitigating potential risks and adverse outcomes.

Ethics in AI pertains to the moral principles that govern the design, development, and deployment of AI systems. It encompasses considerations such as fairness, transparency, accountability, and the potential societal impact of AI technologies. Ethical AI aims to ensure that these systems do not perpetuate biases, infringe on individual rights, or cause harm to society or the environment. It emphasizes the importance of designing AI systems aligned with human values and societal norms, promoting the welfare and dignity of all individuals.

On the other hand, security in AI focuses on safeguarding AI systems from vulnerabilities and threats that could compromise their integrity and reliability, as well as the confidentiality of the data they process. As AI systems increasingly become integral to critical infrastructures and personal applications, ensuring security against malicious attacks, unauthorized access, and unintended malfunctions is paramount. Secure AI practices involve implementing robust security measures throughout the AI life cycle, from data collection and model training to deployment and monitoring.

The balance between innovation and responsibility in AI applications is a delicate one. On the one hand, pursuing innovation drives the development of AI technologies that can solve complex problems and enhance efficiency, and it also opens up new possibilities for advancement. However, the responsibility to ensure that these technologies are developed and used ethically and securely cannot be overlooked. This balance requires a collaborative effort among technologists, ethicists, policymakers, and society to establish guidelines, standards, and best practices that guide the responsible development and use of AI.

As we explore AI's ethical and security implications, it becomes evident that fostering an environment where innovation thrives while upholding ethical standards and security measures is crucial for the sustainable and beneficial advancement of AI technologies. This chapter aims to provide insights into how we can navigate the challenges and opportunities presented by AI, ensuring that its development and deployment are conducted with the utmost consideration for ethics and security.

The landscape of AI ethics

The landscape of AI ethics is both vast and complex, encompassing a range of considerations to ensure that the development and application of AI technologies align with moral principles and societal values. Fundamental to this ethical landscape are the concepts of fairness, transparency, and accountability, each playing a critical role in fostering trust and acceptance of AI systems:

- **Fairness**: Fairness in AI involves the equitable treatment of all individuals, ensuring that AI systems do not perpetuate or exacerbate existing biases. This requires careful consideration during the data collection and model training phases to avoid embedding discriminatory patterns into AI algorithms. Ensuring fairness means actively identifying and mitigating biases related to race, gender, age, or any other characteristic that could lead to unequal treatment.

- **Transparency**: Transparency in AI pertains to the openness and clarity regarding how AI systems operate and make decisions. It involves making the workings of AI algorithms understandable to users and stakeholders, enabling them to grasp the logic behind AI-driven outcomes. Transparency is crucial for building trust in AI systems as it allows individuals to verify the reliability and fairness of AI decisions.

- **Accountability**: Accountability in AI assigns responsibility for the outcomes of AI systems, ensuring that there are mechanisms in place to address any issues or harms that arise from AI decisions. It involves establishing clear guidelines and protocols for auditing AI systems, rectifying errors, and providing recourse for those adversely affected by AI decisions. Accountability ensures that AI developers and deployers are answerable for the ethical integrity and societal impact of their technologies.

The societal impact of AI

The societal impact of AI extends far beyond the immediate applications of the technology, influencing employment, privacy, security, and social dynamics. Ethical AI design requires a proactive approach to understanding and mitigating these broader implications, ensuring that AI technologies contribute positively to society. This includes considering the long-term effects of automation on the workforce, the use of AI in surveillance and its privacy implications, and the potential for AI to influence public opinion and democratic processes.

The importance of ethical AI design

Ethical AI design is not merely a regulatory requirement but a foundational element for the sustainable and beneficial integration of AI into society. It involves embedding ethical considerations into every stage of the AI development process, from initial concept to deployment and monitoring. Ethical AI design prioritizes the welfare and dignity of individuals, ensuring that AI technologies serve to enhance human capabilities and improve societal well-being without causing harm or injustice.

Navigating the landscape of AI ethics is essential for harnessing the full potential of AI technologies while safeguarding against their risks. By adhering to principles of fairness, transparency, and accountability, and by conscientiously assessing the societal impact of AI, developers and policymakers can guide the ethical advancement of AI, ensuring its design and application are aligned with human values and societal goals.

AI security challenges

The integration of AI into various sectors brings not only transformative benefits but also significant security challenges. These challenges range from safeguarding data privacy to protecting AI systems against sophisticated attacks, all of which are crucial for maintaining the integrity and reliability of AI applications.

The following are the key security challenges in AI:

- **Data privacy**: AI systems often rely on vast datasets, including sensitive personal information. Ensuring the privacy of this data against unauthorized access or breaches is a paramount concern, especially in applications involving healthcare, finance, and personal services.

- **Vulnerability to attacks**: AI systems, particularly machine learning models, are susceptible to various forms of attacks, including adversarial attacks where slight, often imperceptible, alterations to input data can lead to incorrect outputs. Protecting AI systems from such manipulations is critical to their reliability.

- **Integrity of AI systems**: The complexity of AI systems can sometimes obscure flaws in their design or function, making it challenging to ensure their integrity. Ensuring that AI systems perform as intended, without being compromised or producing unintended consequences, is essential for user trust and safety.

Now, let's look at a few case studies illustrating security breaches and their implications:

Case study 1 – healthcare data breach

A healthcare provider utilizing AI for patient data analysis experienced a significant data breach, exposing sensitive patient records. The breach occurred due to inadequate security measures around the AI data repository. The implications were severe, including loss of patient trust, legal repercussions, and the imposition of hefty fines for violating patient privacy laws.

Case study 2 – financial AI system manipulation

A financial institution's AI-driven trading system was manipulated through an adversarial attack, leading to abnormal trading patterns and significant financial loss. Attackers subtly altered the input data to the AI system, exploiting vulnerabilities in the model's design. The incident highlighted the need for robust security measures to protect AI systems from such sophisticated attacks.

Case study 3 – autonomous vehicle system compromise

An autonomous vehicle's AI system was compromised, causing erratic vehicle behavior and endangering passenger safety. The breach was traced back to a security flaw in the AI's decision-making algorithm, which was exploited to alter the vehicle's operation. This case underscored the critical importance of ensuring the integrity and security of AI systems, especially in applications with direct safety implications.

The following table provides a structured overview of the significant security challenges faced by AI systems, highlighted through real-world case studies that demonstrate the potential implications of these challenges. Addressing these issues is crucial for the secure and trustworthy deployment of AI technologies:

Security Challenge	Description	Case Study	Implications
Data privacy	Ensuring the protection of sensitive information processed by AI systems	**Healthcare data breach**: A healthcare provider's AI system leaked patient data due to inadequate security measures.	Loss of trust, legal issues, and financial penalties due to privacy violations
Vulnerability to attacks	Protecting AI systems from adversarial and other sophisticated cyberattacks	**Financial AI system manipulation**: An adversarial attack on a financial institution's AI model led to abnormal trading patterns	Financial losses and the need for enhanced model security against data manipulation
The integrity of AI systems	Maintaining the reliable performance of AI systems without compromise or unintended consequences	**Autonomous vehicle system compromise**: A security flaw in an autonomous vehicle's AI algorithm was exploited, causing unsafe behavior	Safety risks and the critical need for thorough security audits of AI algorithms in safety-critical applications

Table 10.1 – Overview of the security challenges faced by AI systems

This section on AI security challenges underscores the paramount importance of addressing the myriad security concerns accompanying AI technology integration across various domains. The case studies presented illustrate the potential risks and vulnerabilities associated with AI systems and the far-reaching implications of security breaches, ranging from financial losses and privacy violations to safety hazards.

As AI continues to permeate more aspects of our lives, from healthcare and finance to transportation and personal services, the imperative to fortify these systems against threats becomes increasingly critical. The lessons drawn from these case studies highlight the necessity for a multifaceted approach to AI security, encompassing robust data protection measures, resilience against adversarial attacks, and the assurance of system integrity.

Moving forward, the development and deployment of AI systems must prioritize security as a foundational component, ensuring that these advanced technologies are both beneficial and safe for users. Collaborative efforts among technologists, policymakers, and industry stakeholders are essential to establish comprehensive security standards and practices that can keep pace with the rapid evolution of AI. By doing so, we can harness the transformative potential of AI while safeguarding against the risks, paving the way for a future where AI technologies can be trusted to operate securely and ethically in service of society.

Regulatory frameworks and standards

The realm of AI ethics and security is increasingly governed by a complex tapestry of regulatory frameworks and international standards. These guidelines play a crucial role in ensuring that AI technologies are developed and deployed in ways that uphold ethical principles and maintain robust security measures.

Existing and emerging regulatory frameworks

Across the globe, governments and regulatory bodies are crafting policies to address the unique challenges posed by AI. These frameworks often focus on ensuring transparency, fairness, accountability, and security in AI systems. Notable among these are the European Union's **General Data Protection Regulation** (**GDPR**), which includes provisions for AI and data privacy, and the AI Act, a comprehensive set of rules proposed by the European Commission to regulate AI use within the EU, focusing on high-risk applications.

In the United States, regulatory initiatives are more sector-specific, with guidelines emerging in healthcare, autonomous vehicles, and finance. The **National Institute of Standards and Technology** (**NIST**) is also working on developing standards and tools to foster innovation and ensure the trustworthiness of AI technologies.

Emerging economies are not far behind, with countries such as India and Brazil proposing frameworks to balance AI innovation with ethical considerations and data protection.

The role of international standards and guidelines

International organizations play a pivotal role in harmonizing AI ethics and security standards across borders. The **Organization for Economic Co-operation and Development (OECD)** has established Principles on AI, which many countries have endorsed, outlining values such as inclusivity, transparency, and accountability.

The IEEE Global Initiative on Ethics of Autonomous and Intelligent Systems offers detailed guidelines and recommendations for ethically aligned design in AI, focusing on areas such as transparency, accountability, and user data rights.

The **International Organization for Standardization (ISO)** and the **International Electrotechnical Commission (IEC)** are also active in this space, developing standards that address various aspects of AI, from terminology and data management to ethical design and use.

The landscape of regulatory frameworks and international standards for AI ethics and security is dynamic and evolving. As AI technologies advance, so must the policies and standards that guide their ethical and secure development and use. The collaboration between governments, international bodies, and industry stakeholders is essential in shaping a global approach to ethical AI, ensuring that these powerful technologies contribute positively to society while safeguarding.

Best practices for ethical AI development

Developing AI systems with ethical considerations at the forefront is crucial for ensuring that these technologies are beneficial and do not inadvertently cause harm. Adhering to best practices in ethical AI development can guide organizations in creating AI solutions that are responsible, transparent, and aligned with societal values:

- **Stakeholder engagement**: Involve a diverse group of stakeholders in the AI development process, including ethicists, legal experts, potential users, and representatives from affected communities. This ensures a broad range of perspectives and concerns are considered, making the AI system more inclusive and equitable.

- **Establish ethical guidelines**: Develop a set of ethical guidelines specific to the AI project, outlining the core values and principles that the development will adhere to. These might include commitments to fairness, non-discrimination, transparency, and privacy.

- **Conduct ethical impact assessments**: Implement a process for conducting regular ethical impact assessments at various stages of the AI life cycle. These assessments should evaluate the potential ethical implications of the AI system, including its impact on privacy, individual rights, and societal norms.

- **Transparency and explainability**: Strive for transparency in AI algorithms, data usage, and decision-making processes. Whenever possible, use **explainable AI (XAI)** techniques that allow users and stakeholders to understand how and why decisions are made.

- **Privacy by design**: Incorporate privacy considerations into the design and architecture of AI systems from the outset. Employ data minimization techniques and secure data storage and transfer methods, and ensure that data usage complies with relevant privacy regulations.

- **Bias detection and mitigation**: Actively seek out and mitigate biases in AI datasets and algorithms. Implement fairness measures and regularly audit AI systems to ensure they do not perpetuate or exacerbate biases.

- **Ensure accountability**: Establish clear accountability mechanisms for AI decisions. This includes delineating the roles and responsibilities of those involved in the development and deployment of AI systems and creating channels for recourse if the AI system causes harm.

- **Foster an ethical culture**: Cultivate an organizational culture that prioritizes ethics in AI development. Encourage ongoing education and dialog on ethical AI practices among team members.

- **Engage in public discourse**: Participate in broader discussions on AI ethics within the industry, academia, and policymaking circles. Share insights, challenges, and best practices to contribute to the collective understanding of ethical AI.

- **Continually review and improve**: Ethical AI development is an ongoing process. Regularly review and update AI systems, ethical guidelines, and impact assessments to adapt to new insights, technologies, and societal expectations.

By adhering to these best practices, organizations can navigate the complex ethical landscape of AI development, ensuring that their AI systems are not only innovative but also responsible and aligned with the greater good. The following table will help you gain more understanding of what we've just discussed:

Practice	Description	Implementation Tips
Stakeholder engagement	Involve diverse stakeholders in AI development	Include ethicists, legal experts, users, and community representatives in the design and review process
Establish ethical guidelines	Create a set of ethical principles for AI projects	Outline core values such as fairness, transparency, and non-discrimination
Ethical impact assessments	Evaluate the ethical implications of AI systems	Conduct assessments at multiple stages of the AI life cycle to identify and mitigate potential ethical issues
Transparency and explainability	Ensure AI decisions are understandable	Use XAI techniques and make data usage and algorithms transparent
Privacy by design	Integrate privacy considerations from the outset	Employ data minimization, secure data practices, and comply with privacy laws

Practice	Description	Implementation Tips
Bias detection and mitigation	Actively address biases in AI	Implement fairness measures, audit AI systems regularly, and correct detected biases
Ensure accountability	Establish accountability for AI decisions	Clarify roles and responsibilities and provide channels for recourse if harm occurs
Foster an ethical culture	Prioritize ethics in organizational culture	Promote ethical AI practices and encourage ongoing education among team members
Engage in public discourse	Participate in broader AI ethics discussions	Contribute to industry, academic, and policy discussions on ethical AI
Continually review and improve	Update AI systems and practices regularly	Adapt to new technologies, insights, and societal expectations through continuous review

Table 10.2 – Best practices for ethical AI development

In the next section, we'll delve into the critical aspects of safeguarding AI systems to ensure data integrity and protection in the evolving landscape of accounting information systems.

Implementing AI security measures

Implementing robust security measures is crucial for safeguarding AI systems against potential threats and vulnerabilities. This section provides an overview of effective strategies that organizations can employ to enhance the security of their AI infrastructure.

Strategies for implementing AI security measures

Let's discover actionable strategies and best practices for implementing comprehensive security measures in AI systems that encompass data encryption, access controls, regular audits, secure algorithm design, incident response plans, and more:

- **Data encryption**: Protect data at rest and in transit to prevent unauthorized access and ensure confidentiality. Employ strong encryption standards for data stored within AI systems and for data that's communicated between AI components and users.

- **Access controls**: Implement stringent access control policies to ensure that only authorized personnel can interact with AI systems. This includes using authentication mechanisms, role-based access control, and the principle of least privilege to minimize exposure to sensitive functionalities.

- **Regular security audits**: Conduct periodic security audits to assess the security posture of AI systems. These audits should evaluate both the technical aspects, such as software vulnerabilities and network security, and the operational aspects, including user access patterns and compliance with security policies.

- **Secure AI algorithms**: Ensure that AI algorithms are designed with security in mind, taking into account potential vulnerabilities to adversarial attacks. Techniques such as input validation, anomaly detection, and adversarial training can help improve the resilience of AI models.

- **Threat modeling**: Engage in threat modeling exercises to identify potential security threats to AI systems. By understanding the attack vectors and the system's vulnerabilities, organizations can implement targeted defenses to mitigate identified risks.

- **Update and patch management**: Keep AI systems, including the underlying software and hardware components, up to date with the latest security patches and updates. Regular maintenance helps protect against known vulnerabilities that could be exploited by attackers.

- **Incident response plan**: Develop and maintain an incident response plan specifically tailored for AI systems. This plan should outline the steps to be taken in the event of a security breach, including containment, investigation, and recovery processes.

- **Employee training and awareness**: Educate employees about the potential security risks associated with AI systems and the best practices for mitigating these risks. Promoting security awareness among staff can help prevent accidental breaches and improve the overall security culture.

- **Secure development life cycle**: Incorporate security considerations throughout the AI development life cycle, from initial design to deployment and beyond. This includes conducting security reviews and assessments at each stage of development to identify and address security issues early.

- **Collaboration and information sharing**: Collaborate with industry peers, security experts, and academic institutions to stay informed about emerging security threats and best practices. Participating in information-sharing initiatives can help organizations learn from others' experiences and strengthen their security measures.

By implementing these strategies, organizations can build robust defenses for their AI systems, protecting them from various security threats and ensuring their integrity and reliability in serving business and societal needs. The following table provides a structured overview of key strategies for securing AI systems, along with brief descriptions and practical tips for their implementation:

Strategy	Description	Implementation Tips
Data encryption	Protect data within AI systems through encryption	Use strong encryption standards for data at rest and in transit
Access controls	Restrict access to AI systems to authorized personnel only	Implement authentication, role-based access control, and the principle of least privilege

Strategy	Description	Implementation Tips
Regular security audits	Periodically assess the security posture of AI systems	Evaluate technical and operational security aspects, including software vulnerabilities and compliance with policies
Secure AI algorithms	Design AI algorithms to be resilient against attacks	Employ input validation, anomaly detection, and adversarial training techniques
Threat modeling	Identify potential security threats to AI systems	Conduct threat modeling exercises to understand attack vectors and vulnerabilities
Update and patch management	Keep AI systems updated with the latest security patches	Regularly update software and hardware components to protect against known vulnerabilities
Incident response plan	Prepare for potential security breaches in AI systems	Develop a comprehensive incident response plan outlining containment, investigation, and recovery steps
Employee training and awareness	Educate staff about AI system security risks and best practices	Promote security awareness to prevent accidental breaches and improve security culture
Secure development life cycle	Integrate security throughout the AI development process	Conduct security reviews at each development stage to address issues early
Collaboration and information sharing	Engage with the broader community on AI security matters	Participate in industry groups and forums to share insights and learn from others' experiences

Table 10.3 – Strategies for implementing AI security measures

Adhering to these strategies can help organizations enhance the security of their AI infrastructure, safeguard against potential threats, and ensure the reliable operation of AI applications. Next, we will delve into the future horizons of ethical and secure AI, exploring emerging trends and predictions for ethical and security considerations.

Future directions in ethical and secure AI

As AI continues to permeate various aspects of our professional and personal lives, ethical and security considerations are increasingly coming to the forefront. These concerns not only influence the ongoing development of AI technologies but also shape public perception and regulatory frameworks around them. This section will explore future directions in ensuring AI remains ethical and secure.

Predictions for ethical and security considerations in AI development

The following list highlights key predictions for ethical and security considerations in the development of AI, shedding light on anticipated trends and measures that are poised to shape the ethical and security landscape of AI technologies in the realm of accounting information systems:

- **Increased regulatory oversight**: As AI technologies become more sophisticated and their applications more widespread, we can expect a corresponding increase in regulatory oversight. Governments and international bodies are likely to introduce more comprehensive guidelines and standards to ensure AI systems are developed and used ethically, with a strong emphasis on transparency, accountability, and fairness.

- **Ethics by design**: The concept of "ethics by design" will gain prominence. This is where ethical considerations are integrated into the AI development process from the outset. This approach ensures that AI systems respect privacy, ensure fairness, and are transparent in their decision-making processes.

- **Enhanced security protocols**: Security will continue to be a critical concern, particularly as AI systems handle increasingly sensitive and personal data. Advanced encryption techniques, secure data handling practices, and robust cybersecurity measures will be integral to AI development, ensuring data integrity and user trust.

Emerging technologies and methodologies for AI ethics and security

The following list highlights cutting-edge technologies and methodologies that are paving the way for enhanced ethics and security in AI systems within the realm of accounting information systems:

- **Federated learning**: This approach allows AI models to learn from decentralized data sources without the data leaving its original location, thereby enhancing data privacy and security. Federated learning enables AI systems to train on diverse datasets while minimizing the risk of data breaches.

- **XAI**: XAI focuses on making AI decision-making processes transparent and understandable to humans. This not only aids in building trust but also facilitates the identification and correction of biases within AI systems.

- **Differential privacy**: This technique adds "noise" to datasets, allowing AI systems to learn from data without compromising individual privacy. Differential privacy will become increasingly important as AI systems are applied to more sensitive areas such as healthcare and finance.

- **Blockchain for AI security**: Blockchain technology can provide a secure and transparent framework for AI operations, particularly in areas such as data exchange and model training. Its decentralized nature and immutable ledger can enhance the security and integrity of AI systems.

- **AI Auditing Frameworks**: As AI systems become more complex, auditing frameworks will be developed to assess and certify the ethical and security aspects of AI applications. These frameworks will provide standardized benchmarks for AI systems, ensuring they meet ethical and security standards.

The future of AI is inextricably linked with ethical and security considerations. As technology advances, so will the methodologies and frameworks that are designed to ensure AI remains a force for good, rooted in ethical principles and safeguarded against security threats. These developments will enhance the reliability and trustworthiness of AI systems and ensure they contribute positively to society.

Summary

In exploring the ethical and secure advancement of AI, we've traversed a landscape marked by innovation, challenge, and opportunity. This chapter illuminated the pivotal role that ethical considerations and security measures play in developing and applying AI technologies. As we conclude, let's summarize the key points and reflect on the journey ahead:

- **Ethical imperatives**: We've underscored the necessity of integrating ethical principles into AI development, emphasizing fairness, transparency, and accountability. Ethical AI ensures that technological advancements benefit society without causing harm or perpetuating inequalities.

- **Security essentials**: The critical importance of robust security protocols in AI systems has been highlighted, addressing the need to protect sensitive data and maintain user trust in an era of increasing cyber threats.

- **Regulatory frameworks**: The evolving landscape of AI regulation has been examined, predicting a future where increased oversight and international standards guide the ethical and secure deployment of AI technologies.

- **Innovative technologies for ethics and security**: Emerging technologies such as federated learning, XAI, and blockchain have been identified as key enablers for enhancing the ethical use and security of AI systems.

- **The role of education and awareness**: This chapter has advocated for the continuous education of AI developers, users, and policymakers regarding ethical and security considerations, ensuring a well-informed ecosystem that fosters responsible AI development.

Reflective thoughts on the path forward

As we stand at the cusp of a new era in AI, the path forward is cautious optimism. AI has immense potential to revolutionize industries, enhance our lives, and solve complex global challenges. However, this potential can only be fully realized if we navigate the journey while steadfastly committed to ethical principles and security imperatives.

The collaborative effort among technologists, ethicists, policymakers, and society will be paramount in shaping an AI-driven future that respects human rights, protects individual privacy, and secures our digital landscape. As we advance, let's champion the cause of ethical and secure AI, ensuring that technology serves as a beacon of progress, inclusivity, and safety.

The road ahead for AI has its challenges. Still, with a concerted focus on ethics and security, we can pave the way for a future where AI technologies innovate, inspire trust, and uphold the highest standards of moral and security excellence.

Further reading and resources

For those looking to delve deeper into the realms of AI ethics and security, the following books and resources are highly recommended. These materials offer insightful perspectives and in-depth analysis, providing a comprehensive understanding of the ethical and security challenges presented by AI technologies:

*   *AI Ethics*, by Mark Coeckelbergh, provides an accessible synthesis of ethical issues raised by AI, moving beyond the typical hype to address concrete questions about the moral status of AI, privacy concerns, responsibility, transparency, and bias. It's a valuable resource for understanding the philosophical and practical aspects of AI ethics. More information is available at *MIT Press* (`https://mitpress.mit.edu/search-result-list/?keyword=AI+E thics"+by+Mark+Coeckelbergh`).

*   The edited volume *The Oxford Handbook of Ethics of AI* explores the intersecting domains of AI and ethics, offering a multidisciplinary perspective on the ethical implications of AI technologies. It's an essential read for those interested in the broader ethical considerations surrounding AI applications. Details can be found at *Oxford Academic* (`https://academic.oup.com/ edited-volume/34287`).

*   *Everyday AI Newsletter*, by Jordan Wilson, is an online resource that offers insights and updates on AI developments, focusing on making AI understandable and accessible to a general audience. It's an excellent way to stay informed about the latest in AI. Subscribe at *Everyday AI* (`https://www.youreverydayai.com`).

*   *AI Ethics, Security, and Privacy* is a collection of articles and papers that delves into the ethical considerations of AI, including privacy, monitoring, automation's impact on employment, and the moral agency of robots. It's a comprehensive resource for academic and professional research on AI ethics and security. Explore more at *SpringerLink* (`https://link.springer.com/ search?query=AI+Ethics%2C+Security+and+Privacy`).

These resources provide a broad spectrum of knowledge, from addressing fundamental ethical questions to exploring advanced security measures in AI. They suit professionals, academics, and anyone interested in AI technologies' ethical and secure implementation.

Q&A

In the evolving landscape of managerial accounting, the integration of AI poses thought-provoking ethical and security challenges. This section delves into reflective queries and insights, exploring how AI redefines traditional accounting roles, the ethical considerations it brings to the forefront, and the adaptations professionals must embrace. Through a series of questions and answers, we aim to shed light on these complexities, providing a nuanced understanding of AI's impact and the path forward in ensuring its ethical and secure application in the field.

Here are four thought-provoking questions, along with concise answers, so that you can delve deeper into ethical and secure AI practices:

1. How does AI challenge traditional ethics in managerial accounting?

    AI introduces complex ethical challenges, such as algorithmic transparency and accountability, necessitating a reevaluation of traditional ethical frameworks in managerial accounting to ensure fairness and integrity.

2. What role does data privacy play in AI-driven accounting systems?

    Data privacy is crucial as AI systems often process sensitive financial information. Protecting this data from breaches is paramount to maintaining company confidentiality and client trust and adhering to legal standards.

3. How can AI systems be designed to avoid biases in managerial decisions?

    AI systems must be carefully designed and continuously monitored to identify and mitigate biases, ensuring that decision-making processes remain objective and equitable.

4. What are the key considerations for secure AI implementation in accounting?

    Key considerations include robust data encryption, secure access protocols, and regular security audits to prevent unauthorized access and ensure the integrity of financial data.

11
Revolutionizing Corporate Governance with AI

"AI governance must be about more than just algorithms. It's about ensuring that human judgment, values, and accountability remain at the core of decision-making, even as AI systems become more sophisticated."

- (Stuart Russell, Professor of Computer Science, UC Berkeley, and author of "Human Compatible: Artificial Intelligence and the Problem of Control")

This chapter examines **artificial intelligence** (**AI**)'s transformative role in reshaping corporate governance's landscape. As organizations navigate an increasingly complex global business environment, adopting AI technologies presents remarkable opportunities and unique challenges. AI's sophisticated analytical tools and unparalleled data processing capabilities stand at the forefront of this change, offering new pathways to refine decision-making processes, bolster transparency, and enhance accountability within corporate frameworks.

This chapter begins by examining how AI's ability to analyze vast datasets in real time can lead to more informed and strategic decision-making at all levels of an organization. By leveraging AI's predictive analytics and machine learning algorithms, companies can anticipate market trends, identify risks, and uncover opportunities with a degree of precision previously unattainable. This proactive approach to decision-making drives competitive advantage and aligns with the principles of good governance by fostering informed and forward-looking leadership.

We'll explore AI's role in promoting transparency within organizations. AI systems can automate tracking and reporting of key performance indicators, ensuring stakeholders have access to timely and accurate information. This transparency is critical to building trust among investors, regulators, and the public, as it provides a clear view of the organization's operations and its adherence to governance standards.

Accountability, a cornerstone of effective governance, is also significantly impacted by AI integration. Organizations can ensure adherence to legal and ethical standards by implementing AI-driven audit and compliance tools. These tools can detect deviations from expected behaviors or norms, facilitating timely corrective actions and demonstrating the organization's commitment to responsible governance practices.

Integrating AI into corporate governance also introduces ethical considerations and regulatory challenges. This chapter addresses the need for a robust ethical framework to guide the deployment of AI in governance, ensuring that AI systems operate transparently, fairly, and without bias. It discusses the evolving regulatory landscape as policymakers seek to establish standards that govern AI's use in corporate settings, balancing innovation with protecting stakeholder interests.

This chapter provides a comprehensive overview of AI's impact on corporate governance, highlighting its potential to revolutionize traditional governance models. By embracing AI's capabilities, organizations can navigate the complexities of the modern business environment with greater agility, integrity, and foresight, setting new benchmarks for excellence in governance.

AI-driven enhancements in corporate governance

AI revolutionizes corporate governance by enhancing decision-making, risk assessment, and compliance. It enables real-time data analysis, predictive modeling for strategic planning, and automated regulatory compliance checks. These advancements lead to more informed decisions, proactive risk management, and adherence to complex legal frameworks, significantly impacting how corporations are governed in the digital age. AI-driven enhancements in corporate governance extend beyond decision-making and risk assessment to fostering an environment of continuous compliance. By leveraging AI's capabilities, corporations can dynamically align with global regulatory changes, ensuring governance practices remain up-to-date and within legal frameworks. This proactive approach to compliance, powered by AI, marks a significant shift in managing and executing governance responsibilities, promising greater efficiency and reliability in corporate operations.

In corporate governance, the advent of AI marks a pivotal shift toward more dynamic and responsive governance models. AI's contributions to corporate governance are multifaceted, significantly elevating the processes of decision-making, risk assessment, and compliance to unprecedented levels of efficiency and effectiveness.

Enhanced decision-making processes

AI's impact on decision-making in corporate governance is profound. By harnessing the power of real-time data analytics and advanced predictive modeling, AI empowers decision-makers with deep insights that were previously unimaginable. This capability enables executives to make more informed, data-driven decisions that align with the organization's strategic objectives and market dynamics. AI systems can sift through vast amounts of data to identify patterns, trends, and anomalies, facilitating a more nuanced understanding of the business landscape and helping leaders anticipate future challenges and opportunities.

Revolutionizing risk assessment

Risk assessment in the corporate sector is transforming thanks to AI's predictive analytics and machine learning algorithms. These technologies allow organizations to identify risks with greater precision and speed, from financial uncertainties to operational vulnerabilities. AI's ability to analyze complex datasets and predict potential outcomes enables corporations to adopt a more proactive stance toward risk management. By foreseeing potential issues before they arise, a company can devise strategic measures to mitigate risks, safeguarding its assets, reputation, and stakeholder interests.

Automating compliance and regulatory adherence

In an era where regulatory landscapes are constantly evolving, AI-driven solutions offer a reliable beacon for ensuring compliance. AI technologies streamline the process of monitoring and adhering to a myriad of regulations across different jurisdictions. Automated compliance checks, powered by AI, can continuously scan for regulatory updates and assess the company's compliance status in real time. This reduces the risk of non-compliance and its associated penalties and significantly lowers the operational burden on compliance teams.

Continuous compliance and dynamic governance

AI revolutionizes the concept of continuous compliance, enabling corporations to remain agile and aligned with global regulatory changes. AI's dynamic monitoring and adaptive learning capabilities ensure that governance practices are current and predictive of future regulatory trends. This agility is crucial to maintaining a competitive edge and upholding corporate integrity in the fast-paced digital economy.

Implications for corporate governance

Integrating AI into corporate governance has challenges, including ethical considerations and the need for robust data governance frameworks. However, the potential benefits—enhanced decision-making, advanced risk assessment, and streamlined compliance—herald a new era in corporate governance. As AI-driven enhancements become increasingly ingrained in governance frameworks, they promise to elevate the standards of corporate conduct, accountability, and transparency, ultimately leading to more resilient and trustworthy organizations in the digital age.

In conclusion, the integration of AI-driven enhancements in corporate governance not only streamlines decision-making processes but also fosters greater transparency, efficiency, and accountability, ultimately leading to sustained organizational growth and resilience in an ever-evolving business landscape.

As we discuss ethical considerations in AI governance in the next section, it becomes imperative to address the potential ramifications of integrating AI into decision-making frameworks.

Ethical considerations in AI governance

Integrating AI into governance frameworks raises many ethical considerations that warrant careful examination. At the core of these ethical debates are concerns regarding accountability, transparency, and the equitable treatment of all individuals under the governance system.

One of the primary ethical considerations is the accountability of decisions made by AI systems. In governance, where decisions can have wide-reaching impacts on public welfare, the opacity of AI algorithms can obscure the rationale behind decisions, making it challenging to attribute responsibility. This raises the question of ensuring that AI systems are held to the same accountability standards as human decision-makers.

Transparency is another crucial ethical aspect. For AI to be ethically integrated into governance, the processes by which AI systems make decisions must be understandable to the public and policymakers alike. This transparency is essential for trust and the effective oversight and regulation of AI technologies.

The ethical use of AI in governance must address the potential for bias and discrimination. AI systems learn from historical data and can perpetuate and amplify existing biases if not carefully designed and monitored. Ensuring equitable treatment necessitates rigorous bias detection and mitigation strategies to prevent discriminatory outcomes.

The ethical deployment of AI within governance frameworks demands a balanced approach that respects individual rights and societal norms. It requires establishing robust mechanisms for accountability, enhancing transparency in AI decision-making processes, and actively combating biases to ensure fair and just outcomes for all citizens. The ethical implications of AI in governance underscore the need for a collaborative effort among technologists, ethicists, policymakers, and the public to navigate the complex landscape of AI ethics effectively.

Case studies – AI in action

Introducing case studies showcasing AI in action offers examples of how AI technologies are being leveraged across various industries to drive innovation, optimize processes, and achieve business objectives.

Case study 1 – Transforming risk management in financial services

Industry context: In the fast-paced financial services sector, where milliseconds can equate to millions of dollars, the ability to swiftly identify and mitigate risks is paramount. A leading international bank was grappling with the challenge of managing the vast array of financial risks inherent in its global operations, from credit and market risks to fraud and compliance breaches.

AI integration strategy: The bank embarked on a transformative journey by implementing an advanced AI-powered risk management framework. This framework utilized a sophisticated array of machine learning algorithms, capable of parsing through terabytes of transactional data and market indicators in real time. The system was equipped with deep learning capabilities to discern intricate patterns and correlations that elude traditional analytical methods.

Implementation challenges: Adapting the AI system to the bank's intricate data infrastructure and ensuring its alignment with various regulatory standards posed significant challenges. Rigorous training datasets, representative of real-world scenarios, were curated to fine-tune the AI's predictive accuracy.

Transformative outcomes

This uncovers the transformative outcomes in financial services:

- **Predictive risk insights**: The AI system offered real-time analysis and predictive insights, forecasting potential risk scenarios before they materialized

- **Customized risk solutions**: The AI framework provided tailored risk mitigation strategies by understanding the unique risk profiles of different business units and geographical regions

- **Strategic decision-making**: Armed with AI-driven analytics, the bank's executives could confidently make strategic decisions backed by data-driven risk assessments

Case study 2 – Automating compliance in the global healthcare industry

Industry context: The healthcare industry is characterized by its stringent regulatory environment, designed to ensure patient safety and data privacy. A global healthcare corporation operating across multiple countries faces the daunting task of staying compliant with an ever-evolving array of healthcare laws and regulations.

AI integration strategy: The corporation implemented a state-of-the-art AI-driven compliance management system to address this challenge. This system harnessed the power of **natural language processing** (**NLP**) to decipher complex regulatory texts and extract pertinent compliance requirements. Coupled with machine learning algorithms, the system adapted to changes in regulatory landscapes, learning from new regulations as they were enacted.

Implementation challenges: Ensuring the AI system's accuracy in interpreting and applying diverse regulatory standards was a key challenge. The system required extensive training on regulatory documents from various jurisdictions, necessitating collaboration with legal experts to validate the AI system's interpretations.

Transformative outcomes

This lists the transformative outcomes achieved through automation:

- **Real-time compliance monitoring**: The AI platform continuously monitored the regulatory environment, alerting the corporation to any changes that impacted its operations

- **Proactive policy adjustment**: With AI-generated insights, the corporation could swiftly update internal policies and procedures to align with new regulations, fostering a culture of continuous compliance

- **Enhanced stakeholder confidence**: Demonstrating a commitment to rigorous compliance standards, the corporation reinforced its credibility and trust among patients, healthcare providers, and regulatory bodies

Transitioning from these successful implementations, let's now explore the strategies and solutions employed when overcoming hurdles on the path to realizing the full potential of AI.

Overcoming challenges

While integrating AI into corporate governance heralds a new era of efficiency, transparency, and strategic acumen, it also presents a constellation of challenges and ethical dilemmas. These obstacles necessitate a thoughtful and deliberate approach to ensure that the benefits of AI are harnessed responsibly and equitably.

Navigating ethical waters

The ethical use of AI is at the forefront of these challenges. The potential for AI systems to perpetuate biases, infringe on privacy, and make opaque decisions raises profound ethical concerns. Ensuring that AI systems operate fairly and transparently requires a robust ethical framework prioritizing human rights and dignity. This involves implementing bias detection and mitigation strategies, ensuring the explainability of AI decisions, and safeguarding privacy through secure data practices.

Data integrity and security

Data is the lifeblood of AI systems. Ensuring the integrity and security of this data is paramount, particularly when sensitive corporate information and personal data are involved. Establishing stringent data governance policies, employing advanced cybersecurity measures, and fostering a culture of data literacy within the organization are critical steps in protecting against data breaches and ensuring the reliability of AI-driven insights.

Regulatory compliance and standardization

As AI continues to evolve, so does the regulatory landscape governing its use. Staying abreast of regulatory changes and ensuring AI compliance presents a dynamic challenge to corporations. It requires a proactive approach to governance, where AI systems are designed with flexibility and adaptability in mind, enabling swift alignment with new regulatory requirements. Engaging with policymakers and contributing to developing AI standards can also facilitate a more harmonious regulatory environment.

Bridging the skill gap

Successful integration of AI into governance structures necessitates a workforce equipped with the necessary skills and knowledge. Bridging the skill gap involves recruiting talent with expertise in AI and data science and upskilling existing employees to work effectively alongside AI systems. This dual approach ensures that the organization can fully leverage AI capabilities while fostering an environment of continuous learning and adaptation.

Cultivating stakeholder trust

The adoption of AI in governance also hinges on the trust of stakeholders, from employees and shareholders to regulators and the public. Building and maintaining this trust requires transparent communication about how AI is used, the benefits it brings, and the measures in place to mitigate risks. Demonstrating a commitment to ethical AI use, prioritizing stakeholder engagement, and showing accountability in AI-driven decisions are essential to cultivating a positive perception of AI integration.

Overcoming the challenges associated with AI integration in corporate governance demands a multifaceted strategy, underscored by a commitment to ethical principles, data security, regulatory vigilance, skill development, and stakeholder trust. By navigating these challenges with foresight and responsibility, organizations can unlock the full potential of AI to revolutionize governance, driving innovation and integrity in equal measure. As we advance through the digital age, the path forward is continuous learning, adaptation, and ethical vigilance, ensuring that AI serves as a force for good in the governance landscape.

Future outlook

As we peer into the horizon of corporate governance, the trajectory of AI integration suggests a future where governance structures are more efficient, transparent, adaptive, and inclusive. The evolution of AI in this realm is poised to redefine the paradigms of decision-making, risk management, compliance, and stakeholder engagement.

Predictive and adaptive governance models

In the future, AI-driven governance models will likely be responsive and predictive. Advanced AI algorithms will enable organizations to foresee shifts in market dynamics, regulatory changes, and emerging risks with remarkable accuracy. This forward-looking approach will allow corporations to adapt their strategies proactively, ensuring resilience and sustainability in an ever-evolving business landscape.

Enhanced decision-making with augmented intelligence

AI's role in decision-making processes will evolve from supportive to symbiotic. Augmented intelligence, where AI enhances human intelligence rather than replacing it, will become a cornerstone of corporate governance. By integrating AI's analytical capabilities with human judgment and ethical considerations, organizations can make more nuanced, informed decisions that balance profitability with social responsibility.

Seamless compliance in a dynamic regulatory environment

As regulatory environments become increasingly complex, AI's ability to dynamically interpret and comply with global regulations will be indispensable. Real-time compliance systems powered by AI will ensure that organizations can swiftly adapt to new laws and standards, minimizing legal risks and fostering a culture of integrity and transparency.

Empowering stakeholder engagement

The future of AI in governance will also see a shift toward greater inclusivity and engagement with stakeholders. AI-driven platforms will facilitate more interactive and transparent communication channels, allowing stakeholders to be more active in governance processes. This increased engagement will enhance trust and alignment between organizations and their diverse stakeholders, from employees and shareholders to customers and communities.

Ethical AI at the core of governance

The emphasis on ethical AI will intensify as AI becomes more ingrained in governance. Organizations will adopt comprehensive ethical frameworks that guide the development and deployment of AI systems, ensuring they uphold fairness, transparency, and accountability. Ethical AI will become a key differentiator in corporate reputation and trustworthiness.

Navigating talent transformation

The integration of AI in governance will drive a transformation in the workforce. There will be an increased demand for professionals who possess expertise in AI and data science and understand corporate governance's intricacies. Continuous education and reskilling programs will be vital in equipping the workforce for the AI-augmented governance landscape.

The long-term impact of AI on corporate governance is poised to be profound and multifaceted. As organizations navigate this transition, the focus will be on leveraging AI to enhance governance effectiveness while ensuring ethical considerations are at the forefront. The future of corporate governance in the AI era promises to be more agile, inclusive, and aligned with broader societal values, heralding a new age of corporate responsibility and innovation.

Summary

As we stand on the cusp of a new era in corporate governance shaped by AI, it is imperative for organizations to navigate this transition with a keen sense of responsibility and foresight. The integration of AI offers unprecedented opportunities to enhance governance practices, but it also presents complex ethical and operational challenges. The path forward requires a balanced approach that harnesses the capabilities of AI while remaining steadfast in the commitment to ethical principles and human-centric values.

In the journey toward AI-augmented governance, continuous learning, adaptation, and ethical vigilance will be key. By embracing these principles, organizations can unlock the full potential of AI to foster governance models that are not only more efficient and effective but also more transparent, equitable, and aligned with the broader societal good.

This chapter has explored AI's transformative potential in corporate governance, examining its benefits, ethical considerations, and integration challenges. As we reflect on the insights and questions raised, it is clear that the future of corporate governance will be deeply intertwined with AI's evolution. Embracing this future requires a commitment to ethical integrity, continuous innovation, and a deepened understanding of the complex interplay between technology and governance.

Further reading and resources

To complement the insights provided in this chapter and facilitate a deeper understanding of AI's role in corporate governance, the following curated selection of books, articles, and online resources is recommended. These resources will enrich your knowledge base, offering diverse perspectives on the implications, challenges, and future directions of AI integration in governance structures.

Books

- *AI Superpowers: China, Silicon Valley, and the New World Order* by Kai-Fu Lee (https://www. amazon.com/AI-Superpowers-China-Silicon-Valley/dp/132854639X)"

  Lee's book offers a compelling look into how AI shapes global economic and political landscapes, with insights into how corporate governance can adapt and thrive in this new world order.

- *The Future of Leadership in the Age of AI by Marin Ivezic and Luka Ivezic* (https://www.amazon. com/s?k=The+Future+of+Leadership+in+the+Age+of+AI%22+by+Marin+Ive-zic+and+Luka+Ivezic&i=stripbooks&crid=21ZG75F8854W1&spre-fix=the+future+of+leadership+in+the+age+of+ai+by+marin+ive-zic+and+luka+ivezic%2Cstripbooks%2C98&ref=nb_sb_noss)

  This book addresses the evolving role of leadership in organizations transformed by AI, providing valuable perspectives on navigating governance in an era where technology and human oversight intersect.

- *The Ethical Algorithm: The Science of Socially Aware Algorithm Design* by Michael Kearns and Aaron Roth (https://www.amazon.com/s?k=The+Ethical+Algorithm%3A+The+Sci-ence+of+Socially+Aware+Algorithm+Design%22+by+Michael+Kearns+a-nd+Aaron+Roth&i=stripbooks&crid=QZ2SJZU5OUPP&sprefix=the+ethi-cal+algorithm+the+science+of+socially+aware+algorithm+design+by+michael+kearns+and+aaron+roth%2Cstripbooks%2C101&ref=nb_sb_noss) Kearns and Roth delve into the ethical considerations crucial to AI implementation in any field, including corporate governance. Their work is instrumental in understanding how to design and deploy AI systems that uphold ethical standards.

Online resources

- *MIT Sloan Management Review: AI and Business Strategy* (`https://sloanreview.mit.edu/big-ideas/artificial-intelligence-business-strategy/`) This is a resource hub featuring a collection of articles, research findings, and case studies on AI's impact on business strategies and governance.

- *World Economic Forum: Shaping the Future of Technology Governance: Artificial Intelligence and Machine Learning* (`https://www.weforum.org/videos/how-are-the-forum-and-partners-shaping-the-future-of-artificial-intelligence-and-machine-learning/`) This platform offers reports, insights, and guidelines on AI governance, focusing on global perspectives and the collaborative effort required to harness AI responsibly.

- *Responsible AI - Maturing from theory to practice by PwC* (`https://www.pwc.com/gx/en/issues/data-and-analytics/artificial-intelligence/what-is-responsible-ai/pwc-responsible-ai-maturing-from-theory-to-practice.pdf`) PwC's whitepaper presents a practical framework for embedding ethical principles into AI development and deployment, and is essential reading for those involved in AI governance.

Integrating AI into corporate governance is multifaceted and fraught with challenges, yet brimming with opportunities. The resources listed here provide diverse perspectives and deep dives into the critical aspects of AI in governance. By engaging with these materials, you can gain a more nuanced understanding of how to navigate the complexities of AI implementation, ensuring that their governance practices are practical, ethically sound, and aligned with future advancements in AI technology.

Q&A

In this concluding section of this chapter, we dive into reflective queries and insights, exploring the nuanced dimensions of AI's integration into corporate governance. This exploration aims to foster a deeper understanding and critical thinking among readers about the role, ethics, and future of AI in corporate governance.

1. What is the fundamental role of AI in transforming corporate governance?

   AI fundamentally transforms corporate governance by enhancing decision-making processes, risk management, compliance, and stakeholder engagement. Its ability to process vast amounts of data in real time, provide predictive analytics, and automate complex tasks positions AI as a pivotal tool in making governance structures more responsive, informed, and efficient.

2. How can organizations ensure ethical AI use in governance?

    Ensuring ethical AI use involves several key strategies:

- **Adopting ethical frameworks**: Organizations should adopt comprehensive ethical guidelines that govern AI development and deployment, emphasizing fairness, transparency, and accountability

- **Bias mitigation**: Implementing robust mechanisms to detect and mitigate biases in AI algorithms is crucial to preventing discriminatory outcomes and ensuring equitable decision-making

- **Transparency and explainability**: AI systems should be designed to provide transparent and understandable explanations for their decisions, fostering trust among stakeholders

3. What challenges do organizations face in integrating AI into governance, and how can they be addressed?

    Challenges in AI integration include data privacy concerns, regulatory compliance, ethical dilemmas, and the skill gap. Addressing these challenges requires a multifaceted approach:

- **Enhancing data security**: Implementing advanced cybersecurity measures and strict data governance policies to protect sensitive information

- **Regulatory agility**: Staying abreast of and adapting to evolving regulatory landscapes to ensure compliance

- **Ethical leadership**: Cultivating a leadership ethos that prioritizes ethical considerations in AI deployment

- **Workforce development**: Investing in training and development to equip employees with the necessary AI and data literacy skills

4. What does the future hold for AI in corporate governance?

    The future of AI in corporate governance is marked by continued innovation and deeper integration. We can anticipate more sophisticated AI systems that offer greater predictive capabilities, more nuanced risk assessments, and more dynamic compliance mechanisms. Ethical AI will become increasingly central, with a growing emphasis on creating AI systems that not only enhance efficiency but also uphold the highest ethical standards.

12
GPT Store Feature in ChatGPT

"People hate searching."

– Sam Altman

The introduction of custom and accessible **generative pre-trained transformer** (**GPT**) models within ChatGPT has revolutionized the realm of **artificial intelligence** (**AI**), marking a significant milestone in the evolution of conversational agents. These GPTs have replaced the plugins that were originally available with GPT-4. This chapter explores the transformative impact of GPTs, emphasizing their role in enhancing interaction capabilities and automating responses in conversational AI. Their advanced natural language understanding allows for more intuitive and context-aware conversations, effectively bridging the gap between human and machine communication.

By enabling the creation of customized GPTs, users can import resources and tailor AI to perform specific tasks or focus on particular topics, enhancing the utility and application of ChatGPT across various domains. From assisting in language learning to providing technical support, GPT can be as simple or as complex as needed, offering a flexible tool for both personal and professional use.

The GPT store, available to all ChatGPT users, irrespective of whether they're a paid or free user, represents a pivotal development in this ecosystem. It not only facilitates the discovery and utilization of these custom AI models by providing a centralized platform where users can find and deploy GPTs tailored to diverse needs but also encourages innovation by allowing creators to share their specialized GPTs with a broader audience.

This introduction sets the stage for a deeper exploration of GPT capabilities and their potential to transform industries and individual interactions with technology, underscoring the importance of adaptability and innovation in the rapidly evolving field of AI.

GPT innovations in ChatGPT

The integration of GPT into ChatGPT has ushered in a new era of conversational AI by introducing several key innovations. These advancements are designed to improve the functionality, accessibility, and customization of ChatGPT, making it a more versatile tool in various applications. Here are some of the most notable innovations:

- **Adaptive response generation**: GPT technology enables ChatGPT to generate responses that are not only contextually aware but also highly relevant to the user's input. This is achieved through deep learning models that process vast amounts of data, learning the nuances of human language and conversation patterns. The result is an AI that can participate in complex conversations, provide informed responses, and maintain coherence throughout interactions.

- **Enhanced customization capabilities**: With the advent of custom GPTs, users now can fine-tune the model to specific needs or areas of expertise. Whether for educational purposes, customer service, or niche topics such as legal advice or medical information, these tailored versions of ChatGPT can provide more specialized assistance. This customization extends the utility of ChatGPT, making it a valuable tool for professionals across different fields.

- **Scalable learning and memory**: GPT models in ChatGPT have improved scalability in learning and memory. Unlike earlier models, which had limited capacity and retention, the latest GPT versions can remember extended conversations within a session. This capability allows for more meaningful and sustained interactions, particularly in scenarios where the continuity of dialog is crucial.

- **Multilingual support**: The GPT framework has significantly enhanced ChatGPT's multilingual capabilities. It can understand and generate text in multiple languages, making it an invaluable tool for global communication. This multilingual support is crucial for businesses operating in international markets and for users seeking assistance in languages other than English.

- **Ethical and responsible AI usage**: Innovations in ChatGPT also include improvements in ethical AI practices. Efforts have been made to reduce biases in the AI's responses, ensure fairness, and increase transparency in how the AI models make decisions. These steps are critical in building trust and ensuring that ChatGPT adheres to ethical guidelines in its interactions.

- **Integration with external data sources**: Recent upgrades allow ChatGPT to access and retrieve information from external databases or the internet (with user permission), providing responses that are not only contextually accurate but also up to date. This integration enhances the tool's usefulness in dynamic environments where real-time data is crucial.

Collectively, these innovations represent a significant leap forward in the capabilities of ChatGPT, transforming it from a simple chatbot into a sophisticated AI system capable of handling a range of complex tasks. As GPT technology continues to evolve, we can expect further enhancements that will continue to redefine the boundaries of what conversational AI can achieve.

Challenges in custom GPT adoption

The launch of the GPT store by OpenAI marks a significant advancement in making customizable AI more accessible. Adopting these GPTs from the GPT store comes with unique challenges that developers and users must navigate. Understanding these challenges is crucial for maximizing the potential of this innovative platform. Here are some of the primary hurdles:

- **Quality control and standardization**: Ensuring the quality and consistency of the GPTs that are available in the store poses a significant challenge. With numerous developers contributing their GPTs, there can be vast differences in quality, reliability, and performance. Establishing a robust review and standardization process is crucial to maintaining user trust and ensuring that all GPTs meet a certain standard.

- **User understanding and expectations**: There can be a gap between user expectations and the actual capabilities of GPTs. Users may not fully understand how to utilize these AI models effectively or might have unrealistic expectations about their functionality. This discrepancy can lead to dissatisfaction and underutilization of the technology.

- **Integration complexities**: Integrating GPTs into existing systems and workflows can be technically challenging, especially for users who are not technologically adept. Compatibility issues with existing software or platforms can hinder the seamless adoption of GPTs from the GPT store.

- **Security and privacy concerns**: When deploying AI models, especially in environments that handle sensitive data, security and privacy become paramount. Users need assurance that the GPTs they adopt adhere to stringent data protection standards to prevent data breaches and maintain compliance with regulations such as GDPR or HIPAA.

- **Economic accessibility**: While the GPT store aims to democratize access to AI, the cost associated with deploying and maintaining GPTs can still be prohibitive for smaller businesses or individual developers. Ensuring economic accessibility remains a challenge in truly democratizing advanced AI tools.

- **Maintenance and updates**: GPTs require regular updates and maintenance to stay relevant and effective. Developers must continuously refine their models based on user feedback and changing data landscapes. Users must also stay engaged with the platform to benefit from updates and improvements, which demands ongoing time and resource investment.

- **Ethical use and bias mitigation**: Ensuring that GPTs are used ethically and that biases are adequately mitigated is a significant concern. Developers need to design GPTs that promote fairness and inclusivity while also providing mechanisms to address and correct any emergent biases or unethical uses.

- **Market saturation and differentiation**: As more GPTs become available, standing out in a crowded market becomes challenging for developers. Differentiating GPTs in terms of features, performance, and specific use cases is crucial to attracting and retaining users.

Addressing these challenges requires concerted efforts from both OpenAI as the platform provider and the community of developers and users. Through collaboration, continuous improvement, and responsive governance, the GPT store can achieve its full potential, empowering users with customizable AI solutions tailored to their specific needs.

Case studies – GPTs in action

This section presents detailed examples of how GPTs have been successfully implemented across various industries and applications, showcasing their utility and transformative impact.

Customer service enhancement

Company: A major telecommunications provider.

Challenge: The company faced high customer service costs and needed to improve response times and satisfaction rates.

Solution: They implemented a custom GPT tailored for customer service that could handle routine inquiries, troubleshooting, and account management tasks.

Impact: The GPT reduced response times from several minutes to seconds, handled up to 50% of incoming queries without human intervention, and improved customer satisfaction rates by 20%. This allowed human agents to focus on more complex customer needs, optimizing overall operational efficiency.

Educational tutoring

Organization: A leading online educational platform.

Challenge: The platform needed to scale its tutoring services to support a growing global student base without compromising the quality of education.

Solution: They developed a custom GPT that was designed to provide personalized tutoring in subjects such as mathematics, science, and language.

Impact: The AI tutor was accessible 24/7, providing instant feedback and explanations, which significantly improved students' learning outcomes. It also allowed the platform to expand its reach to under-resourced regions, democratizing access to quality education.

Content creation for digital marketing

Company: A digital marketing agency.

Challenge: The agency struggled to keep up with the content demands of its clients across various digital channels.

Solution: They employed a GPT specialized in content creation to generate high-quality, engaging text for blogs, social media, and advertising copy.

Impact: The GPT was able to produce diverse content styles tailored to different target audiences, increasing campaign engagement rates by 30% and reducing content creation time by 50%.

Legal document automation

Firm: A corporate law firm.

Challenge: The firm needed to streamline the generation and review of legal documents to reduce turnaround times and free up attorneys for high-value tasks.

Solution: The firm introduced a GPT customized for legal writing that could draft and suggest edits to contracts, briefs, and other legal documents based on the firm's extensive database of prior work.

Impact: This GPT application reduced the time spent on document drafting by 40% and improved the accuracy of legal documents by reducing human error.

Real-time language translation for hospitality

Company: An international hotel chain.

Challenge: The chain sought to enhance guest experiences by improving communication barriers between staff and guests speaking different languages.

Solution: They integrated a multilingual GPT capable of understanding and translating multiple languages in real time that's used both on the company's mobile app and as a desktop tool at reception desks.

Impact: The solution improved communication efficiency, significantly enhancing guest satisfaction and streamlining operations, especially in regions with a high influx of international tourists.

These case studies illustrate the diverse applications of GPTs and their capability to revolutionize industries by automating complex tasks and providing scalable solutions. As GPT technology continues to evolve, its adoption across different sectors is expected to drive significant advancements in operational efficiency, customer engagement, and personalized services. The next section offers insights into the future trends and predictions shaping the landscape of conversational AI.

Future trends and predictions

As custom GPT technology continues to evolve, several key trends and predictions indicate its potential trajectory and impact on various industries. Here are some anticipated developments:

- **Widespread integration in customer service**: Custom GPTs are expected to become increasingly prevalent in customer service applications, offering more nuanced and complex interaction capabilities. These AI-driven bots could handle a broader range of customer inquiries with greater autonomy, providing personalized responses and solutions without human intervention, thereby enhancing the customer experience while reducing operational costs.

- **Enhanced virtual assistants**: The number of virtual assistants is likely to increase significantly. Future GPTs might manage more comprehensive tasks, such as complete planning and coordinating events, managing personal finances, or even advising on business strategy. This evolution will make virtual assistants more indispensable to daily business operations and personal life management.

- **A greater role in content creation**: GPTs will play a more significant role in content generation, not just in writing articles or generating images but in creating multimedia content, such as videos and interactive media. These tools will be able to understand and integrate multi-modal inputs and outputs, making them powerful tools for marketers, educators, and content creators.

- **Improvements in training and customization**: As the technology matures, the process of training and customizing GPTs will become more streamlined and user-friendly. This will lower the barrier to entry, allowing more users without technical expertise to create effective and powerful custom GPTs for their specific needs.

- **Expansion in education and learning**: Custom GPTs are set to revolutionize education by providing personalized learning experiences. These AI models could adapt to individual learning styles and paces, potentially offering students a more tailored educational journey that enhances understanding and retention of knowledge.

- **Ethical and regulatory developments**: As GPTs become more capable and widespread, ethical and regulatory considerations will come to the forefront. This will likely result in more stringent guidelines and standards governing the use of AI, particularly in sensitive areas such as privacy, bias mitigation, and transparency.

- **Economic models based on AI engagement**: The monetization strategies surrounding GPT usage will evolve, with more platforms likely adopting models where creators are compensated based on the engagement and utility their GPTs provide to users. This could spur innovation and diversification in the types of GPTs developed.

- **Interoperability between different AI systems**: There will be a greater emphasis on making GPTs interoperable with other AI systems and platforms. This interoperability will enable more complex systems where GPTs can work in concert with other AI technologies, leading to more integrated and powerful applications across sectors.

- **AI for social good**: There will be a growing emphasis on leveraging AI for social good, addressing pressing global challenges such as healthcare, education, climate change, and poverty alleviation. AI models will be used to analyze complex data, identify patterns, and inform decision-making in these critical areas.

These trends suggest a future where GPT technology not only becomes more embedded in our daily digital interactions but also drives significant advancements in how we engage with and leverage technology for personal and professional use. The following table summarizes the future trends and predictions in custom GPT technology:

Trend	Description	Impact
Widespread integration in customer service	GPTs are used to handle complex customer service interactions autonomously	Improves efficiency, personalizes customer interactions, and reduces operational costs
Enhanced virtual assistants	GPTs are used to manage more comprehensive tasks with greater autonomy	Increases productivity and offers more personalized assistance
A greater role in content creation	Expansion of GPTs into creating multimedia content	Enhances marketing and educational tools with creative and diverse content formats
Improvements in training and customization	Streamlined processes for training and customizing GPTs	Lowers barriers to entry and allows non-technical users to leverage AI tools effectively
Expansion in education	Personalized learning experiences tailored by AI	Revolutionizes educational methods, providing more adaptive learning experiences

Table 12.1 – Future trends and predictions in custom GPT technology

As we peer into the future, anticipate groundbreaking trends and predictions reshaping the landscape of AI.

Preparing for a GPT-driven future

As GPT technology continues to advance and become more integrated into various sectors, both individuals and organizations must be well-prepared to leverage its capabilities effectively. Here are some key strategies to consider:

- **Stay informed about AI developments**: Keeping up to date with the latest advancements in GPT and broader AI technologies is essential. Subscribe to AI-focused publications, follow leading AI research institutions, and participate in relevant webinars and conferences. This will help you understand emerging trends, capabilities, and limitations of AI technologies.

- **Invest in AI and technology education**: Enhance your technical skills or your team's skills through structured learning. This can include courses on AI, machine learning, data analytics, and ethical AI use. Many online platforms offer specialized courses that cater to various proficiency levels, from beginners to advanced practitioners. Investing in continuous learning will enable you to effectively develop, manage, and utilize GPTs.

- **Consider the ethical implications of AI deployment**: Engage with the ethical aspects of AI implementation. This involves understanding the potential impacts of GPT technology on privacy, bias, and transparency. Develop or update ethical guidelines and participate in industry discussions about responsible AI use. Ensuring ethical deployment will help mitigate risks and enhance the credibility and acceptance of AI solutions.

- **Develop a strategic AI implementation plan**: Formulate a clear strategy for integrating GPT technology into your business or personal projects. Identify specific areas where AI can add value, set realistic goals, and outline the steps needed to achieve these goals. This plan should also consider the infrastructure and resource requirements to support AI initiatives.

- **Foster a culture of innovation**: Cultivate an environment that encourages experimentation and innovation within your organization. Encourage team members to explore AI capabilities and think creatively about solving existing problems or creating new opportunities with AI. A culture that's supportive of innovation will facilitate more effective adoption and utilization of GPT technologies.

- **Collaborate and build partnerships**: Engage with other companies, tech developers, and academic institutions to share knowledge and resources related to AI. Collaborations can provide access to additional expertise, technology, and data, enhancing your ability to develop and apply GPT effectively.

- **Prepare for future workforce changes**: Anticipate and plan for the changes that GPT and AI will bring to the workforce. This may involve reskilling employees whose jobs may be transformed by AI, as well as hiring new talent with skills in AI management and development. Being proactive in workforce planning will help ensure that your organization remains resilient and competitive.

By embracing these strategies, individuals and organizations can not only prepare for a GPT-driven future but also actively shape how this technology impacts their operations and industries. This proactive approach is crucial for maximizing the benefits of GPT while effectively navigating the associated challenges. The following table summarizes how to prepare for a GPT-driven future:

Strategy	Action Items	Goal
Stay informed about AI developments	Subscribe to AI publications and attend webinars and conferences	To keep stakeholders updated on the latest AI trends and technologies
Invest in AI and technology education	Take courses on AI, machine learning, and more	To enhance skills to effectively develop, manage, and utilize GPTs
Consider the ethical implications of AI deployment	Engage with ethical AI use and develop guidelines	To ensure responsible use of AI while maintaining trust and integrity in practices

Strategy	Action Items	Goal
Develop a strategic AI implementation plan	Identify needs, choose tools, and formulate integration strategies	To streamline AI adoption and maximize its impact across operations
Foster a culture of innovation	Encourage experimentation and support technological adaptation	To promote a proactive approach to utilizing AI, driving innovation and growth

Table 12.2 – Preparing for a GPT-driven future

With that, let's summarize this chapter.

Summary

This chapter emphasized the significant advancements brought about by customizable GPTs and the introduction of the OpenAI GPT store. These developments mark a pivotal evolution in the landscape of conversational AI, highlighting the shift toward more personalized and user-driven AI experiences.

Customizable GPTs allow users from various sectors – whether they're educators, developers, or hobbyists – to tailor conversational models to their specific needs without requiring deep technical knowledge. This democratizes access to advanced AI capabilities, enabling more people to create solutions that are finely tuned to their unique requirements and contexts.

The OpenAI GPT store further enhances this ecosystem by providing a platform where these custom GPTs can be shared and discovered. It fosters a community of innovation, where creators can showcase their GPTs, and users can find and employ specialized models with ease. This store not only amplifies the utility of custom GPTs but also encourages a collaborative approach to AI development, where sharing and feedback drive continuous improvement and creativity.

As we look to the future, the potential for these customizable GPTs and the GPT store to influence various industries is immense. From transforming customer service with highly specialized bots to revolutionizing education with personalized tutoring systems, the possibilities are as varied as they are impactful. This evolution promises to make our interactions with technology more efficient, effective, and aligned with individual needs, paving the way for a future where AI is more integrated and responsive within our daily lives.

Further reading and resources

For those interested in exploring the capabilities and broader implications of custom GPTs and the GPT store, the following resources provide valuable insights and practical guidance:

Books

- *Architects of Intelligence*, by Martin Ford, features interviews with prominent AI researchers and industry leaders discussing the future of AI, including topics around custom AI applications

- *New Laws of Robotics: Defending Human Expertise in the Age of AI*, by Frank Pasquale, explores the intersection of AI and professional ethics, which is crucial for understanding the deployment of GPTs in various sectors

Research articles and white papers

Explore cutting-edge research on GPTs and their applications by accessing academic papers available on platforms such as `arXiv.org`.

Online courses

Platforms such as Coursera and Udemy offer courses specifically tailored to understanding and implementing AI, including courses on creating and managing custom GPTs.

Blogs and websites

- OpenAI Blog (`https://openai.com/news/`) provides the latest updates on GPT developments and practical use cases

- AI-focused news sites such as `https://www.theverge.com/` and `https://www.wired.com/magazine/` cover broader trends in AI technology and their societal impacts, including discussions around ethical AI use

By engaging with these varied resources, you can gain a deeper understanding of how custom GPTs can be tailored for specific needs, the operational dynamics of the GPT store, and the broader ethical and societal considerations of deploying advanced AI tools.

Q&A

Here are several thought-provoking questions with comprehensive answers that explore the ethical considerations, benefits, and challenges associated with the adoption of custom GPTs and their integration into the OpenAI GPT store:

1. What ethical considerations should be prioritized when developing custom GPTs for public use?

    When developing custom GPTs, it's crucial to prioritize data privacy, ensuring that personal information that's used to train or interact with GPTs is handled securely and transparently. Developers should also address potential biases in GPT outputs, actively working to identify and mitigate any discriminatory patterns in the AI's responses. Clear guidelines and regular audits should be established to maintain ethical standards and compliance with applicable regulations.

2. How can custom GPTs transform customer service and educational sectors?

    Custom GPTs can revolutionize customer service by providing tailored responses based on the specific needs and contexts of businesses, leading to more efficient and personalized customer interactions. In education, custom GPTs can support personalized learning experiences, offering students interactive tutoring and resources that adapt to individual learning styles and paces, thereby enhancing engagement and educational outcomes.

3. In what ways might the introduction of the GPT store impact the broader AI technology landscape?

    The GPT store is likely to democratize access to advanced AI capabilities, enabling a broader range of users to find and deploy AI solutions that meet their specific needs. This accessibility can stimulate innovation across sectors by encouraging more individuals and companies to experiment with and implement AI solutions, potentially leading to rapid advancements in AI technologies and applications.

4. How can inclusivity and accessibility be ensured in the development and deployment of custom GPTs in the GPT store?

    Ensuring inclusivity involves designing GPTs that are accessible to users with diverse abilities and from various backgrounds. This includes providing multilingual support, ensuring user interfaces are intuitive and accessible to people with disabilities, and considering cultural sensitivities in GPT responses. Developers should engage with diverse focus groups during the testing phase to gather feedback and make necessary adjustments before wide release.

13

Overcoming Resistance and Embracing Change

"Change is the law of life. And those who look only to the past or present are certain to miss the future."

- John F. Kennedy

As organizations increasingly look to **artificial intelligence** (**AI**) to enhance their governance structures, they face a complex landscape of inherent challenges and resistance. The adoption of AI within the intricate frameworks of corporate governance ushers in a transformative era that, while ripe with potential, is fraught with hurdles. These challenges range from technological and logistical obstacles to deeply rooted organizational and cultural barriers. The resistance encountered often stems from a natural human apprehension toward change, particularly one as profound and pervasive as that introduced by AI technologies.

This resistance is not without consequence; it can hinder innovation, delay the realization of AI's full potential within governance, and ultimately compromise an organization's ability to stay competitive in an ever-evolving business environment. Integrating AI into governance processes promises enhanced decision-making, improved risk management, and greater efficiency. However, realizing these benefits requires navigating the multifaceted resistance that comes with any significant organizational change.

Embracing change is not merely a recommendation; it is a critical imperative for organizations aiming to thrive in the digital age. The ability to adapt, welcome new technologies such as AI with open arms, and overcome the inertia that holds back transformation will define the future-ready organization. Such adaptability is essential not just for staying abreast of technological advancements but also for leveraging these innovations to enhance strategic decision-making, operational efficiency, and competitive edge.

This chapter delves into the myriad challenges organizations face as they integrate AI into their governance structures. It explores the sources of resistance, from the fear of the unknown to concerns about data privacy and job displacement, and offers strategic insights into overcoming these barriers. By embracing change, organizations can unlock the transformative potential of AI, ensuring their governance practices are efficient and practical but also resilient and forward-looking, poised to meet the demands of the future head-on.

Understanding resistance to AI integration

The journey toward integrating AI into corporate governance is often met with resistance from various quarters within an organization. This resistance can stem from a myriad of sources, each with its complexities and implications. Understanding these sources is the first step in devising effective strategies to mitigate resistance and foster a conducive environment for AI adoption.

Sources of resistance

Let's understand the challenges and explore the sources of resistance:

- **Fear of job displacement**: One of the most prevalent concerns among employees is the fear that AI will automate tasks traditionally performed by humans, leading to job losses or significant changes in job roles. This fear can create a pervasive insecurity, making the workforce resistant to AI initiatives.

- **Distrust in AI decisions**: Skepticism about the reliability and fairness of AI system decisions is often present. This distrust is fueled by concerns over AI's "black-box" nature, where the decision-making process is not transparent, making it difficult for users to understand how decisions are derived.

- **Data privacy concerns**: AI relies on vast datasets, so concerns about how personal and sensitive information is used and protected are paramount. The potential for data breaches or misuse can lead to resistance from stakeholders who prioritize data privacy and security.

In conclusion, the sources of resistance to AI integration are multifaceted, ranging from concerns about job displacement to ethical considerations and fear of the unknown. By comprehensively examining these factors, we gain insight into the complex landscape surrounding AI adoption. As we move forward, let's take a look at case studies that will help address these sources of resistance.

Case studies – overcoming resistance

Let's delve into compelling case studies that illuminate strategies, challenges, and triumphs in conquering resistance:

- Manufacturing giant embraces AI with employee-centric approach

  - **Background**: A global manufacturing company faced significant resistance from its workforce, who feared job displacement due to AI-driven automation.

  - **Resolution strategy**: The company launched an extensive communication campaign to educate employees about AI's role not as a replacement but as a tool to augment their work. They implemented retraining programs to upskill employees for higher-value tasks facilitated by AI, thereby mitigating fears and gaining workforce buy-in.

- Financial services firm builds trust in AI decision-making

  - **Background**: A leading financial institution encountered skepticism from its decision-makers and clients regarding the reliability of its AI-driven investment algorithms.

  - **Resolution strategy**: The firm initiated a transparency drive, providing detailed explanations of the AI algorithms' workings, the data used, and the rationale behind decisions. They also introduced a human oversight mechanism for AI decisions, ensuring a balance between human expertise and AI efficiency, which significantly increased trust among stakeholders.

- Healthcare organization addresses data privacy concerns

  - **Background**: A healthcare organization looking to implement AI for patient data analysis faced resistance due to concerns over patient confidentiality and data security.

  - **Resolution strategy**: The organization prioritized the establishment of stringent data governance frameworks, adhering to global data protection regulations. They conducted open forums with patients and staff to discuss data use policies, encryption methods, and consent protocols, alleviating privacy concerns and fostering a culture of transparency and trust.

Understanding the root causes of resistance to AI integration in corporate governance is crucial for developing effective countermeasures. By addressing fears of job displacement, distrust in AI decisions, and data privacy concerns head-on, organizations can pave the way for a smoother transition to AI-enhanced governance. The highlighted case studies demonstrate that with thoughtful strategies focused on communication, education, transparency, and ethical considerations, it's possible to overcome resistance and harness the full potential of AI in corporate governance.

Strategic approaches to overcoming resistance

Successfully integrating AI into corporate governance necessitates technological readiness and a strategic approach to change management and leadership. Organizations can employ several frameworks and strategies to navigate the complexities of AI adoption, ensuring a smooth transition and widespread acceptance.

We will delve into the frameworks and strategies for change management:

- **Awareness, Desire, Knowledge, Ability, and Reinforcement (ADKAR) model**: A widely recognized change management model, ADKAR can be effectively applied to AI integration. It starts with creating *awareness* of the need for AI, fostering a *desire* among stakeholders to support and participate in the change, providing the *knowledge* and skills required to operate in an AI-enhanced environment, ensuring stakeholders can implement the change, and using *reinforcement* to sustain the change.

- **Kotter's 8-step change model**: This model offers a comprehensive approach, starting with establishing a sense of urgency around adopting AI. It involves forming a powerful coalition to guide the initiative, creating a vision for change, communicating the vision, empowering others to act on the vision, creating quick wins, consolidating improvements, and anchoring new approaches in the culture.

In overcoming resistance to AI integration, these case studies and strategic approaches to overcoming resistance exemplify the power of strategic planning, effective communication, and a commitment to collaboration, ultimately paving the way for successful adoption and transformative outcomes.

Cultivating an AI-embracing culture through leadership

As organizations increasingly embrace the transformative potential of AI, cultivating a culture that not only welcomes but actively embraces AI requires visionary leadership and strategic guidance:

- **Visionary leadership**: Leaders play a crucial role in setting the direction and tone for AI integration. By articulating a clear and compelling vision of how AI can enhance governance and contribute to organizational goals, leaders can inspire confidence and enthusiasm among stakeholders.

- **Inclusive decision-making**: Involving employees and other stakeholders in the decision-making process regarding AI adoption helps demystify the technology and addresses concerns directly. This inclusive approach fosters a sense of ownership and commitment to the change.

- **Transparent communication**: Leaders must ensure open and continuous communication about the AI integration process, its expected outcomes, and its impact on various stakeholders. Transparency helps mitigate fears and build trust.

- **Investment in education and training**: Providing comprehensive training and upskilling opportunities is vital to prepare the workforce for the transition. Leadership should champion these initiatives, emphasizing lifelong learning and adaptability.

- **Empathy and support**: It is essential to recognize AI adoption's emotional and professional impacts on employees. Leaders should demonstrate empathy and provide robust support systems, including counseling and mentorship programs, to help individuals navigate the change.

- **Reinforcement and recognition**: Encouraging and recognizing efforts to embrace AI, adapt to new roles, or innovate processes reinforces positive behavior. Celebrating successes, even small ones, boosts morale and solidifies the change.

The strategic integration of AI into corporate governance is as much about managing the human aspects of change as it is about technological implementation. Organizations can overcome resistance by employing effective change management frameworks, cultivating leadership that champions transparency, inclusivity, and continuous learning, and creating an environment where AI is accepted and embraced. This cultural shift is the bedrock upon which the successful adoption of AI in governance is built, ensuring that organizations adapt to the digital age and thrive in it.

Communication and transparency

In the journey toward integrating AI into corporate governance, the importance of communication and transparency cannot be overstated. Clear, transparent communication serves as a critical bridge between technological innovation and stakeholder acceptance, playing a pivotal role in mitigating resistance and fostering an environment of trust and understanding.

The role of transparent communication

Transparent communication about AI initiatives helps demystify the technology for all stakeholders, including employees, management, shareholders, and customers. It addresses fears and misconceptions that often surround AI, such as job displacement, loss of control, and ethical concerns. By openly discussing the objectives, capabilities, limitations, and ethical considerations of AI systems, organizations can build a foundation of trust and collaboration, essential for successful AI integration.

In conclusion, fostering a culture of communication and transparency not only enhances organizational trust and collaboration but also paves the way for successful AI integration, ensuring a smoother transition and more impactful outcomes.

Strategies for effective stakeholder engagement

Effective stakeholder engagement stands as a requirement for success, demanding a comprehensive arsenal of strategies to navigate diverse interests and ensure alignment toward shared goals:

- **Tailored communication plans**: Develop communication plans that are tailored to the needs and concerns of different stakeholder groups. Understand the unique perspectives of each group and address them specifically, whether it's job security for employees, **return on investment (ROI)** for shareholders, or privacy and ethical use for customers.

- **Educational initiatives**: Launch educational initiatives that provide stakeholders with a basic understanding of AI and its applications within the organization. Workshops, seminars, and accessible online resources can help demystify AI and highlight its benefits and challenges.

- **Open dialogues**: Foster an environment where stakeholders feel comfortable expressing their concerns and questions about AI. Regular town hall meetings, Q&A sessions, and feedback channels can facilitate open dialogue and contribute to a more inclusive transition process.

- **Transparency in AI decision-making**: Strive for transparency in how AI systems make decisions, significantly when those decisions impact individuals directly. Use **explainable AI (XAI)** techniques to make AI decision processes more understandable to non-expert stakeholders.

- **Success stories and use cases**: Share real-life examples of successful AI integration within the organization and other reputable entities. Highlighting tangible benefits and addressing the challenges can reassure and inspire confidence in the technology.

- **Leadership advocacy**: Leadership should actively advocate for the AI initiative, sharing their vision, the expected outcomes, and how AI aligns with the organization's broader goals. A leader's transparent commitment can be a powerful motivator for stakeholder buy-in.

Transparent communication and effective stakeholder engagement are cornerstone strategies for overcoming resistance to AI. Organizations can pave the way for a smoother transition to AI-enhanced governance by prioritizing clarity, education, and open dialogue. This approach addresses fears and uncertainties associated with AI and highlights the technology's potential to revolutionize corporate governance, fostering an environment of trust and forward-thinking adaptability.

Building trust in AI systems

Establishing trust in AI systems is paramount for their successful integration into corporate governance. Trust is the bedrock upon which stakeholders rely when embracing new technologies, especially AI, with its profound implications for decision-making and operational processes. Building this trust involves a multifaceted approach, emphasizing not only the reliability and performance of AI systems but also their ethical development and deployment.

Fostering trust in AI's decision-making

As AI continues to permeate various facets of our lives, fostering trust in its decision-making processes emerges as a paramount concern, necessitating deliberate efforts to demystify algorithms and instill confidence in their reliability and ethical integrity:

- **Explainability and transparency**: One of the key methods to foster trust is through the explainability of AI systems. Stakeholders are more likely to trust AI decisions if they can understand how those decisions are made. Implementing XAI practices, where the processes and factors leading to a decision are made clear, can significantly enhance stakeholder trust.

- **Reliability and accuracy**: Demonstrating the reliability and accuracy of AI systems through rigorous testing, validation, and continuous monitoring is crucial. Sharing performance metrics, success stories, and case studies where AI has added tangible value can reinforce trust in the system's capabilities.

- **Human oversight**: Incorporating human oversight into AI decision-making processes reassures stakeholders that there is a human element evaluating and validating AI's recommendations. This hybrid approach, often referred to as *augmented intelligence*, ensures that AI aids rather than replaces human judgment.

- **Stakeholder involvement**: Engaging stakeholders in the development and implementation phases of AI projects allows for a sense of ownership and control over the technology. Involvement can range from providing feedback on AI applications to participating in pilot projects.

In essence, by prioritizing transparency, accountability, and ethical considerations, fostering trust in AI's decision-making not only safeguards against potential pitfalls but also lays a robust foundation for the responsible and beneficial integration of AI into our society. Let's explore ethical AI development and deployment and its beneficial integration into society.

Ethical AI development and deployment

The ethical development and deployment of AI systems have emerged as critical imperatives, necessitating a thoughtful and proactive approach to navigate complex moral, societal, and technical considerations:

- **Ethical frameworks**: Developing and adhering to ethical frameworks for AI use within the organization is fundamental. These frameworks should address concerns such as fairness, bias, privacy, and accountability, ensuring that AI systems operate within agreed ethical boundaries.

- **Privacy and security**: Safeguarding the privacy and security of data used by AI systems is essential for building trust. Implementing robust data protection measures and transparency about data usage policies can alleviate concerns about misuse or breaches.

- **Bias mitigation**: Actively working to identify and mitigate biases in AI algorithms is critical for fostering trust. This involves diverse and inclusive training datasets, regular bias audits, and corrective measures to ensure fair and unbiased AI outcomes.

- **Regulatory compliance**: It is crucial to ensure that AI systems comply with relevant laws and regulations, especially those related to data protection and ethical standards. Compliance builds trust and protects the organization from legal and reputational risks.

Building trust in AI systems among employees, shareholders, and other key stakeholders is a complex but achievable goal. Organizations can lay a solid foundation of trust by focusing on explainability, reliability, ethical development, and stakeholder involvement. This trust is essential for the successful adoption and integration of AI in corporate governance, enabling organizations to leverage the full potential of AI while maintaining integrity and stakeholder confidence.

Upskilling and reskilling for an AI-enabled workforce

The integration of AI into corporate governance not only transforms business processes and decision-making frameworks but also significantly impacts workforce dynamics. As AI systems take on both routine and complex tasks, the nature of work evolves, necessitating a shift in the skill sets required from employees. This shift underscores the necessity of workforce development through upskilling and reskilling initiatives, ensuring that employees can effectively synergize with AI technologies and contribute to an AI-enhanced governance environment.

The imperative for workforce development

The adoption of AI in governance brings about a dual need within the workforce: to understand and interact with AI systems (upskilling) and to transition into new roles created by the AI-driven corporate landscape (reskilling). Upskilling equips employees with the knowledge and skills to leverage AI tools in their current roles, enhancing productivity and decision-making. Reskilling, on the other hand, prepares employees for entirely new roles that emerge as AI technologies reshape the industry, ensuring that the workforce remains adaptable and relevant.

Strategies for effective upskilling and reskilling

As industries evolve and technologies advance, the imperative for upskilling and reskilling becomes increasingly evident, prompting organizations to adopt strategic approaches to empower their workforce with the knowledge and capabilities necessary to thrive in the digital age:

- **Assessment of skill gaps**: The first step in a successful upskilling and reskilling strategy is to assess existing skill gaps within the organization. This involves understanding the capabilities of the AI technologies being adopted and identifying skills employees will need to work effectively alongside these systems.

- **Tailored learning pathways**: Create personalized learning pathways for employees, considering their current skill levels, learning preferences, and future role requirements. This approach ensures that training is relevant and impactful, leading to higher engagement and better outcomes.

- **Leveraging multiple learning platforms**: Utilize a mix of learning platforms and methodologies to cater to diverse learning styles. This can include online courses, workshops, webinars, simulation exercises, and hands-on projects. Incorporating AI-driven learning platforms can also provide adaptive learning experiences tailored to individual progress and needs.

- **Partnerships with educational institutions**: Collaborate with universities, technical schools, and online education platforms to design courses that specifically address skills needed for an AI-enabled workforce. These partnerships can provide employees with access to cutting-edge knowledge and certifications that are directly applicable to their evolving roles.

- **Learning culture and continuous development**: Foster a culture that values continuous learning and professional development. Encourage experimentation, allow for failure as a learning tool, and recognize achievements in skill development. A supportive learning environment motivates employees to embrace upskilling and reskilling opportunities.

- **Mentorship and peer learning**: Establish mentorship programs where more experienced employees or external experts can guide others through their learning journey. Peer learning groups can also facilitate knowledge sharing and collaborative problem-solving, enhancing the learning experience.

- **Role redesign and career pathing**: In conjunction with reskilling efforts, redesign roles and career paths to align with the new AI-enhanced corporate landscape. Clear career progression opportunities can motivate employees to engage in reskilling programs and adapt to new roles.

Preparing the workforce for an AI-enabled future is critical to successful AI integration in corporate governance. By implementing comprehensive upskilling and reskilling strategies, organizations can ensure that their employees are equipped to work alongside AI technologies and poised to thrive in the evolving digital workplace. This commitment to workforce development is essential for harnessing the full potential of AI in governance, driving innovation, and maintaining a competitive edge in the rapidly changing business environment.

Ethical considerations in AI adoption

The integration of AI into corporate governance is not just a technological or operational endeavor; it's a venture that is deeply entwined with ethical considerations. As AI systems assume roles in decision-making, risk management, and compliance, the ethical implications of their deployment come to the forefront. Addressing these ethical considerations is paramount, not only to align with societal values and regulatory expectations but also to alleviate resistance from stakeholders who may be wary of AI's impact on fairness, privacy, and accountability.

Unpacking the ethical implications

The ethical implications of AI integration in governance span various dimensions, including the following:

- **Bias and fairness**: AI systems, which learn from historical data, can inadvertently perpetuate and amplify biases present in that data, leading to unfair outcomes. Ensuring fairness involves rigorous testing for bias and implementing corrective measures to prevent discriminatory decisions.

- **Transparency and explainability**: The "black-box" nature of some AI systems, where the decision-making process is opaque, poses significant ethical challenges. Stakeholders have a right to understand how decisions affecting them are made, necessitating efforts to enhance the transparency and explainability of AI systems.

- **Privacy and data protection**: AI's reliance on vast datasets raises concerns about privacy and data security. Ethical AI usage must respect individuals' privacy rights and comply with data protection laws, ensuring that data is used responsibly and securely.

- **Accountability and responsibility**: Determining accountability for decisions made by AI systems is a complex ethical issue. Establishing clear guidelines on accountability and ensuring that human oversight is integrated into AI decision-making processes are critical steps.

Alleviating resistance through ethical AI practices

Addressing these ethical concerns proactively can significantly alleviate resistance to AI integration. When stakeholders are assured that AI systems are deployed ethically, with considerations for fairness, transparency, privacy, and accountability, their trust in the technology is bolstered. This trust is crucial for overcoming skepticism and building a collaborative approach to AI adoption.

Developing and adhering to ethical guidelines

The foundation of ethical AI integration lies in developing and adhering to robust ethical guidelines that govern AI usage within the organization. These guidelines should have the following attributes:

- Be developed in consultation with diverse stakeholders, including ethicists, technologists, legal experts, and representatives of affected groups, to ensure a comprehensive perspective on ethical considerations.

- Clearly articulate the organization's commitment to ethical principles in AI usage, including fairness, transparency, privacy protection, and accountability.

- Outline specific practices for developing, deploying, and monitoring AI systems to ensure they align with ethical standards. This includes bias audits, transparency mechanisms, data protection measures, and processes for human oversight and accountability.

- Be integrated into the organization's broader governance and compliance frameworks, ensuring that ethical AI usage is not a standalone initiative but a core aspect of corporate governance.

- Include mechanisms for continuous review and adaptation, recognizing that the ethical landscape of AI is evolving alongside technological advancements and societal expectations.

Ethical considerations in AI adoption are integral to successfully integrating the technology into corporate governance. By proactively addressing ethical implications and developing comprehensive guidelines for ethical AI usage, organizations can mitigate resistance and foster an environment of trust and collaboration. Ethical AI practices align with societal values and regulatory requirements and enhance the legitimacy and effectiveness of AI systems in governance, paving the way for their responsible and impactful deployment.

Case studies – successful AI adoption and change management

The journey to successfully integrate AI into corporate governance is filled with challenges and opportunities for transformation and innovation. The following case studies from various sectors illustrate how organizations have triumphantly navigated resistance to AI adoption and managed the change effectively, offering valuable insights and takeaways.

Case study 1 – retail giant revolutionizes supply chain with AI

- **Background**: A leading global retail chain faced significant operational inefficiencies in its supply chain, leading to stock discrepancies and customer dissatisfaction. Initial proposals to integrate AI for inventory management and demand forecasting met with resistance from employees, who feared job displacement and mistrusted the technology's accuracy.

- **Strategy**: The company launched an extensive internal campaign to educate employees about AI's role in augmenting their work, not replacing it. It highlighted how AI could eliminate mundane tasks, allowing employees to focus on more strategic aspects of their roles. The company also established a pilot project in a select number of stores, enabling employees to see firsthand the benefits of AI in streamlining operations.

- **Outcomes**: The pilot project demonstrated a significant reduction in stock discrepancies and improved customer satisfaction due to better product availability. Employee feedback sessions post-pilot revealed a shift in perception, with increased openness to AI adoption. The successful pilot led to a company-wide rollout, with continued emphasis on employee training and involvement in the AI integration process.

- **Insights**: Transparent communication and hands-on experience with AI can effectively address resistance, showcasing the technology's practical benefits and directly involving employees in the change process.

Case study 2 – healthcare provider enhances patient care with AI

- **Background**: A healthcare provider aimed to integrate AI into its patient care systems to improve diagnostics and treatment plans. However, healthcare professionals were skeptical about relying on AI for critical healthcare decisions, concerned about ethical implications and the potential for AI to overlook the nuances of patient care.

- **Strategy**: The organization prioritized ethical AI development, involving medical professionals in the design and implementation phases to ensure the AI systems were aligned with healthcare standards and values. It also initiated a series of workshops focusing on the ethical use of AI in healthcare, addressing concerns around bias, transparency, and accountability.

- **Outcomes**: The collaborative approach to AI development resulted in systems that enhanced, rather than replaced, the expertise of healthcare professionals. AI-assisted diagnostics and treatment planning led to more accurate and timely care, garnering support from the initially skeptical healthcare staff. The organization's commitment to ethical AI fostered trust and acceptance among professionals and patients.

- **Insights**: Involving end users in AI development and emphasizing ethical considerations can build trust in AI systems, particularly in fields where human expertise and ethical considerations are paramount.

Case study 3 – financial institution improves risk management with AI

- **Background**: A multinational financial institution sought to integrate AI into its risk management framework to predict market fluctuations better and identify potential financial risks. The initiative faced resistance from analysts and risk managers, who were concerned about the reliability of AI predictions and the potential loss of insight from human analysis.

- **Strategy**: The institution adopted a phased approach to AI integration, starting with AI as a support tool to enhance, rather than replace, human analysis. It provided extensive training for analysts on interpreting AI-generated risk assessments and incorporated AI insights into collaborative decision-making processes.

- **Outcomes**: The combination of AI and human expertise led to more robust risk assessments, with the AI system uncovering risk factors that had previously been overlooked. This approach improved the institution's risk management capabilities and alleviated employees' fears of being replaced by AI, demonstrating the value of augmented intelligence.

- **Insights**: A phased approach to AI adoption that complements human expertise with AI insights can alleviate resistance, demonstrating that AI is a tool for enhancement rather than replacement.

These case studies across retail, healthcare, and finance sectors illustrate critical strategies for overcoming resistance to AI adoption: transparent communication, ethical development, hands-on experience, and a collaborative approach that values both AI capabilities and human expertise. By learning from these real-world examples, organizations can navigate the complexities of AI integration, leveraging the technology to drive innovation and efficiency in corporate governance.

Overcoming challenges

The integration of AI into corporate governance is a journey marked by continuous evolution and adaptation. As organizations navigate this path, they encounter a spectrum of persistent challenges, from technological hurdles and cultural barriers to ethical dilemmas and regulatory complexities. Successfully addressing these challenges requires a proactive, strategic approach focused on resilience, flexibility, and stakeholder engagement.

Persistent challenges in AI integration and change management

In the ever-evolving landscape of AI integration, organizations encounter persistent challenges that demand astute change management strategies to navigate effectively. Let's explore the nuanced complexities and innovative approaches to addressing these hurdles:

- **Technological complexity**: The complexity of AI systems and the need for robust data infrastructure can pose significant challenges, particularly for organizations in the early stages of digital transformation.

- **Cultural resistance**: Organizational culture deeply ingrained in traditional ways of working can resist the shift toward data-driven, AI-enhanced decision-making.

- **Ethical and regulatory concerns**: Navigating the ethical implications of AI use and ensuring compliance with an evolving regulatory landscape remains a continuous challenge.

- **Skill gaps and workforce adaptation**: As AI technologies advance, the need for upskilling and reskilling the workforce to leverage these tools effectively becomes more pronounced.

Strategies for continuous adaptation

Let's delve into effective strategies that facilitate seamless adaptation in the face of change:

- **Embracing agile methodologies**: Adopting agile principles in AI projects allows for flexibility, rapid iteration, and adaptation to changing requirements. This approach fosters a culture of innovation and continuous improvement, essential for navigating the complexities of AI integration.

- **Fostering a culture of learning**: Cultivating a learning-oriented organizational culture is crucial for overcoming resistance and adapting to new technologies. Encouraging curiosity, experimentation, and learning from failures can demystify AI and reduce apprehensions.

- **Investing in ethical AI governance**: Establishing a governance framework that emphasizes ethical AI use can address ethical and regulatory challenges. This involves regular ethical audits, adherence to privacy and data protection standards, and transparent AI decision-making processes.

- **Continuous stakeholder engagement**: Regularly engaging with stakeholders, including employees, customers, and regulatory bodies, helps identify emerging concerns and resistance points. Open dialogue and collaboration can foster a sense of ownership and alignment with AI initiatives.

- **Leveraging cross-industry partnerships**: Collaborating with other organizations, industry consortia, and academic institutions can provide valuable insights into best practices for AI integration and change management. These partnerships can also offer resources for workforce development and ethical AI practices.

- **Innovative workforce development programs**: Implementing forward-thinking workforce development programs that focus on the future of work can help bridge skill gaps. This includes partnerships with educational institutions, investment in digital literacy programs, and creating career pathways in AI and data science.

Overcoming emerging resistance forms

As AI technologies and their applications evolve, new forms of resistance may emerge, driven by concerns about advanced automation, AI autonomy, and the implications for employment and societal norms. Addressing these requires the following:

- **Proactive communication**: Anticipating potential concerns and addressing them proactively through transparent communication and education.

- **Inclusive decision-making**: Involving a broad range of stakeholders in decision-making processes related to AI deployment ensures diverse perspectives are considered, mitigating the risk of overlooking potential resistance factors.

- **Ethical leadership**: Leadership committed to ethical standards in AI use can set a tone that balances innovation with responsibility, reassuring stakeholders of the organization's commitment to ethical practices.

Overcoming challenges associated with AI integration and change management is an ongoing process that demands resilience, strategic foresight, and a commitment to ethical principles. Organizations can navigate the complexities of AI adoption by adopting flexible methodologies, fostering a culture of continuous learning, and engaging stakeholders in open dialogue. Continuous adaptation and a proactive approach to emerging challenges and resistance forms are essential for harnessing the transformative potential of AI in corporate governance.

Future outlook

As we gaze at the horizon of corporate governance, the interplay between AI and organizational structures is poised to deepen, presenting both challenges and unparalleled opportunities for innovation. The future outlook for AI in corporate governance is not merely a linear extension of current trends but a dynamic landscape shaped by rapid technological advancements, evolving regulatory frameworks, and shifting societal expectations. Organizations that navigate this landscape successfully will do so by embracing change, fostering a culture of continuous innovation, and maintaining a steadfast commitment to ethical principles.

Evolving with AI in corporate governance

Let's explore how organizations are navigating this paradigm shift and leveraging AI to optimize their governance frameworks:

- **Adaptive governance models**: Organizations will increasingly adopt more adaptive and responsive governance models powered by AI's predictive analytics and real-time data processing capabilities. This will enable more agile decision-making processes that are capable of anticipating and responding to market changes and operational challenges with unprecedented speed and accuracy.

- **Augmented decision-making**: The role of AI in enhancing human decision-making will become more pronounced, with AI systems providing deeper insights and foresight into complex governance issues. This augmented approach will leverage the best human intuition and ethical judgment and AI's computational power to make more informed, balanced, and forward-looking decisions.

- **Integrated ethical AI frameworks**: As AI becomes more embedded in governance processes, developing and integrating ethical AI frameworks will be critical. These frameworks will guide the deployment of AI technologies, ensuring they uphold principles of fairness, transparency, accountability, and respect for privacy, thereby building trust among stakeholders and society at large.

- **Regulatory co-evolution**: The regulatory landscape for AI in corporate governance will continue to evolve, with a likely increase in global cooperation to establish common standards and practices. Organizations will need to stay agile, adapting to new regulations while actively engaging with policymakers to shape a conducive regulatory environment for ethical AI use.

Embracing change and innovation

Let's explore how embracing change can catalyze innovation and drive transformative growth:

- **Cultivating a culture of innovation**: Organizations will need to cultivate a culture that not only embraces technological innovation but also encourages creative thinking and problem-solving across all levels. This involves empowering employees to experiment and take risks, fostering an environment where learning from failures is valued as a step toward innovation.

- **Continuous learning and workforce development**: The need for continuous learning and workforce development will become even more critical as AI technologies and applications evolve. Organizations will invest in lifelong learning initiatives, upskilling and reskilling programs, and collaborative learning ecosystems to prepare their workforce for the AI-augmented future.

- **Stakeholder engagement and collaboration**: Engaging with a broad spectrum of stakeholders, including employees, customers, regulators, and society, will be essential in shaping the future of AI in corporate governance. Collaborative approaches to AI development and deployment can ensure that diverse perspectives are considered, aligning technological advancements with societal values and needs.

The future of AI in corporate governance is marked by a continuous journey toward embracing change and innovation. This journey demands an organization's proactive stance, a commitment to ethical AI use, and an inclusive approach to stakeholder engagement. By fostering a culture of innovation, adaptability, and ethical responsibility, organizations can leverage AI as a tool for operational efficiency and as a catalyst for transformative change, driving enduring success in the ever-evolving corporate governance landscape.

Summary

This chapter navigated the intricate landscape of AI integration within corporate governance, uncovering the multifaceted challenges and opportunities that lie within. The discussions have highlighted the paramount importance of ethical considerations, strategic approaches to overcoming resistance, and the indispensable role of communication and transparency. Furthermore, we explored the necessity of upskilling and reskilling to harmonize the workforce with AI technologies and delved into insightful case studies that illuminate the path to successful AI adoption.

Central to our exploration is the understanding that AI's transformative potential in corporate governance is not without its hurdles. Resistance to AI, stemming from fears of job displacement, ethical concerns, and the opacity of AI decision-making, necessitates a thoughtful and inclusive approach. Strategies to mitigate these challenges have been emphasized, including fostering a culture of empathy, prioritizing bias control, ensuring transparency, and maintaining accountability.

The role of leadership in championing AI integration and change management cannot be overstated. Boards and executive teams are the torchbearers in setting a vision for AI's role in enhancing governance and operational efficiency. Their proactive stance on ethical AI governance, coupled with a commitment to continuous learning and adaptability, sets a precedent for organizational engagement with AI initiatives.

As we look to the future, the continuous journey of AI integration calls for an organizational ethos that values innovation, agility, and ethical integrity. The insights and strategies discussed herein serve as a beacon for organizations navigating the AI landscape, encouraging them to embrace change, tackle resistance proactively, and leverage AI's potential to foster a more resilient, efficient, and forward-looking governance structure.

In embracing AI, organizations are not merely adopting new technologies but are also endorsing a vision for a future where governance is augmented by intelligence, insight, and inclusivity. This chapter urges organizations to stride confidently into this future, armed with the knowledge, strategies, and ethical considerations essential for harnessing the transformative power of AI in corporate governance.

Further reading

For those looking to deepen their understanding of AI in corporate governance and how to navigate the challenges and changes it brings, the following resources offer valuable insights and practical guidance:

- *The Cambridge Handbook of Responsible Artificial Intelligence* delves into the nuances of AI usage within corporate governance frameworks, mainly focusing on supervisory roles and responsibilities. It highlights how AI can aid in auditing accounting and compliance checks, underscoring the importance of monitoring AI applications to ensure they align with corporate governance objectives. This resource is instrumental for understanding the intersection of AI functionalities with corporate governance mandates.

- **IBM's overview of AI governance**: IBM offers a comprehensive look at AI governance, emphasizing the need for responsible governance principles such as empathy, bias control, transparency, and accountability. They also highlight the importance of adapting to regulatory standards for AI safety, security, and privacy. This resource is invaluable for understanding the foundational aspects of AI governance within organizations. Exploring these resources can comprehensively understand the best practices, challenges, and strategies for effectively integrating AI into corporate governance. They provide real-world examples and theoretical frameworks to guide organizations through the complexities of AI adoption and change management.

Q&A

The integration of AI into corporate governance is a multi-faceted journey that raises several pivotal questions. Reflecting on these can provide deeper insights into the process of overcoming resistance and embracing change, enriching our understanding and encouraging critical thinking:

1. How can organizations balance the innovative potential of AI with the need for ethical governance?

   The dual imperative of leveraging AI for innovation while ensuring ethical governance poses a significant challenge. This balance requires a framework that prioritizes transparency, accountability, and fairness within AI systems. As discussed in various forums, including the *Harvard Law School Forum on Corporate Governance* and IBM's insights on AI governance, establishing clear ethical guidelines and engaging in continuous dialogue with stakeholders can help align AI initiatives with core governance principles. Encouragingly, real-world examples, such as AstraZeneca's approach to AI governance, demonstrate that it is possible to navigate this balance through thoughtful policy design and stakeholder engagement.

2. What strategies can be effective in mitigating resistance to AI within organizations?

   Resistance to AI often stems from fears of job displacement, loss of control, and ethical concerns. Strategies to mitigate this resistance include transparent communication about AI's role and benefits, inclusive decision-making processes, and comprehensive education and training programs. These approaches, underscored by IBM's principles of responsible AI governance, emphasize empathy, bias control, and the need for AI systems to be understandable and accountable. By involving employees in the AI integration process and providing clear, accessible information about how AI systems operate, organizations can build trust and reduce resistance.

3. How can continuous adaptation be fostered within organizations to keep pace with evolving AI technologies?

   Fostering an environment of continuous adaptation requires a commitment to lifelong learning and an organizational culture that values agility and innovation. As AI technologies evolve, organizations must remain flexible, reassessing and updating their governance frameworks, ethical guidelines, and workforce skills. The iterative approach to AI governance, as seen in

AstraZeneca's case, where policies and practices are continuously refined in response to emerging challenges and insights, exemplifies how organizations can remain adaptive. Leveraging agile methodologies and maintaining an open, learning-oriented culture is key to ensuring that governance practices keep pace with technological advancements.

4. In what ways can boards and executive teams lead the charge in AI integration and change management?

Boards and executive teams play a crucial role in setting the tone for AI integration and change management. Their leadership is pivotal in establishing a vision for how AI can enhance governance and operational efficiency. As highlighted in discussions around **generative AI (GenAI)** and corporate boards, executive teams should be proactive in acquiring knowledge about AI, setting strategic priorities for its use, and overseeing the development of robust governance frameworks. By demonstrating a commitment to ethical AI use and fostering a culture of innovation and adaptability, boards and executive teams can lead by example, encouraging organization-wide engagement with AI initiatives.

Reflecting on these queries and insights underscores the complexity of integrating AI into corporate governance. It is clear that a multi-pronged approach, encompassing ethical frameworks, stakeholder engagement, continuous learning, and strong leadership, is essential for navigating challenges and embracing opportunities presented by AI. As organizations venture further into this territory, fostering a culture that values ethical considerations, transparency, and adaptability will be crucial for harnessing the transformative potential of AI in governance.

14
Lifelong Learning in the Age of AI

"Education is not the filling of a pail, but the lighting of a fire."

- W.B. Yeats

Advancements in **artificial intelligence** (**AI**) have significantly transformed the educational landscape. This revolution has made lifelong learning an essential personal and professional development pillar. In today's era of rapid technological progress, continuously learning and adapting is paramount.

AI is not just a tool for automating tasks but also a catalyst for personalized and inclusive learning experiences. It offers opportunities for students and educators to enhance teaching practices and learning outcomes. For instance, AI can provide personalized support to teachers at scale, helping them refine their teaching methods with real-time feedback and suggestions based on expert pedagogy. This kind of support can be particularly beneficial in simulating student interactions for new teachers, allowing them to practice and improve their teaching strategies in a controlled environment.

The potential of AI to change the focus of what is important for learners is significant. By alleviating the need for complete proficiency in certain skills, AI allows learners to engage more deeply with the material, fostering a more creative and analytical approach to learning. This shift could lead to a greater emphasis on soft skills such as critical thinking and problem-solving, which are increasingly valuable in the modern workforce.

The role of AI in education also extends to creating a judgment-free environment for learning, where students can engage and take risks without fear. This is particularly important for building self-confidence in learners who may be hesitant to participate in traditional classroom settings. AI-driven interfaces can offer constructive feedback in a manner that encourages more active engagement from students.

The integration of AI into education also brings forth significant challenges, such as ensuring cultural diversity in AI-generated content and optimizing AI responses for student learning rather than just providing quick answers. The rapid adoption of AI tools such as ChatGPT in education settings has highlighted the need for careful consideration of these technologies' pedagogical implications.

As we navigate this new era, the necessity of continuous education becomes ever more evident. The dynamic nature of AI and technology means that the job market is constantly evolving, with new skills and competencies becoming relevant overnight. To stay competitive and thrive in this changing landscape, individuals and organizations must embrace lifelong learning as a core strategy for growth and development.

The new paradigm of learning with AI

The integration of AI into the educational realm is setting the stage for a revolutionary shift in how learning experiences are designed and delivered. Moving beyond the traditional one-size-fits-all model, AI is ushering in an era of personalized and adaptive learning tailored to each learner's needs, interests, and pace.

AI-powered, personalized learning approaches are pivotal in addressing student disengagement by offering adaptive content, interactive experiences, and data-driven insights to optimize learning outcomes. This student-centric approach ensures that education is more engaging and aligned with each learner's unique aspirations and career paths. It is essential to navigate challenges such as privacy concerns and algorithm biases to fully realize AI's potential in education.

Innovations such as simulating student interactions provide new teachers with a risk-free environment to practice and refine their teaching strategies. AI's capacity for real-time feedback can enhance teaching methods by offering live advice based on expert pedagogy. This level of support is unprecedented in traditional education systems and represents a significant leap toward more effective and dynamic teaching practices.

AI's role in education extends to changing the learning focus. By reducing the need for proficiency in specific skills, AI allows students to engage more deeply with the material, fostering a more creative and analytical approach to learning. This shift is likely to emphasize developing critical thinking and problem-solving skills, which are invaluable in today's rapidly evolving job market.

AI also presents an opportunity to create a learning environment free from the fear of judgment, enabling students to take risks and engage more actively in their learning journey. Such an environment is conducive to building self-confidence and encouraging exploratory learning, which is a critical component of lifelong learning.

As we navigate this new paradigm, it's clear that AI has the potential to make learning more accessible, engaging, and aligned with individual learner needs. Embracing this change requires a thoughtful approach to integrating AI into education, ensuring that it enhances rather than replaces traditional teaching and learning methods.

Lifelong learning as a strategic imperative

The shift from traditional education models to a paradigm where learning extends throughout an individual's life is significant, driven by the rapid advancements in technology, particularly AI. This new model emphasizes learning as a continuous, lifelong journey that is essential to both personal fulfillment and professional development in an ever-evolving digital era.

The concept of a learning society, as discussed by UNESCO, places lifelong learning at the core of societal development, transforming education and skills development to meet the challenges and opportunities of the Fourth Industrial Revolution. This approach is not only about enhancing talent but also about embedding a culture of learning within the fabric of society, making education and skill development accessible and relevant to all, regardless of one's stage in life or socio-economic background.

The digital transformation of education in emerging markets is creating new opportunities for collaboration among all stakeholders. The integration of digital technologies in education is seen as a pathway to a digital lifelong learning ecosystem that is more modular and affordable. This ecosystem is vital for developing fluid digital skills at scale and for providing historically excluded populations with access to quality education and training.

In the digital age, where digitalization and automation are reshaping the workplace, the skills required for success are also changing. Skills such as problem-solving, communication, curiosity, adaptability, and emotional agility are becoming increasingly important. These skills not only contribute to an individual's resilience and success in a changing work environment but also foster an atmosphere that's conducive to lifelong learning.

The transition to lifelong learning is not just an educational reform; it's a transformation that requires a collective effort from governments, educational institutions, industries, and communities. By fostering a mindset geared toward continuous improvement and adaptability, individuals and organizations can navigate the challenges and seize the opportunities presented by technological advancements, ensuring relevance and success in the digital age. This table outlines the key themes of lifelong learning, highlighting the critical concepts and principles:

Theme	Description	Implications for individuals	Implications for organizations
Personalized learning	AI enables learning experiences tailored to individual needs and pace	Enables more effective and engaging learning paths	Facilitates the development of a more skilled and adaptable workforce
Continuous education	The rapid evolution of AI and technology necessitates ongoing learning	Encourages a mindset of curiosity and adaptability	Promotes a culture of innovation and continuous improvement
Access and inclusion	AI has the potential to make education more accessible to diverse populations	Increase opportunities for personal and professional development	Enhance social responsibility and broaden talent pools
Ethical considerations	Addressing ethical issues in AI-powered education is crucial	Foster awareness of data privacy, bias, and equity	Ensure responsible use of AI and build trust among stakeholders

Table 14.1 – Key themes of lifelong learning

Lifelong learning is not a luxury or an option; it's a necessity. By embracing the ethos of continuous growth and development, individuals, organizations, and societies can navigate the complexities of the modern world and unlock their full potential.

AI-driven tools and platforms for lifelong learning

The following is an overview of various AI-powered tools and platforms that facilitate lifelong learning, from language apps and online courses to virtual simulations and interactive learning environments:

AI tool	Function	Benefits for learning	Example platforms
Adaptive learning platforms	Adjust content and pacing based on learner performance	Personalize learning, improve engagement and outcomes	Khan Academy, Coursera
Virtual simulations	Simulate real-world scenarios for hands-on learning	Enhance practical skills and real-world application	Labster, SimScale
AI tutors	Provide personalized tutoring and feedback	Offer individual support and address specific learning gaps	Duolingo, Quizlet

Table 14.2 – Overview of AI tools and platforms

In essence, AI-driven tools and platforms stand poised to revolutionize lifelong learning, empowering individuals to embark on a journey of continuous growth and discovery in an increasingly dynamic and interconnected world.

Overcoming barriers to continuous learning

Engaging in lifelong learning is essential to personal and professional growth, especially in an era dominated by rapid technological advancements such as AI. However, several common obstacles can hinder this continuous learning journey. Understanding and addressing these barriers is crucial to fostering a culture of ongoing education.

Common obstacles to lifelong learning

While the benefits of lifelong learning are undeniable, several common obstacles can hinder individuals from fully embracing this transformative journey:

- **Emotional barriers**: Emotional factors such as fear of failure and low self-esteem can significantly deter individuals from pursuing learning opportunities. These barriers often stem from negative past experiences or the daunting prospect of stepping out of one's comfort zone.

- **Motivational barriers**: A lack of clear goals or understanding of the practical benefits of learning can lead to diminished motivation. With a clear purpose or end goal, individuals may be able to see the value in dedicating time and effort to acquiring new skills or knowledge.

- **Learning environment challenges**: The format of learning content and the overall learning experience can also pose significant barriers. Traditional text-based or one-size-fits-all courses may not cater to diverse learning styles, leading to disengagement and poor learner experiences.

Strategies to overcome these barriers

Navigating the challenges of lifelong learning requires proactive strategies to overcome the barriers that may impede progress and hinder personal growth:

- **Addressing emotional barriers**: Creating an open culture of learning within organizations and educational institutions can help mitigate the fear of failure. It's important to communicate that making mistakes is a natural part of the learning process and to provide structured support, such as learning paths, to guide learners toward success. Recognizing and celebrating small achievements can also boost motivation and self-esteem.

- **Tackling motivational barriers**: Setting clear, achievable goals for training programs can enhance motivation. Breaking down larger objectives into smaller, manageable tasks or modules can help learners stay focused and understand the incremental benefits of their efforts. Sharing practical applications and success stories can also illustrate the real-world value of continuous learning.

- **Improving the learning environment**: To cater to various learning styles, incorporating a mix of media such as videos, imagery, and interactive content can make learning more engaging. Leveraging technology to facilitate social learning and peer support can also enrich the learning experience. Providing a flexible and user-friendly learning platform that allows learners to access content at their convenience is crucial to accommodating different schedules and commitments.

AI and digital technologies offer promising solutions to these barriers, making learning more personalized, accessible, and aligned with individual needs. By leveraging AI-driven tools and platforms, educators and organizations can create adaptive learning experiences that address the unique preferences and challenges of each learner.

The role of organizations in promoting lifelong learning

Organizations play a crucial role in nurturing an environment where lifelong learning is not just encouraged but integrated into the fabric of corporate culture. By actively supporting continuous education, businesses and institutions can unlock significant benefits not only for their employees but also for the organization as a whole.

Supporting lifelong learning in organizations

In fostering a culture of continuous development and growth, organizations must prioritize strategies that actively support and promote lifelong learning among their workforce.

Creating learning opportunities

Creating learning opportunities is a fundamental aspect of supporting lifelong learning in organizations, ensuring that employees have access to continuous development and skill enhancement throughout their careers.

- **Structured programs and resources**: Organizations can offer structured learning programs that include workshops, seminars, and access to online courses that cover a wide range of topics relevant to employees' current and future roles. Providing resources such as subscriptions to academic journals and industry publications can also support continuous learning.

- **Learning through collaboration**: Encouraging collaborative projects where employees from different departments work together can lead to shared learning experiences and insight exchange. This can also include partnerships with universities or other educational institutions.

Recognizing and incentivizing learning achievements

Recognizing and incentivizing learning achievements is a fundamental strategy in supporting lifelong learning within organizations, as it motivates employees to continuously enhance their skills and knowledge.

- **Recognition programs**: Implementing recognition programs that acknowledge employees' efforts in pursuing further education or skills development can motivate others to engage in learning activities. These might include awards, certificates, or public acknowledgments during company meetings.

- **Career advancement opportunities**: Linking learning achievements directly to career progression, such as promotions or role enhancements, can serve as a strong incentive for employees to take learning seriously.

Embedding learning into organizational culture

Embedding learning into organizational culture is crucial for supporting lifelong learning in organizations, as it fosters an environment where continuous improvement and development are integral to the company's values and operations.

- **Leadership endorsement**: When organizational leaders actively participate in learning initiatives—either by leading training sessions or by sharing their own learning experiences—this sets a tone that learning is valued at all levels of the organization.

- **Making learning part of the routine**: Integrating short learning sessions into regular work routines can help normalize continuous education. This could be through weekly "learning hours" or by integrating educational content into regular meetings.

In conclusion, cultivating a workplace environment that values and supports lifelong learning isn't just a strategic choice; it's a fundamental necessity in today's rapidly evolving corporate landscape. By investing in employee development, fostering a culture of curiosity, and providing accessible learning opportunities, organizations not only empower their workforce to adapt to change but also position themselves as leaders in innovation and excellence. As we move forward, let us continue to champion lifelong learning as a cornerstone of organizational success, driving both individual fulfillment and collective achievement.

Impact of organizational support on employees

The impact of organizational support on employees' professional development and overall well-being cannot be overstated, as it plays a pivotal role in shaping their performance, satisfaction, and long-term success within the workplace.

- **Enhanced employee engagement**: When employees see that their personal and professional growth is supported, their engagement with the organization increases. Engaged employees are more likely to contribute positively, stay with the company longer, and advocate for the company as a great place to work.

- **Fostering innovation**: Organizations can foster an environment that's ripe for innovation by encouraging learning and exploring new ideas. Employees who are exposed to diverse ideas and can cross-pollinate concepts from different fields are often at the forefront of innovation.

- **Increased adaptability**: Continuous learning helps employees adapt to rapidly changing industries. The ability to quickly acquire new skills and adapt to new roles or technologies is crucial to maintaining organizational agility and competitiveness.

Organizations' support for lifelong learning is a significant determinant of their long-term success and adaptability. Investing in the continuous growth of their workforce not only enhances employee satisfaction and retention but also drives innovation and maintains competitive advantage in fast-evolving markets. By fostering a culture that values and supports ongoing education, organizations enhance their resilience and contribute to the development of a more knowledgeable and adaptable society.

Ethical and inclusive considerations in AI-educational tools

As AI increasingly permeates the field of education, it brings with it a range of ethical considerations that must be addressed to ensure that these tools benefit all users equitably. Addressing concerns such as data privacy, algorithmic bias, and equitable access is essential to creating AI tools that are not only effective but also fair and inclusive.

Addressing ethical concerns

When adopting new technologies or implementing novel practices, it's imperative to acknowledge and address the ethical concerns that may arise to ensure responsible and sustainable outcomes for all stakeholders involved:

- **Data privacy**: With AI systems processing vast amounts of personal data to personalize learning experiences, ensuring the privacy and security of this data is paramount. It is crucial to implement robust data protection measures that comply with legal standards such as the GDPR in Europe or the CCPA in California. Additionally, transparency about how data is collected, used, and protected helps build trust with users.

- **Algorithmic bias**: AI systems can inadvertently perpetuate existing biases if not carefully designed and monitored. To combat this, it's essential to use diverse datasets for training AI models and to regularly audit these models for any signs of bias. Implementing algorithmic audits by independent third parties can also help ensure these systems operate fairly.

- **Equitable access**: Ensuring that AI educational tools are accessible to all students, regardless of their socioeconomic background, is crucial. This includes not only addressing economic accessibility but also ensuring that these tools are usable for students with disabilities. Designing AI systems with universal design principles in mind can help achieve this.

Best practices for developing ethical, inclusive AI tools

In developing ethical and inclusive AI tools, adhering to best practices not only fosters trust and transparency but also ensures that these technologies contribute positively to society while minimizing potential biases and harmful impacts:

- **Inclusive design**: Involve a diverse group of stakeholders, including students and educators from various demographic backgrounds, in the design process of AI tools. This approach helps identify and address potential issues of accessibility and usability early in the development process.

- **Transparency and accountability**: Develop AI tools that provide transparent explanations for their outputs, which is especially important in educational settings where understanding the basis of information provided by AI is crucial. Maintaining accountability for AI decisions, such as providing users with the ability to challenge and receive clarification about AI-generated decisions, reinforces trust.

- **Continuous feedback loops**: Establish mechanisms for ongoing feedback from users to continually improve AI tools. This can include regular surveys, user testing sessions, and forums for users to share their experiences and concerns.

- **Cultural competence**: AI tools should be designed to be culturally competent, recognizing and respecting the diverse cultural backgrounds of users. This involves incorporating a range of perspectives and educational content that is culturally relevant and sensitive.

Ethical considerations are at the heart of developing and deploying AI educational tools. By focusing on inclusivity, transparency, and accountability and rigorously addressing concerns such as data privacy, algorithmic bias, and equitable access, developers can create AI tools that are innovative, effective, ethical, and supportive of diverse learning needs. These best practices ensure that AI technologies contribute positively to the educational landscape, enhancing learning experiences without compromising ethical standards.

Future directions in lifelong learning

The landscape of lifelong learning is poised for a transformative shift as AI continues to evolve and integrate into educational frameworks. This integration is expected to revolutionize how knowledge is acquired, retained, and applied, while also emphasizing the growing importance of interdisciplinary learning and the balanced development of soft and technical skills.

Predictions on the evolving role of AI in lifelong learning

Exploring the evolving role of AI in lifelong learning unveils a list of predictions that forecast its transformative impact on education, professional development, and personal growth in the years to come:

- **Emerging technologies and models**: Future AI technologies are likely to include more sophisticated neural networks that are capable of understanding and predicting learner behaviors and needs with unprecedented accuracy. This could lead to the development of highly adaptive learning environments that adjust in real time to the pace and style of each learner. Moreover, blockchain could be utilized to securely and transparently track educational achievements throughout one's life.

- **Personalized learning journeys**: AI is expected to enhance personalized learning by using data from diverse learning interactions to tailor content, challenge levels, and learning pathways that suit individual career goals and learning styles. This personalization will make learning not only more effective but also more engaging, helping learners to stay motivated over longer periods.

- **Augmented and virtual reality**: As AR and VR technologies become more refined and accessible, they will increasingly be integrated into lifelong learning models. These tools can offer immersive learning experiences that are particularly effective for complex skill acquisitions, such as surgical procedures and advanced engineering concepts, by simulating real-world environments.

Importance of interdisciplinary learning and soft skills

The importance of interdisciplinary learning and soft skills has emerged as a crucial aspect of preparing individuals for success in a rapidly changing world:

- **Interdisciplinary approaches**: The complex problems of today's world require solutions that draw on multiple fields of knowledge. AI's role in facilitating access to cross-disciplinary resources and experts can help learners combine diverse fields into cohesive study paths, enhancing creativity and innovation.

- **Soft skills development**: Alongside technical skills, the future of lifelong learning will also emphasize the development of soft skills such as critical thinking, emotional intelligence, and adaptability. AI can support this by providing scenarios and simulations that challenge learners to apply these skills in varied contexts, preparing them for the nuanced demands of modern workplaces.

- **Continuous feedback and improvement**: AI systems can offer continuous feedback, allowing learners to see real-time progress and identify areas needing improvement. This instant feedback is crucial to adult learners who must balance the demands of education with personal and professional responsibilities.

The future directions of lifelong learning are deeply intertwined with the advancements in AI, promising a more dynamic, responsive, and personalized educational landscape. As these technologies continue to develop, they will play a pivotal role in shaping a new era of education that is flexible, interdisciplinary, and inclusive, providing learners with the tools they need to succeed in an increasingly complex world. Integrating soft skills alongside technical training will ensure that learners are well-rounded and capable of navigating the challenges of a changing global economy.

Lifelong learners – success stories and inspirations

The journey of lifelong learning is replete with inspiring stories of individuals and organizations that have harnessed the power of continuous education and make significant contributions to society. These stories not only serve as a testament to the benefits of lifelong learning but also inspire others to embark on their own learning journeys.

Individual success stories

Reflecting on individual success stories offers invaluable insights into the transformative power of lifelong learning:

- **Susan Wojcicki**: As the former CEO of YouTube, Susan Wojcicki has emphasized the importance of continuous learning in her career. Starting as Google's first marketing manager, Wojcicki's path to becoming a leading figure in tech was paved by her commitment to learning and adapting in a rapidly evolving industry. She advocates for ongoing education and technology mastery, illustrating how continuous learning can lead to significant career advancements and leadership roles.

- **Sal Khan**: The founder of Khan Academy, Sal Khan, turned a tutoring project for his cousin into a global educational resource, impacting millions. Khan Academy started as a series of YouTube tutorials, which evolved into a platform offering free courses on a wide range of subjects. Khan's journey highlights how a passion for education and commitment to lifelong learning can lead to innovations that transform the educational landscape for others.

Organizational success stories

Organizational success stories serve as inspiring examples of how a commitment to lifelong learning can drive innovation, foster growth, and propel businesses to new heights of success:

- **Accenture**: Known for its commitment to empowering its employees through education, Accenture has invested heavily in learning platforms that provide training in various technical and business skills. This investment in lifelong learning is integral to the company's strategy, helping to keep its workforce relevant and innovative in the face of changing industry demands. Accenture's approach not only improves employee skills but also drives growth and adaptability within the organization.

- **General Electric (GE)**: GE has long been celebrated for its GE University, which plays a crucial role in employee development. This institution is part of a broader culture that encourages continuous improvement and learning. By fostering an environment where employees are continually challenged to learn and innovate, GE has maintained its position as a leader in multiple industries, from aviation to digital technologies.

Impact on society

These stories of lifelong learners demonstrate that continuous education can lead to personal fulfillment, career success, and broader societal impacts. They reflect a range of benefits, from enhanced personal capabilities and professional qualifications to contributions to global education and corporate innovation. The inspirational journeys of these individuals and organizations underscore the transformative power of lifelong learning and its role as a cornerstone of personal and professional development in today's dynamic world.

Summary

This chapter has explored the transformative potential of AI in reshaping the landscape of lifelong learning. AI's integration into educational frameworks is not just enhancing traditional learning methods but also revolutionizing how we approach personal and professional development through continuous education. By personalizing learning experiences, making education more accessible, and supporting the development of both technical and soft skills, AI is playing a pivotal role in preparing individuals for the future.

As we stand on the brink of this transformative shift, it becomes imperative for individuals, organizations, and societies to embrace lifelong learning as a fundamental component of success and fulfillment in the age of AI. For individuals, continuous learning is the key to staying relevant and competitive in a rapidly evolving job market. For organizations, fostering a learning culture is crucial to innovation and adaptability, ensuring they remain at the cutting edge of their industries.

As lifelong learning becomes increasingly integrated with AI, it offers significant opportunities for growth, innovation, and resilience. It allows for a more inclusive and equitable distribution of learning opportunities, breaking down barriers that traditionally limit access to education.

Therefore, the call to action for embracing lifelong learning is evident. We must actively participate in and promote educational practices that support continuous learning and adaptability. By doing so, we not only enhance our lives but also contribute to broader societal advancements, positively impacting the world around us.

Embracing lifelong learning in the age of AI presents an exciting pathway to a future where education is more dynamic, personalized, and impactful. Let us move forward with the resolve to harness these opportunities, continually adapt to new challenges, and thrive in an ever-changing global landscape.

Further reading and resources

For those looking to delve deeper into the topics of AI in education, lifelong learning, and the impact of continuous education on personal and professional growth, the following books, articles, and online resources are highly recommended:

- *Drive: The Surprising Truth About What Motivates Us by Daniel H. Pink* (`https://www.amazon.com/Drive-Surprising-Truth-About-Motivates/dp/1594484805`): While not exclusively about education, this book is essential to understanding what motivates us to learn and grow. Pink's insights are particularly relevant to designing learning environments that motivate and engage lifelong learners.

- *NEW-HBRs 10 Must Reads on Lifelong Learning by Harvard Business Review* (`https://www.amazon.com/NEW-HBRs-Must-Reads-Lifelong-Learning/dp/B09W2W141V`): This series of articles from HBR offers practical advice on how individuals and organizations can foster a culture of continuous learning. It includes strategies for keeping skills fresh and adapting to new challenges and opportunities in the workplace.

- *EdSurge* (`https://www.edsurge.com/`): This educational technology website provides articles, research, and news on the latest trends and innovations in education technology, including the use of AI in education. It is a valuable resource for educators and administrators looking to stay abreast of the latest developments in the field.

- *Coursera* (`https://www.coursera.org/en-IN`) *and edX* (`https://www.edx.org/`): These **massive open online course** (**MOOC**) platforms offer various courses on AI, education technology, and personal development topics. They are excellent resources for anyone looking to expand their knowledge and skills through self-directed learning.

- For more detailed insights into how AI is transforming education and the implications for lifelong learning, you can explore discussions and findings from sources such as the World Economic Forum and the Stanford Institute for Human-Centered AI:

  - Explore the World Economic Forum's perspective on AI in education: `https://www.weforum.org/agenda/2023/05/ai-accelerate-students-holistic-development-teaching-fulfilling/`

- Delve into Stanford's research on AI's potential in education: `https://hai.stanford.edu/news/ai-will-transform-teaching-and-learning-lets-get-it-right`

- Understand UNESCO's viewpoint on AI enhancing education: `https://www.unesco.org/en/articles/how-can-artificial-intelligence-enhance-education`

These resources blend theoretical knowledge and practical insights, suitable for educators, technology professionals, and lifelong learners. By exploring these materials, you can better understand how AI and digital technologies are shaping the future of education and continuous learning.

Q&A

In exploring the profound impact of AI on lifelong learning, several key questions arise that challenge our understanding and approach to education in the digital age. This section addresses these queries, offering insights that can help educators, learners, and organizations navigate the evolving educational landscape:

1. How can AI personalize learning without compromising privacy?

    AI offers the potential to tailor educational experiences to individual needs, but this personalization relies on data that must be handled responsibly. Best practices include using anonymized data when possible, implementing stringent security measures, and ensuring transparency with users about how their data is being used. Continuous dialogue about ethical standards and privacy regulations is crucial to maintaining trust.

2. What strategies can ensure that AI tools are accessible to all learners?

    Ensuring that AI educational tools are accessible requires a commitment to universal design principles. This means that AI platforms should be usable to people of all ages, backgrounds, and abilities. Strategies include providing multiple ways to engage with content (e.g., text, audio, visual), ensuring compatibility with assistive technologies, and offering content in multiple languages.

3. How can organizations foster a culture of lifelong learning?

    Organizations can foster a lifelong learning culture by integrating learning into the daily routines of employees, providing ongoing professional development opportunities, and recognizing and rewarding educational achievements. Leadership should model learning behaviors and advocate for continuous growth and adaptation as core values.

4. What role does interdisciplinary learning play in a technology-driven world?

    Interdisciplinary learning is increasingly important when complex problems require multifaceted solutions. Integrating **science, technology, engineering, arts, and mathematics (STEAM)** with soft skills such as communication and problem-solving prepares learners to think broadly and apply their knowledge creatively. Encouraging project-based learning and collaboration across different fields can enhance this approach.

5. How can educators balance the use of AI with traditional teaching methods?

    Balancing AI with traditional teaching involves using AI to enhance, not replace, human instruction. AI can take on repetitive tasks, provide data-driven insights, and support personalized learning paths, allowing educators to focus more on interactive, critical thinking and creative activities that foster deeper understanding and student engagement.

These reflections underline AI's transformative potential in education while highlighting the thoughtful considerations necessary to harness its benefits effectively. They also emphasize the need for ongoing research, policy-making, and community engagement to address the challenges and opportunities presented by AI in lifelong learning.

15

The Future is Now – Integrating AI into Accounting

"Artificial intelligence is revolutionizing accounting, automating tasks, boosting efficiency, and empowering accountants to focus on strategic analysis and client insights."

– Idris Nagri (Accountancy Age)

The accounting sector is on the cusp of a significant transformation driven by the rapid advancement and integration of **artificial intelligence** (**AI**). This shift is not just about adopting new technology; it's about redefining the entire profession. AI is streamlining traditionally time-consuming and labor-intensive processes, thus enabling accountants to focus on more strategic functions rather than routine number crunching.

AI technologies are proving indispensable for enhancing the accuracy and efficiency of accounting operations. Automated systems can process large volumes of data with greater precision and significantly less error, reducing the likelihood of costly mistakes. Furthermore, AI-driven analytics provide deeper insights into financial data, allowing accountants to offer more nuanced advice on business strategy and risk management.

The accounting field is undergoing a rapid transformation with the adoption of AI. Firms that harness AI technologies are gaining a significant edge, offering faster, more reliable, and more comprehensive services at a lower cost. This capability not only drives business growth but also reshapes client expectations, setting a new benchmark for what's possible in accounting services.

The integration of AI in accounting practices is not just a matter of maintaining competitiveness. It's about adapting to the demands of a digital age where speed, accuracy, and strategic foresight are paramount. As we explore the role of AI in accounting, it becomes evident that this technology is not merely a tool for enhancement – it is a transformative force that will redefine the future of the accounting profession.

AI innovations in accounting

The integration of AI in the accounting sector is revolutionizing traditional practices, bringing both efficiency and enhanced capabilities that are changing the profession's core functions.

Automation of routine tasks

AI technologies are making significant strides in automating routine accounting tasks that have traditionally consumed considerable time. These tasks include data entry, transaction matching, and financial report preparation. By automating these processes, AI allows accountants to shift their focus from manual data handling to more strategic activities such as financial analysis, decision support, and advisory roles. For instance, AI-powered software can analyze large volumes of invoices and receipts, extract relevant data without human input, and input this data directly into financial systems with high accuracy. This speeds up the process and reduces the likelihood of errors associated with manual entry.

AI's automation capabilities extend to more complex processes, such as the end-to-end handling of accounts payable and receivable, where AI systems can match payments to invoices and manage discrepancies independently. These advancements free up valuable resources, allowing accounting professionals to focus on areas that add greater value to their organizations, such as strategic planning and growth analysis.

Enhanced fraud detection and regulatory compliance

AI is also crucial in transforming fraud detection and regulatory compliance within accounting. Advanced AI algorithms can analyze patterns in large datasets that would be impossible for humans to evaluate efficiently. These algorithms can identify anomalies, outliers, and patterns indicative of fraudulent activities, such as unusual transactions or inconsistent reporting patterns. By leveraging machine learning, these systems continuously improve their detection capabilities based on new data, staying ahead of sophisticated fraud techniques.

AI systems are instrumental in ensuring compliance with ever-changing regulatory requirements. They can be programmed to stay updated with the latest regulatory changes and automatically adjust financial systems to comply with new rules and regulations. This is particularly valuable in complex regulatory environments where manual monitoring and updates are resource-intensive and error-prone.

These AI innovations enhance the efficiency and accuracy of accounting practices. They also enable firms to manage risks more effectively and provide higher-quality services to clients. The integration of AI in accounting is proving to be a transformative force, heralding a new era where technology and traditional accounting practices converge to create a more dynamic, responsive, and efficient accounting landscape. The following table provides an overview of recent AI innovations in accounting, highlighting their applications, benefits, and potential impact on the industry:

AI Application	Description	Benefits
Automation of routine tasks	AI automates tasks such as data entry, reconciliation, and report generation	Frees up time for strategic work and reduces human error
Fraud detection	AI uses pattern recognition to identify unusual transactions that may indicate fraud	Enhances security and compliance, as well as quickly detects potential issues
Regulatory compliance	AI systems are updated to comply with current laws and automatically apply these rules	Ensures compliance with less manual oversight and reduces the risk of penalties

Table 15.1 – AI innovations in accounting

These AI innovations are transforming the accounting landscape, making processes more efficient, accurate, and insightful, ultimately driving the industry toward a more automated and data-driven future. While AI innovations offer significant advantages, their adoption in accounting also presents several challenges that need to be addressed to fully realize their potential.

Challenges in AI adoption

Integrating AI into accounting processes offers numerous benefits but presents significant challenges that firms must navigate to harness AI's potential fully.

Technical and integration challenges

One of the primary hurdles in adopting AI within accounting is the technical barrier associated with data standardization and integration with existing systems. AI systems require high-quality, standardized data to function effectively, but accounting data often exists in various formats and may be spread across different systems. Ensuring data consistency across an organization is a formidable task that requires robust data management strategies. Additionally, integrating AI solutions into legacy systems without disrupting existing workflows can be complex and costly. Firms need to invest in middleware or develop custom integrations that allow AI tools to communicate seamlessly with these older systems, which often involves significant time and financial resources.

Moreover, the deployment of AI in accounting also demands a robust infrastructure that can handle large volumes of data processing and analysis. Many organizations may find their current IT infrastructure inadequate, requiring upgrades to both hardware and software to support AI capabilities effectively.

Cultural acceptance and training needs

Beyond technical issues, cultural resistance within accounting departments can also impede AI adoption. The transition to AI-driven processes often requires a shift in mindset from traditional ways of working to more technology-centric approaches. This change can be met with skepticism and resistance, particularly from staff who may fear job displacement or feel overwhelmed by the need to learn new technologies.

Addressing these concerns involves clear communication from leadership about AI's role as a tool to enhance, not replace, the capabilities of human accountants. It is crucial to highlight how AI can take over tedious, repetitive tasks, allowing accountants to focus on more strategic and fulfilling aspects of their roles.

Ongoing professional development is essential to equip staff with the necessary AI skills. This training should cover how to use new AI tools to interpret AI outputs and make decisions based on data-driven insights. Creating hands-on training and real-time learning opportunities can help ease the transition and build a more tech-savvy workforce.

Organizations must also foster a culture that values continual learning and adaptability, encouraging employees to view AI adoption as an opportunity for growth and innovation. By addressing both the technical and cultural challenges of AI adoption, accounting firms can pave the way for a smoother transition and fully realize the benefits of AI in enhancing operational efficiency and decision-making. The following table outlines the key challenges in adopting AI in accounting, detailing the specific issues and their implications for the industry:

Challenge Type	Specific Issues	Solutions
Technical and integration	Difficulties in data standardization and system compatibility	Invest in robust IT infrastructure and use middleware for integration
Cultural acceptance	Resistance from staff and fear of job displacement	Training programs and clear communication about AI benefits
Training needs	Lack of AI skills among existing staff	Specialized training sessions and hiring new talents with AI expertise

Table 15.2 – Challenges in AI adoption

Addressing these challenges is crucial for the successful integration of AI in accounting, ensuring that the industry can fully leverage the benefits of these advanced technologies.

Case studies – AI transformations in accounting

Integrating AI in accounting has led to significant operational improvements across various organizations. These case studies highlight successful AI implementations, detailing the processes involved, the challenges faced, and the tangible benefits realized.

Case study 1 – AI-enhanced fraud detection in a major bank

Overview: A major international bank implemented an AI system designed to enhance its fraud detection capabilities. The AI model was trained to identify patterns and anomalies in transaction data that could indicate fraudulent activity.

Process: The bank integrated the AI system with its existing transaction processing platform, allowing for real-time analysis of payment data.

Challenges: Initial challenges included aligning the AI system with the bank's data privacy policies and ensuring it could handle the massive volume of transactions without delays.

Benefits: The AI system significantly improved the bank's ability to detect and prevent fraud, reducing fraudulent transactions by over 25% within the first year of implementation. This enhancement not only saved the bank considerable financial resources but also strengthened its reputation for security among its customers.

Case study 2 – automated financial reporting at a tech startup

Overview: A fast-growing tech startup implemented AI to automate its financial reporting processes, aiming to improve accuracy and timeliness.

Process: The startup used AI tools to automate data entry and reconciliation tasks that were previously done manually, integrating these tools with their financial software.

Challenges: The startup faced difficulties in training the AI system to recognize and categorize financial data from diverse sources accurately.

Benefits: Automation reduced the time required for financial reporting by 40%, allowing the finance team to focus more on analysis and less on manual data handling. The accuracy of financial reports also improved, facilitating better strategic decision-making.

Case study 3 – enhancing compliance and advisory services in an accounting firm

Overview: A large accounting firm deployed AI to enhance its compliance audits and advisory services, using AI to analyze complex datasets for compliance issues and advisory opportunities.

Process: The firm developed a proprietary AI platform that could integrate with client systems to access and analyze financial data.

Challenges: Integrating AI with diverse client systems was initially a hurdle, requiring customized solutions for different types of financial systems.

Benefits: The AI platform enabled the firm to provide more comprehensive compliance audits and tailor its advisory services based on insights derived from AI analysis. This capability led to a 30% increase in client satisfaction and a significant uptick in advisory service revenues.

These case studies demonstrate the power of AI in transforming accounting practices, showcasing not just the efficiency gains but also the enhanced capabilities that AI brings to fraud detection, compliance, and financial reporting. Through careful integration and overcoming initial challenges, these organizations have realized significant benefits from AI, setting a precedent for its broader adoption in the industry.

Strategic implementation of AI in accounting

Implementing AI in accounting requires careful planning and strategic execution. This section covers the foundational steps for AI integration and strategies to cultivate AI expertise within accounting teams.

Foundational steps for AI integration

The following foundational steps outline the essential actions that organizations should take to effectively integrate AI into their accounting processes, ensuring a smooth and successful transition:

1. **Needs assessment**: Begin by assessing the specific needs of your accounting department. Identify which processes could benefit most from automation or enhanced analytics. This could involve streamlining transaction processing, improving accuracy in financial reporting, or enhancing fraud detection.

2. **Tool selection**: Choose the right AI tools that align with your identified needs. Consider factors such as compatibility with existing systems, ease of use, scalability, and support provided by the vendor. Popular AI tools for accounting include machine learning platforms for anomaly detection and chatbots for handling routine inquiries.

3. **Technological partnerships**: Partner with AI technology providers who have expertise in the financial sector. These partnerships can provide access to advanced technologies and expert guidance on integrating AI into existing systems. Look for partners with a track record of successful implementations in accounting.

4. **Pilot testing**: Conduct a pilot test with a selected AI tool on a small scale before a full rollout. This approach helps identify potential issues and ensures that the AI solution meets the needs without disrupting existing operations.

5. **Integration and scaling**: Once the pilot test is successful, integrate the AI tool into your accounting systems. Plan for a gradual rollout and be prepared to scale the implementation as the team becomes more accustomed to the new technology.

Cultivating AI expertise

To maximize the benefits of AI in accounting, it is crucial to cultivate expertise within the organization. The following strategies focus on developing the necessary skills and knowledge among accounting professionals to effectively leverage AI technologies:

- **Training programs**: Develop training programs to upskill existing employees. Training should focus on how to use AI tools effectively, interpret AI-generated insights, and integrate these insights into decision-making processes. Training can be conducted internally or through external courses offered by AI experts.

- **Hiring practices**: Incorporate AI proficiency as a criterion in the hiring process for new accounting personnel. Consider candidates with a background in data science or experience with AI tools as they can bring valuable skills to your accounting team.

- **Continuous learning**: Encourage continuous learning and development in AI by providing regular updates on new AI technologies and methodologies. This could include subscribing to relevant journals, attending industry conferences, and participating in webinars focused on AI in accounting.

- **Cross-functional teams**: Create cross-functional teams that include IT and accounting professionals. These teams can work together to ensure that AI implementations are aligned with both technical standards and accounting needs.

- **Leadership and culture**: Foster a culture that embraces innovation and change. Leadership should actively support AI initiatives by promoting AI's benefits and strategic importance in accounting, addressing any resistance, and celebrating successful AI integration milestones.

By following these steps and strategies, accounting firms and departments can effectively implement AI technologies, enhance their capabilities, and stay competitive in an increasingly digital landscape. The next section highlights key considerations and strategies to ensure the ethical use and effective governance of AI technologies in the field.

Ethical considerations and AI governance

The integration of AI in accounting raises several ethical considerations that need to be addressed to ensure trust and integrity in financial practices. Establishing robust AI governance frameworks is crucial to managing these ethical challenges effectively.

Ethical issues in AI

In this section, we'll explore the ethical considerations surrounding AI adoption in accounting practices, shedding light on important issues and potential implications for stakeholders:

- **Data privacy**: Data privacy is paramount, especially given the sensitive nature of financial information. AI systems often require access to vast amounts of data, and there is a risk that this data could be mishandled or exposed. Ensuring that AI applications comply with data protection laws such as GDPR in Europe or the CCPA in California is essential. Encryption, access controls, and regular security audits are necessary measures to safeguard data integrity.

- **Potential biases in AI algorithms**: AI algorithms can inherit biases from the data used to train them, which can lead to unfair or discriminatory outcomes. For example, if an AI system is used for credit scoring and the training data has historical biases against a particular demographic, the AI could unfairly disadvantage individuals from that group. Regularly reviewing and updating the AI algorithms to correct for biases and implementing transparent methodologies for AI decision-making are critical steps in mitigating these issues.

- **Transparency and accountability**: There must be transparency in how AI systems make decisions, particularly in accounting, where such decisions can have significant financial implications. Stakeholders should be able to understand and question the AI's decision-making process. Establishing clear accountability for AI-driven decisions is also essential, ensuring that there are protocols in place for addressing any issues that arise.

Strategies for establishing AI governance frameworks

Here, we'll explore strategies and best practices for establishing robust governance frameworks that address key considerations:

- **Governance structure**: Create a governance structure that includes a diverse range of stakeholders, including AI experts, ethicists, legal advisors, and end users. This structure should oversee the development, deployment, and ongoing management of AI technologies to ensure they are used ethically and responsibly.

- **Ethical AI guidelines**: Develop and implement a set of ethical guidelines for AI use that aligns with the organization's values and ethical standards. These guidelines should address issues such as data privacy, bias mitigation, transparency, and accountability.

- **Regular audits and compliance checks**: Conduct regular audits of AI systems to ensure they comply with both internal ethical guidelines and external legal requirements. Compliance checks should be an ongoing process to adapt to new regulations and changes in the operational environment.

- **Stakeholder engagement**: Engage with all stakeholders, including employees, clients, and regulatory bodies, to gain insights into their concerns and expectations regarding AI use. This engagement should inform the AI governance process and help build trust in AI systems.

- **Training and awareness programs**: Implement training and awareness programs to educate all relevant stakeholders about the ethical use of AI. These programs should focus on understanding AI capabilities, limitations, and the ethical considerations associated with its use.

By addressing these ethical considerations and implementing robust AI governance frameworks, accounting professionals can leverage AI technologies effectively while maintaining high standards of ethical practice and compliance. This approach ensures that AI is used as a force for good, enhancing the efficiency and accuracy of accounting services without compromising ethical values or stakeholder trust. The following table presents an overview of ethical considerations and strategies for establishing AI governance frameworks in accounting practices, providing insights into key principles, challenges, and recommended approaches for responsible AI integration:

Ethical Issue	Strategy to Address	Implementation
Data privacy	Implement robust data protection measures and comply with legal standards	Securely handling sensitive information and trust from stakeholders
Algorithmic bias	Regular audits of AI algorithms use diverse datasets for training	Fair and unbiased AI operations.
Transparency and accountability	Develop clear guidelines for AI decision-making and ensure stakeholders can question AI logic	Transparent operations and increased stakeholder confidence in AI decisions

Table 15.3 – Ethical considerations and AI governance

In conclusion, addressing ethical considerations and implementing robust AI governance frameworks are essential steps in ensuring responsible and beneficial AI integration in accounting practices. By prioritizing transparency, fairness, and accountability, organizations can foster trust, mitigate risks, and maximize the value of AI technologies in the accounting industry.

Future trends and predictions

As AI continues to evolve, its impact on the accounting profession is expected to grow, bringing significant changes to traditional practices and the broader industry landscape. Here are some insights into emerging AI technologies and their potential implications for the field of accounting:

- **Advanced predictive analytics**: Future AI developments will likely enhance predictive analytics capabilities, allowing for more accurate forecasting and financial planning. These tools can predict cash flow scenarios, assess risk, and provide insights that inform business strategy. The ability to anticipate financial outcomes with greater precision will be invaluable for accountants in advisory roles.

- **Increased automation of complex processes**: While current AI applications focus on automating routine tasks, emerging technologies are expected to handle more complex accounting functions such as tax preparation, audit processes, and cross-border financial transactions. This shift will further free up human accountants to focus on strategic decision-making and complex problem-solving.

- **Integration of AI with blockchain**: The convergence of AI and blockchain technology holds significant promise for enhancing transparency and security in accounting. Blockchain can provide a secure and immutable record of transactions, while AI can analyze these records for patterns, anomalies, or compliance issues. This integration could revolutionize areas such as real-time auditing and secure, decentralized financial management.

- **AI-driven regulatory compliance**: As financial regulations become more complex and varied across jurisdictions, AI systems equipped with machine learning algorithms will increasingly be used to ensure compliance. These systems will be able to update themselves in real time as new regulations emerge and automatically provide accountants with guidance on compliance.

- **Personalized client interactions**: AI is expected to personalize the interaction between accountants and their clients by providing tailored advice based on deep learning of individual client profiles. This will enhance the client experience, making it more interactive and responsive to individual needs.

- **Ethical AI and governance**: With the increasing role of AI in sensitive areas, there will be a greater emphasis on developing ethical AI systems and robust governance frameworks. This will involve establishing clear guidelines and standards for AI applications in accounting to ensure they are used responsibly and ethically.

These trends suggest that AI will transform how accountants work and redefine their roles within organizations and the services they offer clients. The future accounting landscape will likely be characterized by greater efficiency, deeper insights, and enhanced decision-making capabilities driven by sophisticated AI technologies. As these changes unfold, accountants must adapt by acquiring new skills and embracing new technologies, positioning themselves as strategic advisors in an increasingly automated and data-driven environment.

Preparing for an AI-driven future

As AI continues to reshape the accounting landscape, both individual accountants and firms must adopt strategies to thrive in this evolving environment. Here are the key aspects you must consider when preparing for an AI-driven future in accounting:

- **Embrace lifelong learning**: The field of accounting is undergoing rapid change due to technological advancements. Accountants must commit to continuous education to keep pace with new AI technologies and methodologies. This could involve participating in professional development courses, workshops, and seminars on AI and its applications in accounting.

- **Develop technical skills**: Besides traditional accounting skills, gaining proficiency in data analytics and machine learning and understanding AI software tools will become increasingly important. Accountants should seek hands-on experience with AI platforms and tools that are becoming prevalent in financial analysis, reporting, and auditing.

- **Cultivate a culture of innovation**: Firms should foster a culture that embraces change and innovation. Encouraging experimentation with new technologies and processes can help with discovering more efficient ways to manage workloads and client needs. This culture should support risk-taking and learning from failures, both of which are crucial for innovation.

- **Update business models**: Firms need to reassess their business models to integrate AI effectively. This may involve redefining service offerings, incorporating AI-driven insights into client services, and using AI to enhance decision-making processes. Updating business models also means considering new pricing strategies for services that leverage AI technologies.

- **Strengthen ethical standards and practices**: As AI is adopted, ethical considerations must be at the forefront to ensure that it is used responsibly. Accountants should understand the ethical implications of AI, particularly regarding data privacy, security, and the potential for bias. Firms should establish clear guidelines and provide training on ethical AI use.

- **Promote agility and flexibility**: The ability to adapt quickly to new technologies and market conditions is vital. Firms should cultivate an agile working environment where technological adaptability is a core competency. This includes being open to changing traditional workflows and embracing digital transformation strategies.

- **Engage in strategic partnerships**: Building relationships with tech companies and AI solution providers can provide access to cutting-edge technologies and expertise. These partnerships can help accountants better understand how AI can be applied effectively within their specific contexts.

By taking these steps, accountants and accounting firms will not only be better prepared for the current changes but also for future advancements in AI. This proactive approach will ensure they remain competitive and continue to provide value to their clients in a technologically advanced marketplace.

Summary

Throughout this chapter, we have explored the transformative impact of AI on the accounting profession, highlighting how AI is reshaping traditional practices and introducing efficiencies that redefine the role of accountants. As we've discussed, AI not only automates routine tasks but also enhances capabilities in fraud detection, financial analysis, and regulatory compliance. This evolution is setting a new standard in the industry, driving accountants toward more strategic and advisory roles.

The potential of AI to revolutionize accounting is clear, but realizing this potential requires more than just technological integration. It demands a proactive approach to embracing new skills, continuous learning, and adapting business models to leverage AI's capabilities fully. Accountants and firms must recognize that staying abreast of AI advancements is no longer optional but essential for maintaining relevance and competitiveness in a rapidly evolving field.

As we look to the future, the call to action for the accounting profession is unequivocal: **embrace AI technology**. This involves not only implementing AI systems but also fostering a culture that values innovation, ethical standards, and ongoing education. By doing so, accountants can ensure they remain valuable, resilient, and capable of delivering superior insights and services in the digital age.

The journey toward an AI-integrated accounting landscape is filled with challenges, yet it is also replete with opportunities for growth and transformation. Let's move forward with the resolve to harness these opportunities, continually adapt to new developments, and thrive in the dynamic world of accounting. Embracing AI is not just about keeping up with technology – it's about leading the charge in defining the future of the profession.

Further reading and resources

To deepen your understanding of AI applications in accounting and stay updated on the latest advancements, this section outlines some recommended books, articles, and online resources, along with links to professional courses and webinars.

Books

- *Artificial Intelligence for Audit, Forensic Accounting, and Valuation*, by AI Naqvi, is a comprehensive guide that explores how AI can transform auditing, accounting, and valuation practices
- The Big Data Opportunity in Our Driverless Future, by Evangelos Simoudis, although focused on big data, provides insights applicable to AI in accounting, particularly around data management and analytics

Articles

- How artificial intelligence can help save accounting - Journal of Accountancy provides regular features and updates on how AI is being integrated into accounting practices, with practical case studies and expert opinions.
- The Business of Artificial Intelligence (hbr.org) offers a collection of articles discussing the strategic implications of AI across different sectors, including accounting.

Online platforms

- **Coursera** provides various courses on AI and data analytics that can be applied to accounting. Specific courses to look out for include *AI For Everyone*, by Andrew Ng, and *AI in Finance*. Coursera
- **edX** offers courses such as *Data Science and Machine Learning Essentials*, which can help accountants understand the technical aspects of AI. edX

Professional courses and webinars

- **AICPA and CIMA**: The **Association of International Certified Professional Accountants** (**AICPA**) offers courses and webinars on AI in accounting, helping professionals understand the implications of AI for financial management and reporting

- **AI CPA webcasts**: These webcasts provide up-to-date information on how AI technologies are affecting the accounting industry, directly from experts in the field

These resources provide both foundational knowledge and advanced insights into how AI can be leveraged in accounting to drive efficiency, accuracy, and strategic decision-making. Whether you are looking to understand the basics of AI or apply advanced AI strategies in your accounting practices, these resources offer valuable learning opportunities.

Q&A

As we explore the integration of AI in accounting, it is crucial to address both the transformative aspects and the challenges. The following are some thought-provoking questions along with insights that delve into the ethical implications, potential benefits, and obstacles of AI in accounting:

1. What ethical considerations are necessary to ensure AI in accounting upholds data privacy and security?

    Implementing robust encryption practices, strict access controls, and regular audits can help safeguard sensitive data. Additionally, adhering to legal standards such as GDPR and involving ethics experts in AI development can further strengthen ethical practices.

2. How could the long-term application of AI redefine the accounting profession in the coming years?

    AI is expected to automate routine tasks, allowing accountants to focus more on strategic advisory roles. This shift could enhance the value accountants bring to business decision-making, emphasizing predictive analytics and financial insights.

3. What major challenges might organizations face when integrating AI into existing accounting systems?

    Key challenges include the high cost of implementation, the complexity of integrating AI with legacy systems, and potential resistance from staff. Addressing these issues requires strategic planning, investment in training, and a gradual integration approach.

4. In what ways might AI impact your day-to-day responsibilities as an accountant?

    AI could automate tasks such as data entry and compliance checks, freeing up time for more complex and rewarding work, such as analysis and consulting. This shift would require accountants to develop new skills, particularly in data interpretation and strategic thinking.

5. What cultural shifts are necessary within accounting teams to facilitate the acceptance and effective use of AI?

    Cultivating a culture that embraces change, prioritizes continuous learning, and supports technological innovation is crucial. Leadership should actively promote these values, demonstrating the benefits of AI and providing resources for staff to adapt to new tools and methodologies.

    These reflections are designed to help accounting professionals understand the implications of AI and prepare for the changes it will bring. Emphasizing proactive learning and adaptation will be key to leveraging AI effectively in the accounting sector.

Index

S

T

V

packtpub.com

Subscribe to our online digital library for full access to over 7,000 books and videos, as well as industry leading tools to help you plan your personal development and advance your career. For more information, please visit our website.

Why subscribe?

- Spend less time learning and more time coding with practical eBooks and Videos from over 4,000 industry professionals

- Improve your learning with Skill Plans built especially for you

- Get a free eBook or video every month

- Fully searchable for easy access to vital information

- Copy and paste, print, and bookmark content

Did you know that Packt offers eBook versions of every book published, with PDF and ePub files available? You can upgrade to the eBook version at packtpub.com and as a print book customer, you are entitled to a discount on the eBook copy. Get in touch with us at customercare@packtpub.com for more details.

At www.packtpub.com, you can also read a collection of free technical articles, sign up for a range of free newsletters, and receive exclusive discounts and offers on Packt books and eBooks.

Other Books You May Enjoy

If you enjoyed this book, you may be interested in these other books by Packt:

Mastering QuickBooks 2024

Crystalynn Shelton

ISBN: 978-1-83546-995-8

- A crash course on basic accounting concepts
- Overcome challenges encountered during migration from QBD to QBO
- Record income and expenses, pay vendors, and manage payroll
- Streamline client billing with invoicing and quoting templates
- Use QuickBooks Online for tax filing and deadline management
- Plan cash flow, profits, and revenue with the Report Center
- Customize financial reports and sales forms for your requirements
- Calculate depreciation and automate workflows with QBO Advanced

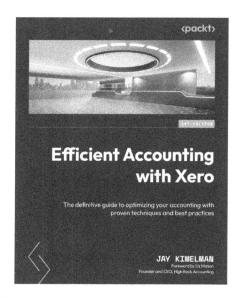

Efficient Accounting with Xero

Jay Kimelman

ISBN: 978-1-80181-220-7

- Understand why Xero is the best choice in accounting software for your SMB
- Easily set up or convert to Xero for a service- or product-based business
- Reconcile cash and related transactions effortlessly
- Track and depreciate capital assets purchased by and used in the business
- Produce customized reports tailored to your specific need
- Use Xero to make informed and timely decisions and become a better business owner or advisor

Packt is searching for authors like you

If you're interested in becoming an author for Packt, please visit `authors.packtpub.com` and apply today. We have worked with thousands of developers and tech professionals, just like you, to help them share their insight with the global tech community. You can make a general application, apply for a specific hot topic that we are recruiting an author for, or submit your own idea.

Share Your Thoughts

Now you've finished *ChatGPT and AI for Accountants*, we'd love to hear your thoughts! Scan the QR code below to go straight to the Amazon review page for this book and share your feedback or leave a review on the site that you purchased it from.

`https://packt.link/r/1835466532`

Your review is important to us and the tech community and will help us make sure we're delivering excellent quality content.

Download a free PDF copy of this book

Thanks for purchasing this book!

Do you like to read on the go but are unable to carry your print books everywhere?

Is your eBook purchase not compatible with the device of your choice?

Don't worry, now with every Packt book you get a DRM-free PDF version of that book at no cost.

Read anywhere, any place, on any device. Search, copy, and paste code from your favorite technical books directly into your application.

The perks don't stop there, you can get exclusive access to discounts, newsletters, and great free content in your inbox daily

Follow these simple steps to get the benefits:

1. Scan the QR code or visit the link below

https://packt.link/free-ebook/9781835466537

2. Submit your proof of purchase
3. That's it! We'll send your free PDF and other benefits to your email directly

www.ingramcontent.com/pod-product-compliance
Lightning Source LLC
Chambersburg PA
CBHW080632060326

40690CB00021B/4900